The Social Economy
of Single Motherhood

Some Recent Titles from the *Perspectives on Gender* Series

The Social Economy of Single Motherhood

of Single Motherhood

Raising Children in Rural America

Margaret K. Nelson

ROUTLEDGE
NEW YORK AND LONDON

Published in 2005 by
Routledge
Taylor & Francis Group
270 Madison Avenue
New York, NY 10016

Published in Great Britain by
Routledge
Taylor & Francis Group
2 Park Square
Milton Park, Abingdon
Oxon OX14 4RN

Printed in the United States of America on acid-free paper
10 9 8 7 6 5 4 3 2 1

International Standard Book Number-10: 0-415-94777-4 (Hardcover) 0-415-94778-2 (Softcover)
International Standard Book Number-13: 978-0-415-94777-0 (Hardcover) 978-0-415-94778-7 (Softcover)

Library of Congress Cataloging-in-Publication Data

Nelson, Margaret K., 1944-
   The social economy of single motherhood : raising children in rural America / Margaret K. Nelson.
      p. cm. -- (Perspectives on gender)
   Includes bibliographical references and index.
   ISBN 0-415-94777-4 (hardcover : alk. paper) -- ISBN 0-415-94778-2 (pbk. : alk. paper)
   1. Single mothers-United States-Social conditions. 2. Single mothers-United States-Economic conditions. 3. Welfare recipients-United States. 4. Rural families-United States. 5. Sociology, Rural-United States. I. Title. II. Series: Perspectives on gender (New York, N.Y.)

HQ759.915.N46 2005
306.874'32'0973091734--dc22   2005016474

Taylor & Francis Group
is the Academic Division of T&F Informa plc.

Visit the Taylor & Francis Web site at
http://www.taylorandfrancis.com

and the Routledge Web site at
http://www.routledge-ny.com

To the memory of
Eve Adler (1945–2004)
and
Joan Smith (1935–2004)

CONTENTS

ACKNOWLEDGMENTS

While Joan Smith and I were writing *Working Hard and Making Do*, we mused about possible sequels, in which we would redo our analysis with a focus either on a more urban region of Vermont or on single parents, in contrast to the married couples we had studied. When the first review of our book included a stern admonition that we consider a more varied group of families, the die was cast. By the time we actually got around to thinking about writing, however, Joan's work as Dean of the Faculty at the University of Vermont had drawn her away from her own scholarship. This book, then, though conceived jointly, became my project alone.

Of course, no more than any other book does this represent a single person's efforts. Most significantly, I am grateful to the many women who patiently tolerated the interviews on which this book is based. Although I cannot thank them by name, I hope that in reading this book, they will find a reward for their contributions and believe that I "got" what they were saying. I want to thank as well my faithful interviewers—Carol McMurrich, Jessica Lindert, and Bethany Johnson—whose perseverance, sensitivity, and adaptability enabled them not just to stand in for me, but often to pursue issues I might well have overlooked. And I especially want to thank two former students—Sarah Theall and Jennifer LaBrecque—who conducted interviews for their own research and allowed me to share their data and their findings.

A number of other people helped me with various details of writing. I am grateful to Carol McMurrich and Melissa Fuller for having the patience to transcribe the interview tapes. Kristin Ryan, Kristin Gray, Kara Bonneau, Melissa Maxwell, Gillian Menza, and Rebecca Schutz all spent time in the library or on the Internet tracking down references. I appreciate their patience and precision. I want to thank as well Laura

Zarchin and Hope Stege, two former students who knew how to gather data from sources that were opaque to me. Among the many students who worked for me, I want to acknowledge especially Marina Zaloznaya, who wrote brief and clear summaries of a number of different significant issues. And I extend special thanks to Valerie Benka, who graduated from patient researcher to superb editor, and to Christopher Ross, who copyedited the manuscript with meticulous care.

On a daily basis, Charlene Barrett graces the Sociology/Anthropology departmental office with astonishing good cheer; she makes the rest of my life run smoothly enough that I can devote time to my writing. Middlebury College has not only given me the support of its remarkable staff, but it has also literally supported the project, both through the Faculty Development Fund and through the enrichment funds associated with the Hepburn Chair. I appreciate as well the sustained encouragement I receive from my departmental colleagues, and especially from Burke Rochford, who believes in me when I begin to doubt myself.

A large number of other colleagues have commented on various parts of this manuscript. Some of these are the "anonymous" reviewers for journals, and as is the case for the women I interviewed, I cannot refer to them by name. They also should know of my gratitude; I hope they also believe I "got" what they had to say. Some, however, I can acknowledge here because they acknowledged themselves. I thank Rob Benford, Rosanna Hertz, Susan Himmelweit, Keith Kilty, Elaine McCrate, and Robert Zussman. I am especially appreciative of the support I have received from Nancy Naples, Karen Hansen, and Naomi Gerstel, women who know well how to combine professional collegiality with good friendship. My debt to Myra Marx Ferree is as enormous as it is longstanding.

This book is dedicated to two dear friends, who died while I was putting the final touches on it. Eve Adler, an inveterate follower of Leo Strauss, is unlikely to have ever read the book, though she would have rejoiced in its publication as she did, throughout our long friendship, in every piece of good fortune it was my pleasure to enjoy. Joan Smith has played a very different role in my intellectual life, and I miss being able to draw on her keen insights. She was also a good friend, and I miss even more the occasions of sociability we shared.

During the years I was writing this book, I was sustained by the love and friendship of many people. Sonja Olson gave sound advice and encouraged me to finish writing so I could get on with my life. Jane Chaplin not only helped me walk away my woes, but also served as a sounding board for ideas that ranged as widely as our rambles themselves. My sister Emily K. Abel, who is always at the other end of the phone when I need her, cares in all the ways that matter. My children, Sam Nelson and Jeff Nelson, and my daughter-in-law, Rebecca Freedman, feed me both literally and figuratively; the anticipation of my first grandchild brightened some difficult days. Last, but not least, I offer enduring gratitude to my husband, Bill Nelson, whose daily presence in my life makes me complete.

INTRODUCTION

It was nine o'clock on a summer's evening when my research assistant arrived at Sarah Stanley's door prepared to interview her about her life as a single parent.[1] A petite, brown-haired, thirty-four-year-old woman, Sarah cheerfully greeted Carol and then, as she set about preparing two glasses of iced tea, apologized for having to meet so late. She explained that she wanted her children to be asleep before she began to describe the events that had landed her in a small town in Vermont.

Sarah began with a brief life history, telling of a childhood spent in Connecticut as the third of four children, of a joyful romance with the man she met in junior college and married soon after graduation, and of a decade of married life on the West Coast, where Sarah pursued her career as an interior decorator and her husband his as an accountant. And, she told Carol, both she and her husband had been delighted when they became parents, first to Zach, now six, and then to Maya, now two.

Although there had been intimations of trouble over the years, problems reached a crescendo during the period immediately following Maya's birth; when the baby was but nine months old, Sarah's husband was hospitalized with a severe mental illness. Knowing that it was unlikely that he would soon—or even ever—resume his role as husband and breadwinner, after several months of internal struggle, Sarah decided on separation and divorce. She also decided to move "back East" and to make her way in the world as a single mother of two small children. Although she knew that this move meant leaving all that was familiar to her at that time, Sarah was persuaded that it was the wisest course: Her brother, a pilot, found her inexpensive plane tickets so that she could move her family, and her parents offered to let her live rent-free in half of a second home they owned

1

in Centerville, Vermont. Here, Sarah believed, she would find the support she needed while making a new start in a "tight community."

Sarah was partly right about both these beliefs. Her family stepped in with regular assistance to fill the gap left by her husband's absence. Her parents came to stay in the other half of the house they owned for two out of every six weeks, and they made themselves available to help with both babysitting and advice. And, at least initially, Sarah was grateful; speaking of her mother, she explained, "[Having her here is] really nice in a lot of ways because she'll watch my kids for me and I really appreciate that." At the same time, however, Sarah discovered that this support generated its own complications. She had been accustomed to more autonomy—"Before I moved here I only saw [my parents] once every two years"—and she found it disconcerting to be subject to their constant appraisal—"I'm not used to living in front of my parents." Sometimes, in fact, she finds her family's presence downright invasive—"I mean, I walk out of my front door and they're there, waving from the kitchen window."

But Sarah does not have to rely on her parents alone. Sarah's sister lives nearby as well and she makes herself available to help out. In addition, with considerable effort, Sarah has expanded her network of support and redefined her notion of community to include a group of friends who help out with daily needs and provide essential sociability:

> *I feel like I have a network of very supportive friends who—I wouldn't say I rely on them—but I know they're there for me, which is great. And I worked really hard to make these friends. It's hard to take the time to even be with friends sometimes, but I always make time—I always make a lot of time for friends. I have friends over; I do a lot of entertaining. Because friends are like our mainstay. We have a great time together and also we know that we're going to be there for one another.*

Sarah has also put energy into a new romance. Although she is now carefully discouraging a man who was originally hired to be a babysitter for her children and has since begun to express more than a casual interest in her, she is responding with more enthusiasm and interest to a man whom she has just begun to date.

Initially, when Sarah had contemplated the issue of how she would survive in these new circumstances, she assumed she would be able to rely on public welfare for financial support. After all, she reasoned, she had no income from her husband, and she was reluctant to work outside the home if it meant day care for her children, who had experienced the recent trauma of their father's illness (and disappearance from the family) and *a move across the country. When Sarah approached the department of social welfare upon arriving in Vermont, she was surprised to learn that her and her husband's years of hard work weighed against her. Since she had approximately $25,000 available to her (derived from their savings and from the proceeds of the sale of their home), she did not "qualify" for any state assistance outside of the Medicaid extension program (fondly called Doctor Dynasaur) for her two children.[2] Even so, Sarah decided not to seek employment outside the home until her children were settled, and she calculated that if she managed carefully, she could stretch her resources over at least a year. It was toward the end of that first year that Sarah and Carol began to talk.*

THE SOCIAL ECONOMY OF SINGLE MOTHERS

This book is about a distinctive set of issues that constitute Sarah's talk, and the talk of sixty-seven other single mothers in Vermont, as they describe how they handle the events of their daily lives. As will be discussed more fully, the women who were interviewed for this study vary widely in income, in the routes that brought them to be single parents, and in their individual attitudes and preferences. But they have in common the fact that they all are white, custodial mothers of at least one child under the age of eighteen, and that they live in a rural state.[3] Most significantly for the issues in this book, all of the women live a life of complex and rich involvement with others as they develop what I call a "social economy" of single motherhood. Like Sarah, they rely on others (family, friends, the state, their own children, and their boyfriends) for help in meeting their daily needs. Also, like Sarah, they have to make sense of their new sociability even as it challenges their desires to be self-sufficient and to protect the privacy of their newly configured families.[4]

Not So Single; Not So Lone

This emphasis on "the social" may come as a surprise in a book about single mothers.[5] The term *single mother* itself focuses attention on a woman's marital status, on the fact that she is raising children without a man; it implicitly suggests that she lacks "romantic companionship."[6] In many other countries the common term is *lone mother*, a description that focuses less on marital status but evokes images of solitude and perhaps even isolation. Both terms give rise to common misconceptions. Many of those who are counted as "single mothers" by our normal accounting procedures are *not* on their own, but are instead cohabiting with a partner;[7] in all likelihood, many more are likely to be "partnered" in the sense of having ongoing romantic relationships (with men or women). Women designated as "lone mothers" live with a child or children and thus are rarely "alone." Moreover, many women who are considered "lone mothers," like those considered "single mothers," live in household configurations that include other adults.[8]

But, whether defined as single mothers or as lone mothers, social interaction may very well extend beyond that arising from living arrangements, and it is these other social connections that are of the greatest interest here.[9] In an essay drawing on her experiences as a lesbian single mother, economist June Lapidus explained that she and her son live within a rich "web of relationships" that includes,[10]

> the friends who have taken him to breakfast every Saturday since he was born; my best friend with whom I struggle around issues of discipline and the theories and practice of raising children; the woman who came into our lives as my lover when my son was three and remains in our lives, though she and I are no longer lovers; the friends who sat in the hospital waiting room providing Thai food to my labor coaches; the teachers at my son's school who continue to think with me about his needs; the fourteen-year-old boy down the street who baby-sits; and the woman who provided love and nurturance in her home so that I could both work and parent. We are part of an extended biological family of grandparents, aunts, uncles, cousins, and nieces and nephews. We are also simultaneously members of many communities, some as mother and son, and some individually.

The Economic and the Social

This book, like Lapidus's essay, looks at the "web of relationships" within which single mothers exist, even though it focuses on women who are not self-defined as being lesbians.[11] Rather than share the concept Lapidus introduces, however, I use the concept of the "social economy" (of single mothers) to describe this complex set of connections because it conveys more fully the issues under consideration here.[12]

The word *economy* carries with it the connotation of material efforts necessary to meet the routine demands of daily life—demands that range from the activities necessary to bring in income, to such mundane tasks as doing the day's laundry, and to the ongoing pleasurable *and* burdensome care mothers provide for their children. As is well-known, and will be discussed further below, the "economy" of single mothers is marked by insufficiency, especially when compared to that of married-couple families: Not only is the median income of single mothers less than 40 percent of that of married-couple families, but single mothers experience a shortage of time and energy, and thus of rest and leisure, as they strive to attend to their everyday needs.[13]

The term *social* carries an equal, if not greater, burden here. As single mothers seek to meet their "economic" needs, they establish connections with, and come to rely on, a broad variety of others: family and friends, the representatives of state agencies, their own children and the fathers of those children, and potential partners. The phrase *social economy* reminds us that the survival strategy of single mothers depends on this vast array of interconnections with individuals who can provide money, goods, and help with the tasks of daily living. It also reminds us that individuals pursue not only "material" needs but also emotional support and ordinary sociability: Single mothers, like others, want and need to talk, to laugh, to love, to care, and to cry. The term also implicitly conveys the notion that when single mothers involve others in their survival strategies, they engage in the *work* of sociability: They locate others who can meet the full range of their needs, and they negotiate, discuss reciprocal obligations, and make compromises. In addition, the term links to the idea that by engaging in "sociability" individuals become members of a community and seek to live by its prevailing values. Most distinct, even though single mothers rely on other individuals (and often on the state), they attempt to abide by the normative requirement that they be independent and self-sufficient. Furthermore, as they endeavor to meet needs that they cannot easily satisfy within the family alone, they also strive to sustain a sense that their family is not deficient, and to protect themselves and their children from denigration, and even stigma.

Sociability and economic interests are often seen as being at odds with each other insofar as the former connotes shared interests while the latter connotes (rational) *self*-interest. As I explore the concept of a social economy throughout this book, I am especially attentive to conflicts, tensions, and contradictions that inevitably emerge as single mothers strive to meet their needs through interactions with others while retaining an ongoing commitment to the values—of self-sufficiency, of what constitutes a "good" family—that prevail in their social worlds.

The Example of Finding Child Care

In considering how Sarah Stanley discusses her strategies for solving the ongoing problem of providing care for her children, I introduce some of the complexities that I discuss in this book. During the interview, Carol asked a straightforward question: "Have you needed to ask for help with babysitting or child care in the last six months?" In an equally straightforward manner, Sarah answered, "Oh yeah, lots," indicating, not surprisingly, that she lived a life that frequently required "material" support from others. Carol then pursued this issue, asking whom Sarah was likely to call for help. Sarah answered,

> I ask my sister because she's free and because she's the auntie so I know my kids love to be with her. And then I basically go for the cheapest babysitter I can.... I go for the high school student who charges five dollars an hour.

In this initial response, Sarah reveals her financial constraints, as she suggests that she looks for the least expensive solution to this ongoing problem of finding child care. But she also indicates that she is conscious of, and values, the emotional link between her sister and her children—both her sister's (assumed) love for her children ("the auntie") and her children's love in return ("I know my kids love to be with her").

As the conversation continued, however, Sarah indicated that seeking to maintain that connection evoked concerns about what she could offer in return:

> Well, I try not to [ask her too often] because I don't—I've got this independent streak where I'd rather pay for it a lot of the times. I only ask her when I'm desperate because I know I can't give anything back to her at this point in my life because I'm overwhelmed with my own responsibilities and I can't give back. I guess I don't want it to be held over my head in any way. But she's not like that; it's just the way I am. She ends up doing about an hour a week.

Sarah thus now implies that reliance on her sister challenges her commitment to the broad social value of wanting to be, as she put it, "independent," and that in her definition being independent includes not only avoiding being indebted to others, but also establishing reciprocity in interpersonal relationships. For that reason, she asks her sister for less help than she needs; her need to be independent competes with, and gets in the way of, her need to have that ongoing assistance.

Indeed, Sarah indicates that reciprocity is a significant concern, not just in relation to her sister, but within the friendship network she has worked to develop during the past several months. Even though drawing on this network has its own burdens (of travel and of "paying" her own way), Sarah values the give-and-take it involves and the evidence that she is part of a mutual arrangement:

> I do a lot of bartering with friends [for child care]. I actually have friends all over the place now who I can leave my kids with. I have a whole variety of resources. Often I'll drive half an hour out of my way and drop them at someone's house.... And they'll leave their kids with me.

But Sarah has to work hard to sustain this mutuality. Not only did she put effort into creating this network, but she now keeps track of the personalities, schedules, and ongoing needs of the diverse people involved, as well as of the demands she has already placed on them. She also worries that she sounds too calculating, too straightforwardly economic:

> Well, each person that I know has a different personality and a different schedule or a different amount of kids, and is available at different times. I might have asked one person too many times.... Wait, let me see, I probably have—one, two, three, four—four different people that I can leave my kids with. But I weigh against, and *this sounds really bad*, but if I need to leave my kids with someone or if I need something from someone, I basically figure out who the last person I asked was and move on to someone else. I try not to overwhelm one particular person with too much. (Emphasis added.)

Even as she weighs these different variables and relies on so many other people, Sarah reiterates her own claim to self-sufficiency:

> The thing is I really don't ask—I'm pretty self-sufficient. I really give back a lot, just as much as I take. I do that willingly because I enjoy my friendships and I don't ask other people unless I'm really up a creek, I really don't. Or I get a babysitter or if my parents—if my mom's here, I'll ask her. I sort of do what my gut tells me to do.

Moreover, Sarah adds to this mix of moral concerns another value. She wants to make up for the losses her children have experienced and she wants to ensure that they are well loved. (As previously noted, she relishes her children's connection with their "auntie.") When Carol asked if Sarah could articulate her feelings about having a range of people involved in her children's daily lives, Sarah responded that she found comfort in having her children exposed to many different loving people. She said, as well, that because she had worried about how her kids were "going to be affected growing up without a strong male presence in the home," she was delighted to be able to include in the mix a man who babysat from time to time.

> I feel good about [the variety] because I believe that that's healthy, especially in a single-parent family. I think it's healthy for them to be close to other loving people of all different ages. And so, [there's also] Jack; he's another guy who does babysitting for me.

Even though she has created these varied resources, Sarah still experiences moments of crisis when her own needs and those of her children clash, and in that clash she finds threats to her own standard of good mothering:

> I take them with me to the dentist. They sit in the hallway. [I take them to my] doctors' appointments... and they make chaos in the doctor's room when I'm desperately trying to have a conversation with the doctor. The dentist is probably the most stressful because there's nobody there to watch them. They could run out of the front door. The receptionist can keep an eye on them but there are no guarantees. That's really stressful.

The complex social economy Sarah has established to meet her ongoing need for child care does not function smoothly or without gaps and flaws. Taken as a whole, however, its creation and daily operation demonstrate the considerable effort Sarah puts into mediating among a broad range of needs and concerns even as these needs and concerns conflict with one another.

SINGLE MOTHERS FROM OTHER PERSPECTIVES

As I explore the concept of a social economy, I fill a gap in the empirical and theoretical literature on single mothers. This group of women has traditionally been the focus of much social analysis and commentary, which can be broadly divided into two groups: liberal and conservative.

A Liberal Perspective: Material Constraints

The first group of scholars, writing from a liberal political perspective, has looked predominantly at those who are poor, those who have had children out of wedlock, those who depend on low-wage work, and, in particular, those who rely on welfare.[14] Sarah Stanley, who has assets sufficient to place her well above the poverty line, might not be included in many of these studies. But the fact that Sarah's assets of approximately $25,000 (even if she spends them all in a single year) place her just slightly above the median for single mothers in the state in which she lives, makes her a particularly emblematic and appropriate object of study. Indeed, when the state estimates that Sarah, as a single parent of two children, would need at the very least $30,000 to make ends meet, it is not surprising to learn that she also contends with serious material struggles.[15] It is also no surprise that although Sarah does not depend on welfare, she does now rely on at least one means-tested program; she anticipated welfare reliance in the past and expects it may enter her picture in the future. And, like more than half of white single mothers in the United States, she arrived at her status through divorce, rather than through having a child out of wedlock.[16]

Other elements of Sarah's struggles are similar to those of the vast majority of single mothers. Not only does she have limited financial resources, but she is experiencing new limitations on her knowledge, time, energies, and abilities. She had never had to accomplish her daily routine of housework and child care without any backup: How, she wants to know, do you shovel a foot of snow off the front walk when two children are asleep inside? How do you cook dinner while meeting the needs of a cranky two-year-old? She also had never bought a car on her own, but she needs one in this community. And she is just learning how to respond to all the things that need doing around the house, including mowing the lawn and putting up storm windows.

Moreover, each day seems to bring a new crisis. During a cold spell the winter before we visited with her, the pipes burst in Sarah's bathroom; the week before we came, both of the children came down with the flu. Sarah described these events in a way that highlighted how difficult she was finding it to manage both within new economic constraints and without the assistance of a partner:

> When I'm sick and I have a fever of 103 and both my kids are sick with fevers of 104, and [I can't] afford a babysitter, and [there is] no family around; and lying on the couch, and having to force yourself to get up; and you're throwing up on the floor and you have to take care of two screaming sick children: That to me has to be the hardest thing...just not having a partner, a backup.... [Or] just little things like floods: We've had a few floods in the basement...and [the children are] running around naked while I'm trying to talk to the plumber....

Even though Sarah is not alone, thanks to the ongoing support of family and friends, she continues her description of her daily life to show that she finds the relentlessness of the ongoing demands on her resources, time, and energy both overwhelming and dispiriting:

> And decision making, and working seven days a week, twenty-four hours a day without a break, ever, ever, ever, fifty-two weeks a year, year after year. And maybe the only time I get to myself is in the evenings after I've put them to sleep. But usually I've already put in a fourteen-hour day and I'm too tired to even relax.... I have a kind of relentless schedule. So those are the hardest things. Not to sound like I'm pitying myself, but realistically, it's hard.

Scholars who draw attention only to these ongoing demands and how they shape the lives of single mothers, implicitly, and often explicitly, argue that when material needs are especially compelling, we should not look too closely at the content of the resulting actions. Some of these scholars suggest that under conditions of enormous deprivation, a different and perhaps even "deviant" culture can emerge. Sociologist Sharon Hays, for example, argues that "it makes perfect sense that the conditions of poverty can produce, in the most general terms, a different culture."[17] Indeed, when liberal scholars argue that "problems of morality that existed among poor families were primarily the result, rather than the cause of economic hardship," they tacitly acknowledge that there *are* problems.[18] Some such scholars also argue that this "different culture" can be the reason for poverty itself, especially because in any given situation, it would be impossible to distinguish between cause and effect. In what follows, I am rejecting neither this possibility of difference (of what appear to be "bad values") nor the possibility that this difference contributes to the ongoing poverty that single mothers experience. However, I stress the commitment that single mothers have, whether or not they live in poverty, to many mainstream values, even as they occasionally transmute and transform those values to serve the ends of survival.

Liberal scholars also argue that when material needs are compelling, individuals have but few choices to make. It is true that Sarah's life offers few opportunities for "agency," and that her circumstances force her on occasion to make hard choices, such as when she believes she takes risks with her children's safety or exploits the goodwill of others so that she can have her teeth cleaned. But, as the accounting of the decisions Sarah makes about child care indicates, she believes she has some options, and when she considers them, she operates within a framework that takes into account both strictly economic needs *and* her commitment to central values: Because she values her self-sufficiency, she wants to pay her own way (through reciprocity or with cash); because she hopes to provide her children with a rich family life, she wants them to be exposed to "loving people of all different ages"; and because she worries about the absence of her children's father, she wants to include a man in that mix of caregivers.

Kathryn Edin and Laura Lein's landmark study *Making Ends Meet: How Single Mothers Survive Welfare and Low-Wage Work* carefully examines the survival strategies of two groups of single mothers and draws our attention primarily to the outcomes of their decisions.[19] With precision and care, the authors demonstrate that single mothers do develop a highly social strategy that draws on resources garnered from work, networks, and agencies. Edin and Lein primarily highlight the financial resources that network members and agencies provide, however, and they give but minimal attention to the process and the reasoning that accompany the development of the support patterns they identify.

In this book I am more attentive to these issues of process and reasoning; I also explore the full range of support single mothers receive from others. In making these shifts I neither mean to deny that Sarah and the other single mothers who constitute the subject of this book have to make choices within a "shared set of constraints," nor do I mean to deny that they might even overstate the degree to which they can make choices.[20] At the same time, I do suggest that if we focus exclusively on those constraints, or on the resulting survival strategy as measured only by economic resources (or on the patterns of assistance received from others), we cannot fully understand the contours of Sarah's daily life. Her limited choices are not simply determined by difficult economic considerations, but rather are framed within, and equally shaped by, a set of complex, and contradictory, *social* concerns, which include commitment to whatever is taken to be self-sufficiency and to meeting the emotional needs that accompany her particular pattern of family life.[21]

Another example, beyond babysitting, might illustrate this point. When Sarah moved to Vermont she initially accepted her father's offer to pay for health insurance. On straightforward financial grounds this made sense: Sarah did not have a job and she could ill-afford the monthly fee the insurance company charged. Sarah described her father's offer as evidence of how lucky she has been in the support she has received: "I've been okay the whole time. I've been really, really fortunate. Because I don't have a job my dad was paying for my family's medical insurance, which is $658 a month." But she told of this good fortune as a way to tell another story, one about the costs of this dependence on her father, and about her eventual decision to forego this economic benefit for the alternative benefit of what she defined as self-sufficiency:

> There was a situation last month where he pulled this little number on me. And he told me that I had to give him some information about…another check that he'd given us a long time ago, and I told him I might not be able to get the information. So, he said, "Well, I might not pay your health insurance." So, I went and I applied for a Dr. Dynasaur for my kids and I qualified, which means I basically met the poverty level, I guess…. That just happened last week. And *my* medical insurance is now $247 a month, and at the moment I can pay that.So my mission, even though my dad agreed to continue paying for health care, I don't have to ask him. I just went and made my own arrangement.

Sarah has clearly made a financially unwise decision: rather than accepting her father's gift of $658 a month, she has "chosen" to spend $247 of her limited resources for her own health insurance and to engage in the time-consuming, and even socially stigmatized, process of applying for means-tested state benefits for her children. But as was the case with babysitting, Sarah shows that she is not *just* driven by economic constraints. When considered within a broader context, for Sarah, this decision makes good sense: Relying on her father jeopardized her sense of autonomy. Moreover, Sarah had noted earlier in the interview that her father "doesn't respect single parenthood" and that although he insisted that he was not "ashamed of the fact that [she was] a single parent," he was "fairly critical about it." In relying on her father Sarah ran the risk of more constant contact with these attitudes. On the other hand, in relying on the state Sarah is now exposed to the possibilities of a different kind of stigma, and as will be explained more fully in what follows, a high level of ongoing surveillance, even if she relishes her newfound self-sufficiency ("I just went and made my own arrangement").

To be sure, my theoretical framework follows that of the liberal scholars discussed above, in that it takes as its starting point significant material constraints as a daily feature of the lives of single mothers. For many such women these constraints are far more crushing than those Sarah faces. Indeed, as Sarah herself acknowledges, she is especially lucky to have the choices she does: She has a father who is both willing and able to help pay for health insurance, and she lives in a state with generous provisions for children such that fewer than 4 percent are without health insurance (as compared to a nationwide figure of more than 12%).[22] At the same time, however, because she is not currently employed and does not have a partner who can purchase insurance through his job, Sarah *is* in a bind that extends beyond that created by limited material resources alone. Within the context of those limitations she still has to make choices among competing options: Should she forgo insurance altogether? Should she accept dependence on her father (who interferes with her autonomy and makes clear his disdain)? Should she accept dependence on the state (and risk having to report her income to the state and face the contempt of medical personnel who might give preferential treatment to those with private insurance)?

I do not mean to suggest that all women would make the same choice as Sarah: In fact, as will be shown, some women view dependence on the family as less threatening to a sense of autonomy than reliance on the state, while others make precisely the opposite determination. My goal throughout this book is to explore *how* a desire for independence and self-sufficiency, combined with a desire to meet one's own and one's children's needs for a satisfactory family life, is enacted through a complex and internally contradictory set of relationships and attitudes that I call the social economy of single motherhood. In this balancing act, wanting to evade the stigma often associated with the single-parent family figures prominently, as does the desire to establish social relations with individuals who will provide material *and* emotional support in equal measure.

A Conservative Approach: Deficient Values

In their analyses of single mothers, scholars from a conservative political perspective are more likely to emphasize values as the cause of actions, and they are more likely to make judgments about both the underlying values and the resulting actions.[23] These scholars believe that as a society we should not lend our support to a pattern of social life that they view as being inherently problematic. Hence, they believe it appropriate not only to stigmatize single mothers but also to deny them those measures of public support that could encourage this lifestyle, and especially those measures that would encourage dependence on the state. At the same time, conservatives often encourage single mothers to be dependent on individuals—on men and on family members—and to rely on informal services offered through neighborhoods and community groups.

When conservative scholars stress the outcomes of mothers' choices—including welfare reliance, marital disruption, and out-of-wedlock childbirth—they often at least tacitly assume that a different set of choices could be made, and that if single mothers simply had the "right" values, they would have opted for staying within a two-parent family, or at least would practice self-sufficiency. Some theories start with the notion that even among the very poor, the choice of welfare represents laziness and inadequate commitment to "personal responsibility," and that those who do make that choice are part of a subculture that disregards traditional values of our society.[24] Still others see in unwed childbirth a willingness to be promiscuous, an inadequate regard for the value of fatherhood, and a desire to "cheat" the government.[25] A substantial body of literature finds in divorce and separation evidence of insufficient concern for the family and thus a breakdown in family values.[26] In fact, it is because some scholars believe that the outcomes they deplore represent a set of deficient or deviant values that they believe it necessary to change the structure of incentives. By making it harder to depend on the state they believe they will make enactment of prosocial choices more likely; they thus tacitly suggest, far more than liberal scholars do, that single women have freedom of choice.

Such scholars might be very surprised to hear Sarah talk about how she made the decisions in her life that led to becoming a single parent, and why she is willing to consider welfare reliance an appropriate means of support. This talk—which is missed if we look at her actions alone—shows that Sarah is very concerned about how she appears to others, about her unexpected entry into what she perceives as being a stigmatized social status, and about her membership in a social community of highly moral actors. Sarah expressed these concerns immediately in the interview, as she explained that wanting the children to be asleep was not just because she wanted the conversation to occur without interruption, but because, as Carol wrote in her notes, Sarah wanted to avoid exposing her children to a discussion of the causes for, and the form of, their current family: "She says she doesn't like talking about being a single parent in front of them." Carol's notes continue with evidence that Sarah herself is also uncomfortable with this issue:

> And before we started taping, or before we even started talking about the interview, she was saying to me about how she hates the words *single parent*. She doesn't call herself a single parent to anyone if she can help it because she just thinks there's such a stigma attached to the words *single parent*. And she says, "I try to say that I'm parenting alone or I don't know how I say it but I just try not to say that I'm a single parent."

As Carol and Sarah continued with the recorded interview, Sarah reiterated not just this awareness of stigma but also her concern about her losses from divorce, even though she believed separation was utterly necessary to ensure "a secure and good kind of future" for her family. She wrapped together a vision of normal family life, a language of citizenship, and even the religious imagery of a fall from a state of grace, to express her fear that she had been expelled from what she took to be a position of legitimacy in society:

> I had a hard time... in the beginning because family to me signi- fies a mother and a father with children and a dog and, you know, big household, balanced, happy, fun.... And initially when you do fall from the America apple pie dream you—someone like me—people look at you and they wonder what happened. And you look at them and you think, "Oh my God, they have what I used to have. And I don't have this anymore." I got a dog to make us feel more—like there were more of us. You know, that's one of the reasons I got the dog.... It just seemed—it seems like a family should have a dog, so we got a dog.

Sarah's efforts to reclaim her place in this "America apple pie dream" have extended beyond getting a dog, and she expresses sentiments that display her commitment to remaining a rightful member of her society as she has defined it. When Sarah talks about her children, she expresses a pride that reveals both her middle-class concern with their intellectual abilities and her more general motherly concern that, in spite of traumas, they enjoy psychological well-being and know the proprieties that will enable them to find a place in a particular social sphere: "They're smart and they've got good manners, and they're happy and at peace for the most part." And she includes herself in the category of *all* mothers (rather than assuming she has been cut off from this moral community) when she explains that she is "proud of my accomplishments with my children so far just like any other mom would be."

Indeed, throughout the interview, Sarah expressed a very deep com- mitment to core contemporary American values, even as she took steps that an outside observer might view as contradicting them. When Sarah talked about *why* she had considered relying on welfare, she explained it in terms of a "future" orientation rather than the "present" orientation that welfare reliance is assumed to reflect: "I would have gone on welfare in a minute to stay home with my kids. I think that's the best invest- ment I could have made." When she talked about her negotiations with the state for health insurance, she insisted on her honesty, even though, like many others, she assumes that dishonesty prevails among those who use means-tested programs: "I was very honest at the risk of not having my children qualify [for Doctor Dynasaur] whereas other people

will basically fib. There are people who will do that. And it's easy to do."
Sarah also spoke in moral terms about her dealings with the men in her
life. She is eager to be married again, but she is not willing to take advantage of a man (the babysitter) she does not love, and she is unwilling
to trade emotional and sexual involvement for his material assistance.
She also is not willing to allow the new man in her life to help her out
or even to introduce him to her children because, as she says, "It's still
the early stages."

As Sarah's story has already indicated, she relies heavily on the state for
health insurance and on a broad variety of friends and relatives for support in her daily life. Nonetheless, Sarah boasts about an independence
that she describes as even more compelling than what she experienced
as a married woman:

> I'm proud just knowing that I'm doing it on my own. I'm just
> getting a lot of satisfaction from knowing that I'm doing a pretty
> good job on my own. When you're sharing it with someone else
> you don't—I don't think you feel it as much as you do when you're
> doing it on your own.... Well, like [that's] normal and this is
> like, "Oh my God, I made it through another day." I'm proud of
> myself, yes.

In short, Sarah's social economy has an internal, albeit often contradictory, logic that accommodates to prevailing social values even though
her actions, from the outside, might appear to challenge those values.
This internal logic is ignored by conservative scholars who examine only
the discrepancy in outcomes between those assumed to be acting from
the right values and those assumed to be morally deficient. It is equally
ignored by more liberal scholars who take for granted that surviving
within narrow economic constraints makes talk of choices and values
irrelevant.[27]

DOING RESEARCH ON THE SOCIAL ECONOMY

In order to explore the social economy of single mothers, I rely on interviews conducted with a nonrandom, snowball sample of sixty-eight
respondents. Initially, I located these respondents by placing notices
describing the research project at various agencies that served the poor,
at a local parent-child center (a resource for young mothers and their
children), and at various day-care centers, preschools, and after-school
programs. Those who agreed to be interviewed were then asked to provide the names of other single mothers. The snowball sample technique

was particularly appropriate for this study because it often allowed my research assistants and me to interview multiple women within a single social support network.

The interviews generally lasted at least two hours; they were all taped and the tapes were subsequently transcribed. Most of the interviews were conducted in a single session; on occasion, however, the interview ran to two separate sessions.[28] As part of the interview, women were asked to discuss their survival strategies, paying particular attention to issues concerning the relationships they had developed with other individuals and the manner in which those relationships revolved around the exchange of necessary goods and services.[29]

We also asked respondents to draw diagrams of their support networks. If they had not already done so, we then asked them to discuss each person named on the diagram, including both a description of the circumstances under which support was exchanged and the kind of relationship that ensued. Most of the respondents drew arrows to indicate the direction of the flow of material and nonmaterial support.[30] The women also generally included a distance element: Those with whom they had less regular or less intense relationships were depicted as being farther away from the center. In short, in these drawings the respondents indicated both the degree of "equality" or reciprocity in their relationships *and* the degree of intimacy or closeness. As many of the quotes below illustrate, respondents found this task, as well as many of the interview questions, thought-provoking and sometimes even irritating; both the thoughtfulness and the moments of irritation guide the analysis that follows.

All interviews were conducted between 1995 and 2000 in Vermont and the vast majority of them were conducted in the rural area Joan Smith and I dubbed Coolidge County when we conducted research there on the survival strategies of married-couple families.[31] This practice ensured that I was familiar with the general demographic and economic characteristics of the area in which I was doing research; it also allowed me to make comparisons between single-parent and married-couple families with respect to specific components of their survival strategies (see chapter 1).

For many decades now the methods of social science have been subject to critiques from a broad range of commentators who argue that these methods are contaminated at every stage.[32] At one end of the research process, it is argued that the processes of data collection shape information gathered so that we cannot believe our evidence; at the other end, it is argued that the individual characteristics of the social scientist tarnish the claims to objective interpretation.[33] Scholars who focus on such claims sometimes tell more about themselves and the dilemmas of the research process than they do about their "substantive" findings.[34] While I do not intend to go in either of these directions, I acknowledge these critiques and I use them to inform the study.

All of those who conducted interviews for this study were white (as were our subjects), and all of us made reference to the fact that we were collecting information for a project that had its origins at a nearby liberal arts college.[35] All of us were committed to a contemporary approach to interviewing: We asked for informed consent, we were open to answering questions about who we were, and we discussed the goals of the research, even as those goals changed. Even so, this was not participant observation or "true" ethnography: We did not live among or befriend the respondents, but we instead walked into our respondents' lives, conducted our interviews, and walked out of those lives once more. And at no point did we equally make ourselves the objects of study.

Thus, no matter how conversational the interview might have become, it inevitably partook of a much maligned power differential.[36] No matter what techniques we employed to equalize the power relationship, and as sympathetic as we might have tried to be, we must have represented, at the very least, the public world that had found single motherhood to be a subject of some curiosity and interest. That is, there was no way around the fact that we wanted to know about our respondents' lives *because they were single mothers*; thus, by definition, we were defining "them" as somehow "different."[37]

This awareness of "difference" serves well the goals of uncovering the meaning attached to the construction and dynamics of the social economy of single mothers. As anthropologist Nicholas Townsend notes, "The more closely behaviors and situations conform to cultural norms, the less people feel the need to explain, account for, or elaborate on those behaviors."[38] And, both by virtue of cultural norms that identify the married-couple family as "normal," and the fact that the interview topic itself focused on deviations from that norm, we would expect that single mothers would offer explanations, accounts, and elaborations that would help reveal the meanings they attached to the dynamics of their daily lives. As Sarah's comments suggest, she is aware that this status *is* stigmatized. Sarah's comments also suggest that she has had to work hard—even beyond the effort of getting a dog—to make her current family form acceptable to her.[39]

There is another reason to expect that interviews will access rich accounts of how single mothers negotiate the prevailing values embedded in their cultural concerns. Being a single mother itself often represents a moment of transition and an episode in a life history. Sarah, for example, was living with her husband a mere eighteen months before we spoke with her; two years after that interview, we ran into her on the street and she was proudly wearing a new wedding ring. Her situation is not unusual, as the median length of time women wait to remarry after their first divorce is just over three years.[40]

Because women who are in transition from a cohabiting or marital relationship to being without a partner (and often back again) and women who are newly accommodating to the demands of single parenting live "unsettled" lives, we expect a rich engagement in "cultural work." As sociologist Ann Swidler writes in *Talk of Love: How Culture Matters*:[41]

> Culture works differently in settled and unsettled lives. In settled lives, culture is intimately integrated with action. Culture is ubiquitous, yet it is difficult to disentangle what is uniquely "cultural" since culture and life experience seem to reinforce each other.... In unsettled lives, in contrast, people use culture to organize new strategies of action and to model new ways of thinking and feeling. Cultural work is more active and its influence is more visible because the new patterns are in tension with previous modes of action and experience.

DESCRIBING SINGLE MOTHERS
Issues of Commonality

The women in this study, like Sarah, are all custodial parents of at least one child under age eighteen, but they differ considerably from the common stereotype of single mothers as members of a minority group who live in an urban ghetto and are extremely poor.[42] The single mothers in this study are all white, and in this they are *not* so atypical, despite the racist stereotype: In 2000, 64 percent of the nation's single mothers with a child under eighteen were white.[43] The women in this study live in the rural areas and small towns and cities of Vermont (most of them live in Coolidge County), and in this they are less typical: In 2000, less than one fifth of all single-mother households were found in nonmetropolitan areas. Although single mothers in Vermont face a range of economic struggles and rely on a range of economic resources, they are generally poorer than married couples in the same region, as is the case for single mothers throughout the country.[44] Each of these factors matters in the analysis that follows (see Table 1 for a description of the sample population compared with all single mothers and all married mothers in Vermont).

Table 1 Comparison of Single-Mother Sample with Single Mothers and Married Mothers in Vermont

	Sample		Single Mothers in Vermont*		Married Mothers in Vermont*	
	N	Percent	N	Percent	N	Percent
Age						
Less than 20	1	2	1	1	2	0
20–29	13	28	12	13	74	13
30–39	15	32	42	44	238	41
40+	18	38	41	43	273	47
Total	47	100	96	100	587	100
Mean		*34.7*		*38.0*		*38.5*
Median		*36.0*		*38.0*		*39.0*
Household Income						
Less than $10,000	5	12	14	15	6	1
$10,000–19,999	14	34	32	33	25	4
$20,000–29,999	7	17	25	26	46	8
$30,000–39,999	9	22	18	19	75	13
$40,000–49,999	4	10	5	5	92	16
$50,000 or more	2	5	2	2	342	58
Total	41	100	96	100	586	100
Mean		*$24,899*		*$22,781*		*$64,704*
Median		*$21,782*		*$21,125*		*$55,000*
Education						
LT HS	1	2	4	4	16	3
HS/GED	15	23	31	32	209	36
Some College	27	42	39	41	167	28
BA or more	22	34	22	23	195	33
Total	65	100	96	100	587	100
Age of Youngest Child						
LT6	34	56	29	30	220	37
6–18**	27	44	67	70	367	63
Total	61	100	96	100	587	100
Mean age		*6.6*		*9.2*		*7.94*
Median age		*5.0*		*9*		*8*
Age of Oldest Child						
LT6	22	36	11	11	117	20
6–18	23	54	79	82	432	74
Over 18	6	10	6	6	38	6
Total	61	100	96	100	587	100
Mean age		*9.5*		*11.8*		*11.1*
Median age		*8*		*12*		*12*

Table 1 Continued

	Sample		Single Mothers in Vermont*		Married Mothers in Vermont*	
	N	Percent	N	Percent	N	Percent
Number of Children						
1	29	44	42	44	187	32
2	22	33	43	45	273	47
3	11	17	8	8	87	15
4 or more	4	6	3	3	40	7
Total	66	100	96	100	587	100
Mean		*1.9*		*1.7*		*2.0*
Median		*2*		*2*		*2*
Marital Status						
Married, spouse present	1	2	4	4	585	100
Separated	1	2	16	17		
Divorced	35	60	52	54	1	
Widowed	2	3	3	3		
Never married/single	19	33	21	22	1	
Total	58	100	96	100	587	100
Living Arrangements						
Lives alone with children	44	73	69	63	503	85
Lives with another adult	16	17	26	27	87	15
Total	60	100	95	100	590	100
Current Welfare Reliance						
Yes	16	24	11	11	15	3
No	50	76	85	89	572	97
Total	66	100	96	100	587	100
Labor Force Participation						
Not in labor force	14	21	15	16	115	20
In labor force	52	79	81	84	472	80
Total	66	100	96	100	587	100

*Statistics for single mothers and married mothers in the state are author's calculations from the 2000 Census 5-Percent Public Use Microdata Sample (PUMS) for Vermont. For more information, see www.census.gov/Press-Release/www/2003/PUMS5.html.
**All single mothers in the sample had at least one child under the age of 18.

Women as the Subject

Much writing about gender focuses on the ways in which men and women differ from one another. These "differences" are especially apparent in the fact that most single parents are women.[45] A biological reality is obviously relevant here, but this fact does not rest on biology alone. The predominance of women among single parents has much to do with how men and women view responsibilities stemming from sexual encounters; it also has to do with their own and their partners' gendered assumptions about who can best provide care for young children (see especially chapter 4) as well as with "public" assumptions. Although in theory the courts are neutral, when custody decisions are made all parties often agree that the best interest of the child is achieved by having the child continue to live with the mother. Even before custody battles, however, gender and gender norms play a significant role in the likelihood of premarital pregnancy, as they do in why relationships fail, and thus in why mothers become single through separation, divorce, and the disruption of cohabiting relationships.[46]

Significant for the issues in this book, gender is also relevant to the material conditions under which women live when they become single parents.[47] The fact that sex segregation exists in the labor force and the related fact that women's wages are, on average, but three quarters of men's wages, do much to explain the low incomes of single mothers.[48] Other forms of income and support are shaped by gender as well: For example, family and friends offer different kinds of assistance to single mothers than to single fathers. And of course, the benefits of the welfare state in the United States, though not necessarily explicitly gendered in terms of provisions (i.e., these benefits are available to single fathers as well as to single mothers, and on occasion, to two-parent families), are in and of themselves the results of gendered (and racist) assumptions in the world.[49]

Gender is also a way to describe norms of appropriate behavior that differ for men and women. When we visited with Sarah she apologized for the messiness of her home, even as she laughed at the fact that hers was a commonplace concern. She also said that her greatest source of pride rests in her children, even as she acknowledged that this, too, was a deeply gendered sentiment ("and I am proud of my children so far just like any other mom would be"). When we asked her about the losses she had endured since separating from her husband, she spoke of her struggles to make up for his prior contributions to a very traditional division of labor, where men's housework efforts are considered "help": "He was a help in a lot, in a hundred million ways. He emptied the trash and fixed the roof. He did a million very helpful things." This gendered division of labor left Sarah without some skills she now requires if she is going to get by on her own; it also left her believing that she was justified in asking for help, from those who had the skills, when need and circumstance arose.[50] This same pattern shapes Sarah's inclination, even if she resists it, to ask the new man in her life to take a look at her leaky faucet. In short, in describing the lives of single mothers, I am describing a deeply gendered experience, even if gender is sometimes invisible in this account.

A Rural Locale

As noted, Sarah chose Vermont for practical reasons and because she believed that in such a setting she could find a "tight community." I have noted as well that, in Sarah's case, this tight community sometimes took the form of the too-close and even overwhelming presence of her parents. As will be discussed further, other women also acknowledged the significance of, and the desire for, community as providing sustenance in their daily lives and in one of life's rich contradictions, simultaneously commented on the fact that a small community can entail an undesired visibility and loss of privacy. The women also made note of the fact that the rural community of Vermont held some very traditional notions about family life and thus made the challenge of finding entry into a sociable world more difficult than it might have been elsewhere. In material ways too, as we will see, the rural environment of Vermont both simplifies some aspects of daily life (e.g., minimal traffic and relatively easy access to social services), and makes others far more burdensome (e.g., dependence on a car and the hazards of severe weather).

Race and Ethnicity

In describing the lives of single mothers in Vermont, I am not only describing a gendered and rural experience, but I am also, as noted above, describing a "white" one.[51] Vermont remains among the "whitest" states in the nation—a whiteness that is symbolically manifest in the state's churches and clapboard houses and in the snow that blankets the landscape during the long months of winter. But, as we will see in what follows, and as Sarah has already suggested, whiteness does not protect single mothers from being seen as inadequate or their families from being seen as deficient. Recall that Sarah noted that her father did not "respect" single parenthood and that Sarah herself has concerns about her legitimacy.

Furthermore, whiteness does not protect single mothers from the stigmas of poverty and welfare reliance. In fact, the language used to characterize the latter stigma—by the general public and by the respondents themselves, whether or not they relied on welfare—was precisely the same language of laziness and lax morals used to describe welfare recipients in the country as a whole (even though the majority of those who are poor are incorrectly assumed to be African-American). The similarity in characterization reminds us that although racism certainly stands behind attitudes toward welfare, at least some of the animus is less about race than it is about who fills a certain position within a capitalist labor force.[52] As anthropologist Karen Brodkin writes, "When immigrants [from Europe] were seen as a necessary part of that working class which did the degraded and driven labor, they were constructed with the stereotypes of blackness—stupid, shiftless, sexual, unable to defer gratification."[53]

At the same time, it should be remembered that the women in this study *were* white and thus preserved at least *some* of the privileges accorded whiteness in our society. As we will see in the next chapter, when Vermonters debated making changes to the existing welfare regime they did so with less of a "social threat discourse," and the resulting Welfare Restructuring Plan *is* kinder and gentler than is the case elsewhere.[54]

Meager Incomes

Finally, the respondents' incomes extended from a low of $5,980 for a woman who was welfare reliant at the time we spoke with her, through the state median for single mothers (in 2000) of $21,175 to an outlier high of $66,000. However, *most* of the women lived *most of the time* below what has been deemed a self-sufficiency level in Vermont (see chapter 1), even if some (9% of the total) had yearly incomes that exceeded that amount.

Differences Among the Women

If the respondents in this study are all women of the same race who all live in a rural locale and struggle with relative poverty, they do differ from one another in some very significant ways. These differences also shape the problems they face and the ways in which they cope.

Marital Status and Living Arrangements

The women in this study became single mothers through a variety of routes. Sarah represents the most common of these: 62 percent of the single mothers in the sample were either separated or divorced. In this, the single mothers in this sample are quite similar to single mothers in the state (71% of whom are separated or divorced) and also to white single mothers in the United States (63% of whom are either separated or divorced).[55] A considerably smaller proportion of single mothers in the study (33%) had never been married; this sample slightly exceeds state averages (22%) even though it is precisely the same as that of white women in the United States as a whole. In addition, 3 percent of the women in the study were widows, as are 3 percent of single mothers in the state, and 5 percent of the national population of white single mothers.

The most commonly used census categories differentiate among four major types of single mothers: never married, spouse absent (which includes those who are separated from their husbands), divorced, and widowed. These categories conceal the complexity of single mothers' lives. For example, three women in this study adopted children on their own (in two cases following a prior childless marriage and in another case without ever having been married). Several women had been married more than once and had children within more than one marriage, and in one case, outside of a marriage as well.

These categories also conceal change. I have already noted that for many women single motherhood represents but an episode in a life history.[56] Although the women included in this sample, on average, had been single for somewhat longer than the average for divorced women, they represent the full range of positions along a continuum. A substantial proportion of the women, like Sarah, had been single mothers for less than two years, and a few were still in the process of separation. At the same time, some of the women had settled into single motherhood and did not plan to remarry; others were actively in pursuit of new relationships (see chapter 5). In some cases, the new relationships were moving toward marriage: Three women identified the person with whom they were living as a fiancé. One woman was already remarried and chose to be interviewed because her new husband played no role in raising her child from her previous marriage. She said, "The mother part about it is definitely a single mother. I mean, single as part of the relationship I'm not, but as far as the motherhood part, I am. There's no ... sharing."

Other Demographic Characteristics

In other ways too, the mothers varied. The women themselves ranged in age from nineteen to fifty-one, with an average of thirty-five, which is close to the average age of single mothers in the state. Their children also ranged in age, from an average of almost seven for the youngest child in the family to just over nine for the oldest. Almost half of the women had only one child, but at least four women in the sample had four or more.

The women varied as well in terms of human capital assets. Although a majority of the women had completed some college or more, one quarter of them had no more than a high school certificate or equivalency, and one woman had not completed high school when we spoke with her. All but one fifth of the women were in the labor force at least part-time when we spoke with them, including some women who were also welfare reliant.

LEARNING FROM DIFFERENCE

I actively sought this diversity among my respondents because it reflects well the variety of single mothers in our society (in turn reflecting the increasingly diverse reasons for this status) and enables me to make a broader argument.

Growing Numbers and Diverse Causes

Because the trends producing single-parent families represent widespread social currents, the probability that a woman will spend some part of her lifetime as a single mother is greater now than it has been at any time in the past.[57] Between 1970 and 2000 the number of single-mother families increased from 3 million to 10 million, from 12 percent of all families to 26 percent;[58] between 1940 and 1999 births to unmarried women rose from almost 4 percent to almost 33 percent.[59] If women in rural (nonmetropolitan) areas once lagged behind in rates of both female-headed households and births to unmarried women, they are now catching up.[60]

Several explanations can be found for the growing number of single-mother families both in Vermont and in the United States.[61] One of these is the disappearance of men's "family wage"—a wage historically developed to be high enough to support a family single-handedly. This disappearance means that men are less able to support their families on their earnings alone, and perhaps less willing to join or make commitments to a family in the absence of that ability.[62] Scholars have written much about this phenomenon as it applies to urban areas and to minority populations; it is a phenomenon increasingly evident in rural areas as well.[63]

The disappearing family wage is also one of the major causes of the growing participation in the labor force by women in all marital categories. In 1960 just over one third (37.7%) of all women and less than one third (30.4%) of mothers with children under 18 were in the labor force; today these numbers have mushroomed to almost two thirds (60.2%) and almost three quarters (72.9%), respectively.[64] As a consequence of *this* trend, women are more able—or, as is more commonly the case, *appear* more able—to support themselves as a result of their own earnings.

Shifts in attitudes toward divorce (e.g., no-fault divorce), sexual practices (e.g., more sexual activity outside of marriage), and living arrangements (e.g., increasing rates of cohabitation) also contribute to the growing numbers of single parents, as do shifts in attitudes toward "unwed" parenting.[65] The pregnant white teenager who, in the 1950s, was either encouraged to get married or to give up the child for adoption, is today likely to raise the child on her own.[66] Older single women as well have not only chosen to keep children born outside of a marital relationship, but a growing number of these women have actively sought to become mothers through artificial insemination and adoption. Perhaps as a result of these shifts, in 1998 the U.S. Census Bureau reported that for the first time the majority of first children (53%) were born to or conceived by an unmarried woman.[67]

In this context of widespread social changes standing behind the "production" of single motherhood, it is particularly ironic that since the mid-1990s there have been few efforts designed to ease the lives of single parents, but instead there have been social changes that increase the challenges single parents face and make such individuals more subject to social disdain. This is no accident: It was both the growing numbers of single mothers *and* the fact that a large proportion of single mothers are poor that led to debates about welfare in the 1990s, culminating in the 1996 Personal Responsibility and Work Opportunity Reconciliation Act (PRWORA), which not only ended welfare as an entitlement, but also proclaimed the moral centrality of marriage as official public policy.[68]

An Argument from Variety

The variety of single mothers included in this book also serves the ends of my argument. Scholarship focusing exclusively on single mothers who are living below the poverty level or are on welfare overlooks problems that transcend extreme poverty or welfare reliance, and it fixes single mothers as if they are always in one situation. Similarly, the literature that focuses on a specific group of single mothers (such as those who have not been married or those who are divorced), both works from, and leads to, the assumption that the most significant issues confronting single mothers are a consequence of the route they took to single motherhood rather than being inherent to or emerging from the daily problems that confront all single mothers.[69] In dealing with a broader range of women, I can attend to struggles that depend on women's particular situations (e.g., the different configurations of the social economies of those who are reliant on welfare and those who are not) while also attending to common themes and issues that accompany a woman's attempt to create a survival strategy that responds to both her ethical *and* her material concerns. This is not to deny the significance of any of the conditions on which women vary: As will be shown below, income matters (and it often matters a great deal), and women who have lived with the father(s) of their child(ren) face some very different issues from those who have had a child outside of a committed relationship (see chapter 4). But in this book I argue that the form and shape of both the challenges faced by single mothers, and the solutions they develop to meet those challenges, transcend their particular position within the social hierarchy as well as their personal histories.

ORGANIZATION AND OVERVIEW

In chapter 1, I explore in more detail both the material and ideological contexts within which single mothers develop their social economy. In the first half of the chapter, I describe the Vermont economy with respect to both its distinctive features and its similarity to the country as a whole. In the second half of the chapter I focus on two central sets of ideological issues facing single mothers. The first concerns issues of self-sufficiency; the second concerns the notion that the single-parent family is inadequate and even defective.

Having set the context for this study, in each of the next four chapters I turn to an arena in which the social economy of single mothers is developed. In chapter 2, I look at the issues that emerge as single mothers make choices—as Sarah did about child care—concerning how to draw on family, friends, and the broader community for ongoing material and emotional support. As I examine these different sets of relationships, I establish a key building block to my broader argument: I characterize the web of relationships from which single mothers derive essential material and nonmaterial support and, even more significantly, I demonstrate how these vital affiliations are adjusted according to concerns about both stigma (through the careful choice of members of their social networks) and independence (through manipulations of the concept of reciprocity).

In chapter 3, I examine how the broad groups of single mothers who have ever relied on any form of means-tested assistance from the state come to view this as an acceptable practice, even as public opinion regards it with moral disapprobation. In the first part of the chapter I show that a common set of concerns about stigma motivate the majority of women who rely on means-tested programs to find justifications for that use. I then compare in more detail the attitudes and explanations of those women who relied on welfare before the 1990s restructuring with the attitudes and explanations of those who received assistance in the more recent past. I argue that notions of reciprocity remain significant even when dealing with state officials.

In chapter 4, I shift to an examination of the specific site in which the social economy is enacted. As I turn to the household of the single mother itself, I emphasize the complexities and contradictions that emerge as single mothers make a purportedly private realm into a very social arena. I first consider the issue of how limited material resources shape enactment of an ideal of being a good mother to one's children. I next show that single mothers assume additional roles in conjunction with their assessments of the father's role in child rearing, and, in the last section of the chapter, I turn to the issue of how single mothers manage the conflicts that emerge as they draw other individuals into their family dynamics.

As was the case for Sarah, many single mothers find that this status constitutes but a relatively brief period in their lives. Chapter 5 examines how romantic partners are incorporated into the ongoing social economy of single motherhood. Finally, in the Conclusion, I consider the range of social policy proposals that have been developed to address the problems single mothers experience, and I examine closely the contributions single mothers themselves make to the ongoing debates about how to improve their daily lives.

1

THE CONTEXT OF SINGLE MOTHERS' LIVES[1]

THE MATERIAL WORLD

When I attended summer camp in Vermont as a child, one of the facts I knew about the place I came to love was that it held within its borders more cows than people. While that is no longer the case—Vermont now boasts slightly more people than cows—the rural image still prevails.[2] A "Made in Vermont" label sells products because it reminds us of a long lost way of life—of "intact" families roused by the rooster; of men, women, and children getting breakfast on the table and putting hay in the stalls; of waits for the yellow school bus; of maple syrup; of barn-studded fields; of white churches in valleys; and of rolling hills leading to green mountains.[3]

If the school buses, churches, valleys, fields, hills, and mountains of Vermont remain, there are now fewer cows and barns, and contemporary families are more likely to be getting children to day care and making their way to offices, factories, and stores than they are to be making maple syrup or feeding the cows. As was the case in many rural areas, Vermont went through a round of industrialization in the second half of the twentieth century which by the 1970s resulted in a greater portion of the labor force being employed in manufacturing than in agriculture. As was also the case in many rural areas, Vermont then went through a round of deindustrialization whereby those new manufacturing jobs were replaced by jobs in the service sector.[4] As a result of that restructuring, the distribution of Vermont's labor force mirrors that of the U.S. labor force as a whole, with few jobs in agriculture, forestry, fishing, hunting, and mining (Vermont, 3%, United States, 1.9%); few jobs in manufacturing (Vermont, 15.1%, United States, 14.1%); and many service jobs

(Vermont, 44.5%, United States, 42%).[5] For many this change has yielded far less predictable employment and a far less secure financial position than was possible in 1980.

Women in the Vermont Economy

Employment Options

Women's jobs are distributed differently from those of men in the Vermont economy of the early twenty-first century: As is the case for women everywhere, service jobs of all types are the single most common industry category followed (at some distance) by trade. Together, these two industries account for almost two-thirds (60.9%) of Vermont's female labor force, as opposed to less than half—45.6 percent—of the male labor force, 73 percent of employed single mothers in the state, and 86 percent of the employed women in this study.[6]

Although these are generally low-paying industries in Vermont, as they are everywhere, Vermont women are "lucky" relative to women in other states insofar as their earnings are high in comparison with those of their male counterparts. In 2001, among those who worked full-time, Vermont women's median weekly earnings ($509) were 82 percent of men's earnings ($622); in the United States as a whole, women's median weekly earnings ($511) were 76 percent of men's earnings ($672).[7] But, as these figures suggest, Vermont's wages are low: In 2001 Vermont workers had, on average, wages that were 83 percent of the national median.[8]

Single mothers in Vermont, like those elsewhere, work hard to earn these wages. Although employment outside the home is the modal experience for all mothers, single mothers in Vermont now slightly exceed married mothers both in their rates of labor force participation (84% vs. 80%) and among those who are employed in the hours they devote to paid work (an average of 33 hours per week vs. an average of 30 hours per week). The comparable figures in the United States are labor force participation rates of 81.4 percent for single mothers versus 73.2 percent for married mothers and work weeks of 33.9 hours for single mothers versus 33.7 hours for married mothers.[9]

Single mothers also have to work hard simply to sustain their labor force involvement. With the exception of the unpaid provisions for family leaves offered through the 1993 Family and Medical Leave Act, neither federal nor state provisions support the formation and continuation of family life. As a result, individual workers can only depend on the benefits their employers provide.[10] Health insurance, paid vacations, and sick leave are crucial for all workers: Without these benefits, for all their best intentions, even married couples with children find it difficult to keep both adults employed.[11] These difficulties are compounded for single parents because they cannot share the costs of employment or divide the penalties of missing work when they or their children are sick.[12] Consider twenty-four-year-old, never married, Kitty Thompson. Now that her daughter is four years old, Kitty is employed full-time outside the home. But she explained that her attempts to join the labor force with a young child failed repeatedly:

> I didn't [work steadily] when [my daughter] was really young. It was always every six months I would have to get a new job, because I would miss work too much because of her asthma, because of court [re. child support], or she was running a high fever and day care wouldn't take her. So that was a very big struggle for me.

Women who had steady employment when married indicated that their work/family conflicts intensified when they became single mothers and, in turn, gave rise to new reliance on their children and on others in their social networks.[13] A recently divorced thirty-three-year-old mother of four sons ranging in age from six to thirteen, Melissa Henry leaves her children alone for an hour each morning as she sets off for work and she asks the older ones to help the younger ones get dressed and ready for the school bus; she also allows these children to return home to an empty house each afternoon, and she asks them to do more chores than they did before their father left. When she puts in overtime on Saturday mornings, Melissa leaves her children with family members and friends. Twenty-nine-year-old Anne Davenport's challenges are compounded by the young age of her children. When she was married Anne worked evenings at her commission-sales job, and, before his alcoholism rendered him unreliable, left her two preschool-age children in her husband's care. Once she separated from him, Anne struggled to come up with alternative appropriate arrangements: "[It's hard] getting used to not having somebody else there," she explained.[14]

Kitty, Melissa, and Anne all want and need to work outside the home, and all of them feel the pinch between the demands of employment and the needs of their children. In Kitty's case, her child's needs briefly "won out" and she relied on welfare for a few years. In Melissa's case, a work-based strategy of survival sometimes jeopardizes her own conceptions of what it means to be a good mother to her children and it sometimes exacerbates her feelings of dependence on others. Anne experiences all of these problems: She now relies on welfare to supplement her income, which is reduced both because of her husband's absence and because she cannot now work as much as she did before her divorce; she sometimes worries about the competence of the teenagers with whom she leaves her sons when she goes to her evening job; and she finds herself calling on her parents far more often than she did when she was married.

Child Care and Transportation

For all of these women, as for their peers, finding and making adequate arrangements for child care are unending struggles.[15] The increased labor force participation of all women, the rise in single-parent families, and the new stipulation that welfare recipients seek employment, have put enormous pressure on the existing supply of day care.[16] Waiting lists, especially for very young children, can be as long as two years (by which time the children are no longer quite so young).[17] Locating care poses special problems for a woman like Anne who does not work regular day-time hours, and for a woman like Melissa, who works most weekends.[18] Women in these types of situations are likely to fall back on less formal arrangements. Susan Barrows, who is twenty-one and has never been married, may be exercising her preference for care by relatives when she leaves her two-year-old son with her parents as she goes off to her evening job as a waitress.[19] But Susan has few other options and when she relies on her parents, she incurs another set of ongoing obligations.

The cost of child care compounds these difficulties. Day care expenses for one child can run to more than $400 per week.[20] Some single mothers find, quite simply, that they cannot afford to work outside the home: Anne Davenport's good friend Joan Meyer, a mother of three children, said two years after her divorce, "I would like to be out working, but working for me is almost impossible because of the day care costs. And so I'm like in limbo." Child care subsidies do exist for those who are poor, and in Vermont subsidies are available on a sliding scale for those with incomes below $31,031.[21] These subsidies, however, rarely cover the full cost of care.[22] And when women like Anne, Melissa, and Susan rely on teenagers, friends, and relatives to watch their children, the possibility of getting any state reimbursement is precluded.

If child care discussions peppered the conversations we had with single mothers, talk about transportation was often the main dish. It came up when the women talked about their criteria for acceptable jobs, which they wanted to be within easy commuting distance, and when they talked about getting young children to day care and older children to and from school and after-school activities. In short, transportation is a major hassle for single mothers regardless of their employment status, and like child care, it draws them into informal arrangements with, and frequently dependence on, others.[23]

Because there is virtually no public transportation in Vermont (outside of the more urban areas), there is no easy or inexpensive solution to this challenge. Transportation costs in Vermont can run to more than $250 a month, even though the overall cost of living in the state is comparatively low.[24] Rural women also have to contend with the unpredictable expense of car repair, especially if they have old cars. Two women, each very recently separated from her partner, made specific reference to these troubles as having cast into disarray their efforts to survive in straitened circumstances: "My car got fixed last week and that was $145"; "Well, just a couple of months ago I had an $850 bill for new brakes and brake pads and stuff, so that really took a chunk out [of my budget]." Two other women, both newly off welfare assistance and trying to make ends meet in the absence of the grants offered by the state's welfare-to-work program (called Reach Up), also cited these expenses as the item most likely to disrupt their careful budgeting: "I needed money more than once [and] it all had to do with my car breaking down, money for repairs"; "I would like to have food stamps but I can do without them, but . . . you know, my car insurance is due, oh my God—or I got a flat tire, I need a new tire, what am I going to do?"

In fact, because the stories surrounding this issue were so very compelling, one of the interviewers for this study offered to ask *her* (male) partner if he would do some repairs for a woman with whom she spoke. As she explains in her field notes, she knew that this repair would be a major expense if purchased from a mechanic, but would be easy enough to accomplish for someone with the appropriate skills:

> Kate Harrington brought up again the problem with her vehicle, and because I had to reschedule this interview to have my brakes fixed, she asked about it, who had done it, and I mentioned my partner had, and so I was drawn into her network myself by offering to ask my partner if he would be willing to do a rather simple repair. Simple, but one that I know will be expensive if she has to go to a mechanic. I will, hopefully, talk [my partner] into doing this good deed.

To be sure, employment in urban areas also often requires long commutes, and urban transportation, without doubt, entails stress. To an urban parent, trying to catch a subway or bus with small children, strollers, briefcases, and knapsacks in tow, it might appear far simpler to get into a car to drive to work and school. But the grass is always greener on the other side and those who rely on cars for daily transportation know well the vagaries of flat tires, unplowed roads, accidents, and inadequate car heating systems. Moreover, there is no way around having to use the car: Almost no facet of daily life can be accomplished when the car is in the shop (including getting to and from the shop) and for much of the year in Vermont the weather is not only cold, but bitterly cold.[25]

The Importance of Infrastructure

Single mothers for whom informal network arrangements already exist can find ways to ease some of the most difficult problems relating to daily work/family conflicts. Melissa Henry tries to save *her* sick days for times when her children are ill. If she runs short of paid time off, she can draw on a variety of friends and relatives in the area (as she does to cover the overtime she puts in on Saturday morning); if her car breaks down, she hitches a ride with a neighbor who works for the same company. Kelly Nye, a twenty-year-old mother of a three-year-old son, lives with her mother and, like Melissa, is embedded in a community rich in extended family members. Consequently, even though she has fewer paid vacation days than Melissa, she too has been able to avoid absences and thus prevent having her pay docked: "I ask my mom to take care of my son if he's sick. If she can't do it, my grandparents will watch him." When Kelly's car breaks down she can catch a ride with her cousin who lives close by and works in the same town as she does. In her interview, Kelly expressed considerable pride that both her "attendance" at work and the evaluation she received for her performance improved over the past year; her explanations for how she manages to show up at work reliably suggest that these achievements rest on an entire network of individuals who are able (and at this point willing) to support her as she makes her way in the world.

Single mothers do not invariably have this infrastructure in place. The work of having to create a network that can be mobilized for regular, but unpredictable, crises constitutes an additional burden. As Sarah Stanley said, "I worked really hard to make these friends." Moreover, as is discussed in chapter 2, both because dependence on others is hard to sustain psychologically and because even close friends and family members might want some return for the support they provide, reliance on others (whether they are readily available or not) requires some form of reciprocal gesture and thus creates work at different times.

Working Hard and Staying Poor

Measuring Poverty

Since 1978 when Diana Pearce coined the phrase "the feminization of poverty," it has become an acknowledged truism that children and adults in families headed by single women live less well than do those in families headed by married couples.[26] The situation for single mothers in the rural state of Vermont is little different from that of single mothers in the rest of the country, even though the former are predominantly white and the latter are more diverse in their race/ethnicity.[27] As noted in the Introduction, the median income for single-mother families in Vermont in 2000 was $21,175; in the United States as a whole, the median income for single mothers was $22,893 (and for white, non-Hispanic single-mother families, it was $27,427).[28] To get some sense of what these income figures mean, we can compare them to both the standard poverty level and the quite different estimates of what is minimally required to make ends meet.

First, the standard poverty level is significant because it is the reference point for access to most means-tested services. In Vermont, for example, some programs serve only clients who fall below the federal poverty line; others, such as Dr. Dynasaur extend to those whose incomes are 300 percent of that level. In 1999, by which time the interviews for this study were essentially completed, the poverty level was $11,060 for a family of two and $13,880 for a family of three, making the median income (of $21,175) almost twice as high as the poverty level.[29] A significant proportion of single-parent families—almost one third of those with related children under eighteen and almost half of those with related children under five years of age—live below the poverty level in Vermont. By way of comparison, for married-couple families with related children under eighteen the poverty rate is just below 10 percent (9.7%) and among those with related children under five it is slightly above that (13%). The situation in Vermont is not anomalous: In the United States as a whole comparable figures show that slightly more than one third of all female-headed families with related children under eighteen live in poverty as do 46 percent of those with related children under five. Among all single-mother families, poverty rates for those with related children under eighteen is 14 percent and for those with related children under five, it is 17 percent[30] (see Table 1.1). These statistics not only indicate that many single mothers are "officially" poor, but they suggest as well that a large percentage of families headed by single mothers will be eligible for means-tested state programs and will have to make a choice about whether or not to take advantage of them (see chapter 3).

Because the poverty level has been subject to enormous political critique, many suggest using an alternative measure such as a "basic needs" or "self-sufficiency budget," which takes into account the real expenses of maintaining daily life.[31] Using this kind of standard, it has been estimated that a single parent with one child living in Vermont would need

Table 1.1 Percent of Single Mothers Living Below Federal Poverty Level

Family Structure	Sample	Percent Below (1999) Poverty Level* Vermont	United States
All families	—	6.3	9.2
With related children under 18 years	—	9.7	13.6
With related children under 5 years	—	12.9	17.0
Families with female head, no husband present	—	24.1	26.5
With related children under 18 years	19.5	31.0	34.3
With related children under 5 years	23.1	49.4	46.4

*In 1999 the poverty level was set at $11,060 for a family of two and $13,880 for a family of three (see U.S. Department of Health and Human Services, "The 1999 HHS Poverty Guidelines"). *Source*: U.S. Census of the Population, "Quick Tables 2002" (http://factfinder.census.gov/).

an annual income of $28,364 to $37,634 in a rural area and $30,288 to $39,653 in an urban area.[32] My calculations from the 5 percent census sample for Vermont indicate that upwards of two thirds of all single-parent families with one child, and upwards of 86 percent of those with two children, have incomes that do not bring them to this level; among the women in this sample, 70 percent of those with one child and 73 percent of those with two children live below the lowest self-sufficiency budget estimates.[33] Economic insufficiency, then, is the modal experience for single mothers in the state, as it is for the sample of single mothers included in this study (see Table 1.2).

But meeting the standard of a self-sufficiency budget does not ensure ready accessibility to needed goods and services. Tiffany Morrow, a thirty-nine-year-old widow, combined her income from wages and Social Security to achieve a total close to that estimated as producing self-sufficiency in her community. Even so she talked about how she constantly had to juggle bills and prioritize among competing needs simply to meet her ongoing expenses; indeed, even as she talked, she juggled these priorities:

> How many [late payment] slips are there? That's unfortunately very serious, because there is never enough money to go around. But basically what I do is find out what needs the most urgent attention. I get lots of calls, unfortunately, from bill collectors. So I make a priority list. One month something gets paid, and then the next month I pay another. Like one month the electric bill will get paid, and then that will have to go because the health

Table 1.2 Income Relative to the (1997) Livable Wage*

Income Relative to Livable Wage	Sample Population		Vermont Population **		
	One Child	Two Children	Single Parent with One Child	Single Parent with Two Children	Married Mothers with Fathers Present (assumes two earners)
Income below lowest livable wage	70%	73%	67%	86%	31%
Income between lowest and highest livable wage estimates	20%	20%	29%	12%	23%
Income above highest livable wage estimate	10%	7%	5%	2%	46%
Total	100%	100%	100%	100%	100%
N	20	15	28	43	273

* Livable wage estimates vary with family size, residential location (urban or rural), and access to health insurance through Medicaid or employers (Ellen Kahler, *The Vermont Job Gap Study, Phase I: Basic Needs and a Livable Wage* [Burlington, VT: Peace & Justice Center, 1997]).
** Author's calculations from 5 percent census data for Vermont.

insurance is due, and then, you know, when there's no health in-surance bill then the electric bill, and the telephone bill, and the mortgage. The mortgage is number one. The mortgage and the car. I make sure those get paid because I can't afford to not have my car to go to work, and I can't afford to not have my house to house my children.

At age forty, Liz Miles's earnings from her job, combined with the child support she receives from the fathers of her two children, bring her income close to the "living wage" level for a family of her size. Still, she talked about the compromises she was forced to make as she sought to meet her own needs and those of her children. As she spoke, she made clear that she weighed the high cost of items such as clothing against other priorities, including her own desire to present herself well in the world, her attempts to meet her daughter's desire to be au courant, and the daily work that goes into sustaining a modest selection of clothing:

I don't buy very much.... In the past I've bought a lot at yard sales and what happened is I'm really tired of wearing other people's clothes. I'm tired of buying clothes because they're cheap at yard sales, that don't quite fit or aren't quite [right]....It's embarrassing to me to go somewhere [wearing something that] may be a little tight, or it's a little stained or it's a little ripped because it was somebody else's. So I guess what I do now is I buy very little and I buy something that's going to last, good quality that's going to last. But we don't have much selection. [For] my son, I still buy [clothes at a discount store] because he isn't conscious of it. But I buy good [brands], like Wrangler....But my daughter wants Gap jeans. So, I'll buy [them] for her. She has, like, two pairs of jeans but they're Gap jeans. But then it's hard because, you know, you have to do laundry in the middle of the week.

Even Poorer

Although a basic needs standard, based on an assessment of what is actually necessary for daily survival, improves our understanding of the economic constraints operating in the lives of those who are poor, even that measure misses several significant features of the economy of single mothers and particularly those features that lead to asking others for help. There are two primary explanations for this fact.

First, many single mothers are not "just" poor, but they are newly poor. Though many researchers have challenged Lenore Weitzman's conclusion that women's standard of living declined by 73 percent following divorce (while men's rose by 43 percent), few deny that divorce has devastating economic consequences for women.[34] When asked what happened to her finances after her divorce, Sarah Stanley, matter-of-factly declared, "Well, there was $50,000 less right there." And many women suggested that equally large shifts in their incomes had led not only to difficulties in meeting basic needs, but also to difficulties in assessing the legitimacy of those needs. For example, Megan Paige, the divorced forty-two-year-old mother of three children, explained:

If I were two people working my job twice, earning the same amount that I have and having these same three kids, we would be fine. I literally need to make twice as much money as I do to be financially stable, pay for all of it, and have enough socked away for my actual retirement. So how can I make it on half? I don't know. I'm not exaggerating when I say that. Because I think this lifestyle that I have—a lot of it is [that] you sort of inherit a lifestyle when you get divorced. I know there's a lot of women with three kids making it with a lot less money than I have, but in a sense you inherit a series of expectations, and the house I'm living in isn't really designed for me to pay for it myself and that kind of thing, so literally if there were two of me I'd be fine.

Second, the novelty of poverty is compounded for those who are simultaneously experiencing the novelty of parenthood. Although many women become single mothers through divorce or through separation from either marital or cohabiting relationships, many become single mothers at the same time that they become new mothers. Not surprisingly, these women—not all of whom are young—find themselves overwhelmed by the new and multifaceted demands on their lives. In chapter 2 we will hear more from Kate Harrington, who gave birth to her first child at age thirty-six. In explaining how difficult she was finding her new life, Kate elided her two statuses—of a single woman with a child and of a new mother—into one: "Everything is pretty much going into learning how to be a single mother. And handling this like, 24-7, just me."

Unpredictable Change and Intersections

If novelty weren't strain enough, single mothers also have to contend with a high degree of ongoing, and often unpredictable, change in their daily lives. Because most of our usual measurements of economic well-being rely on a snapshot image, they miss this fact. Studies that identify single mothers as living below the poverty level, for example, generally ignore variations in income over time. Even Kathryn Edin and Laura Lein's detailed examination of the financial resources of single mothers focuses on income and expenditures for a single month and thus, because an individual's income in one month may not be at all indicative of her income the previous or subsequent months, cannot assess how each of these varies throughout a year.[35] Expenditures also vary widely: A single car repair or broken furnace can disrupt all attempts to plan. To be sure, the statistics that Edin and Lein offer represent a meaningful assessment of the *average* life of single mothers. But, variations in income and expenditures constitute their own source of anxiety, especially because they occur in the context of already straitened resources.

A key reason for the highly unpredictable income of single mothers has its roots in the simple fact that a substantial portion of it comes from child support. In the United States as a whole, many women do not receive any child support at all.[36] But even those who do receive child support rarely get the full amount they are supposed to receive in a given year. When Melissa Henry and her husband separated she painstakingly constructed a budget that would allow her to meet her major expenses and provide what she believes is appropriate care for her four sons. Her ex-husband has not paid regularly, however, and he owes her more than $5,000 in back payments. As a result, she has now found herself deeply in debt and she is having trouble meeting her monthly house and car payments (each more than $200), especially because a recent disaster with the clutch on her car entirely wiped out her modest savings.

A second source of unpredictability comes from commonplace features of women's employment. Not only does economic restructuring continue in Vermont, with substantial layoffs occurring regularly in the manufacturing sector, but as service workers, women are especially likely to have jobs subject to seasonal fluctuations and the whims of tourists. When asked whether she had ever relied on unemployment insurance, one woman asserted that it was a regular part of her annual survival strategy, and she had used it "every off-season" for the past three years. Off-season, she further explained, was "twice a year—in the spring and in the fall."

A third source of unpredictability emerges as earnings meet benefit cliffs. Many social programs designed to offer support for the poor operate not on a sliding scale (although some, like the child care subsidies do), but rather as an on–off switch. As individuals experience even modest increases in their earnings (through such means as getting a better job or receiving a bonus at work), they are suddenly excluded from programs on which they had been relying. Since increased earnings rarely substitute adequately for lost support, individuals who have more "income" may well be *less* able to make ends meet. Liz Miles described her frustration with having to make calculations that pitted her own need to feel accomplished and self-sufficient against her overall economic status: "I feel like every step of the way that I have gotten raises, I have lost programs to help support me. So it's been a real struggle. I mean, I had to sort of put aside my family's needs for my own needs for becoming autonomous. So that's been frustrating." Liz also suggested that, from time to time, she made different decisions to ensure that she did not lose her most significant economic supports, including the state's Medicaid extension program for children. When asked whether she ever engaged in moonlighting, Liz said, "I don't [take on other work] because…I'm right on the edge of losing Doctor Dynasaur."

These several sources of unpredictability can intersect in frustrating ways. On paper, thirty-four-year-old Amy Phelps's total income, which includes the amount her ex-husband is obligated to pay in child support, places her just over the level at which she would qualify for the Vermont Health Access Program (VHAP). However, Amy rarely receives the full amount of income her ex-husband owes her, forcing her to devote numerous hours to trying to make a delicate balance work:

[The state] really gave me a hard time about the child support.…
I had to appeal [the termination] and say to them, *that* is what I'm
entitled to, [but] *this* is what I [actually] get, and they had a hard
time understanding that.… They were very concerned that if I did
get a full amount for a month then I'd be over that month, so they
only set up a month-to-month basis. I told them, "You know, it's
hardly ever I get on a monthly basis [what I'm supposed to get].
On a yearly income you'll see that.…" Now we've worked that
out and [I'm] back on an annual-report-type thing.

Though Amy does not state as much, the paperwork, travel, and meetings associated with these appeals cut into her work time. She is fortunate to have a flexible job where she can make up for hours lost at her
workplace by taking work home; otherwise, she might well find that
her income varied as a result of shifts in her own earnings in addition
to those variations occasioned by her husband's unreliability in paying
child support.

Multiple Income Sources

Amy's troubles are shared by many single mothers, the majority of whom
rely on more than a single source of income for their livelihood (see Table
1.3). Among the women in this study, for example, only 26 percent of
those who had employment outside the home (84 percent of the total in
the sample), relied on wage or salary income alone; another 30 percent
relied on both employment and child support; 23 percent combined these
two incomes with assistance through means-tested programs; 2 percent
combined paid employment, child support, means-tested programs,
and Aid to Families with Dependent Children (AFDC)/Temporary
Assistance to Needy Families (TANF); and the remaining 19 percent
combined some form of income from employment with means-tested
assistance but received no child support. The complexity of managing
separate income streams also holds true for those AFDC/TANF recipients who do not work outside the home, insofar as they also rely on a
variety of means-tested programs and occasionally on child support.
Single mothers have to coordinate these various sources of income and
handle crises caused by each one's instability. These burdens compound
the difficulties of daily survival.

As Liz Miles's comments about clothing and benefits suggest, women
do exercise a limited agency within these significant constraints. A single
mother might choose, as Liz did, to purchase fewer but better clothes,
or to cut back on work to ensure that she does not render herself ineli-
gible for the significant benefits of means-tested programs. Others cut

Table 1.3 Income Sources for Sample Population

A. Percent of Sample That Relies on Each of the Major Sources of Income (Excluding Assistance from Others)

Income source	N	Percent of Total (N = 51)
Paid employment	43	84
Child support	25	49
ANFC/TANF*	12	24
Other means-tested programs	24	47
Other (e.g., inheritance, SSI, etc.)	3	6

B. Distribution of Multiple Sources of Income
Individuals with Paid Employment

Income Source	Number	Percent of those with Paid Employment	Percent of Total Sample (N = 51)
Only paid employment	11	26	22
Paid employment and child support	24	56	47
Paid employment and child support	13	30	25
Paid employment, child support, and means-tested programs	10	23	20
Paid employment, child support, means-tested Programs and ANFC/TANF	1	2	2
Paid employment without child support	8	19	16
Paid employment and means-tested programs	2	5	4
Paid employment, means-tested programs, and ANFC/TANF	6	14	12
Total job holders	43	100	83

Individuals Without Paid Employment

Income Source	Number	Percent of those without Paid Employment	Percent of Total Sample (N = 51)
ANFC/TANF	5	63	10
ANFC/ TANF and means-tested programs	4	50	8
ANFC/TANF, means-tested programs, and child support	1	13	2
No ANFC/TANF	3	38	6
Total without paid employment	8	100	16

*Aid to Needy Families with Children (the Vermont name for what was traditionally called Aid to Families with Dependent Children); Temporary Assistance for Needy Families.

back on employment possibilities to ensure more time and energy for their children. Sheila Davis, the forty-year-old divorced mother of two children, for example, made a decision to "downsize" shortly after her marriage dissolved, even though it meant that she would have to try to get by on a reduced income:[37]

> I'm going to be very challenged in this next year because I'm making a job change. I'm taking a big pay cut. And I decided I needed to make that job change because my job is really stressful and it's compromising my life and the energy I have for my children.

Some women also make choices in the opposite direction and increase their waged work hours, even though doing so means more time away from their children. Still others weigh the needs of their children, their own energies, and the amount they could earn from waged work, and then opt, on a temporary basis, for welfare reliance. This is what Kitty Thompson did and what Sarah Stanley would have preferred to do.

I do not mean to overemphasize the issue of "choice" here. Numerous studies have shown that the movement between welfare and work—and back again—is often located not in choice, but rather in material constraints. This is especially the case for those welfare recipients who face numerous barriers to employment, whether as a result of their own characteristics or the characteristics of the communities in which they live.[38] But even if the women are exercising a very limited degree of agency, they often believe there are choices to be made. This belief increases, rather than diminishes, the psychic pain of measuring survival needs against both a desire for self-sufficiency and a profound interest in tending to the emotional needs of their children.

Poorer Still: No Way to Make Ends Meet

In addition to overlooking change, normal accounting procedures pose a second problem. When census takers ask about income, they look only at those aspects of the standard of living that can be easily quantified. Because cash can be counted, it is counted. But some activities are less amenable to quantification, such as the efforts individuals make to substitute their own labor for goods and services they would otherwise have to purchase in the market. As a result, these efforts rarely show up in our accountings of the cost of living or the well-being of families. However, these efforts can make an enormous difference in the standard at which individuals live, and they may be especially important in a rural area. That is, those who can rely on their own labor to supply necessary foodstuff, fuel, and car repair can make their cash incomes stretch further than those who have to purchase all of these goods and services from the formal economy; they may thus live better than income levels alone would predict.

In studying this kind of activity, my colleague Joan Smith and I found that what we called self-provisioning was common among the married-couple families we interviewed in Coolidge County: Seventy-two percent of families grew some vegetables; 83 percent changed the oil in their vehicles; 46 percent gathered some of their wood for heating; 62 percent took care of their own snow plowing; and 22 percent raised animals for meat (see Table 1.4).[39]

In looking at these same activities again among single-mother families, however, I found that the *only* activity occurring with any frequency was growing vegetables. No woman told an interviewer that she changed the oil in her car herself (even though all but two of the women interviewed did own a car); only one said she actually gathered her own wood (although several said that they used wood to heat their homes); and only one woman raised an animal to supply meat. Moreover, the number of *different* women who participated in these activities is smaller yet since Melissa Henry was the *only* woman in the sample who, with the assistance of the oldest of her sons, engaged in three different self-provisioning practices. All of the remaining self-provisioners engaged in but one of these activities. By way of sharp contrast, in 30 percent of married-couple households, family members engaged in four or more such activities.[40] This comparative evidence suggests that in the absence of a second adult in the household, the possibility of enjoying savings from self-provisioning recedes dramatically. As a result, in comparison

Table 1.4 Self-Provisioning in Coolidge County, Vermont

Self-Provisioning	Married-Couple Households*			Single-Mother Households
	All	Without Children	With Children	
Activity	(N = 158)	(N = 67)	(N = 89)	(N = 40)
Percent who change oil	83%	81%	83%	0%
Percent who cut own wood	46%	42%	50%	2%
Percent who grow meat	22%	16%	26%	2%
Percent who garden	72%	68%	75%	30%
Percent who plow	62%	53%	68%	**
Percent with high rates of self-provisioning (4 or more)	30%	30%	38%	0%

* Recalculated from Nelson and Smith, *Working Hard and Making Do* (Berkeley: Univ. of California Press, 1999).

** Not asked of single mother sample.

with their married peers, single mothers—even at the same income levels as those who are married—live considerably less well than income levels alone indicate.

The preconditions for engagement in these activities also differed in the two sets of households. Among the married-couple households Joan Smith and I studied we found more participation in these activities when incomes were lower. This finding suggested that self-provisioning had become a significant mechanism for stretching modest earnings.[41] But the exact opposite appears to be the case among single mothers: Participation in these activities is strongly associated with having a higher income (20% of those with low incomes grow some of their own vegetables compared with 60% of those with higher incomes).

Three explanations can be found for this difference. First, self-provisioning at even basic levels costs money and single parents at the lowest income levels might not be able to afford those expenses. As Karen Kelly, a welfare-reliant woman with two daughters, noted, "Canning vegetables involves putting out money to have a garden first. I don't have the money to do that." Joan Meyer, also welfare reliant, expressed still greater desperation about being able to manage even the simplest money-saving activities: "I'd like to see a clothesline up here so I can cut costs. I can't even afford the supplies to get a clothesline. So there's a lot of things I know I can do to cut costs but I can't cut costs because I can't afford the things to cut the costs."[42]

Second, self-provisioning takes time and energy, and single mothers face a paucity of both. As Tiffany Morrow, the widow who had such difficulty paying her bills, said, "I use coupons occasionally, but not really to save. All the other things you mentioned [such as gardening or changing the oil in the car], they're all great ideas, but I don't have the time or the energy." In addition, since many self-provisioning activities depend on the skills men have mastered more easily than women, single mothers find themselves at a loss when it comes to assuming those tasks on their own. Sheila Davis, the woman who "downsized" her employment, commented on her ignorance about how to feed the wood stove after her husband left, not to mention the chopping and splitting of wood he used to do: "I knew how to do things like mow the lawn but I didn't know how to deal with the wood stove [and] I didn't take care of any of the stuff in the basement."

No Help with the Daily Work of Survival

The absence of a second adult has other consequences for well-being, particularly when we look at the more routine and essential activities of maintaining a home and caring for children. Qualitative studies sometimes argue that single mothers find housework itself easier than they did when they were married, especially because they no longer have to cope with their anger at a partner who does not do his share of the work, and they do not have to pick up after him.[43] Samantha Stuart, a forty-three-year-old divorced mother of two children could still say, almost three years after she and her husband parted ways, "[After we were separated] it seemed like a great relief not to have *three* children." But these comments competed with those reflecting the simple fact that as single mothers, the women had no ready-made relief from the ongoing responsibility for certain duties and they had to be skilled at multitasking.[44] Diana Spender, who was never married to the father of her daughter, described how hard it was to clean house with a toddler running around: "It's just really impossible to get anything done, like because you do the dishes, and she's just destroying another room. That's why there's two parents, I'm sure. It's just very hard [alone]."

Much of the research on housework among married and cohabiting couples emphasizes inequities in the division of labor and, as a result, has had the impact of trivializing the work men do around the home.[45] But, even as it castigates men for not doing enough, this scholarship also provides concrete evidence that men *do* make significant contributions to the maintenance of a home, albeit lesser and different contributions than those made by women. To take just one example, Suzanne M. Bianchi and her coauthors used data from the National Survey of Families and Households to estimate that although married women in the United States spend, on average, approximately twenty-seven hours a week on core housework tasks (cooking meals, meal cleanup, housecleaning, laundry, and ironing), married men devote seven and a half hours a week to them (see Table 1.5A).[46] Similarly, in Coolidge County, Vermont, Joan Smith and I found that although among married couples child care and cleaning (whether or not there were children in the household) were more common activities among wives than among husbands, many men did contribute to them (see Table 1.5B).[47] In married-couple households, then, women's work of caring for children and of cleaning and maintaining the house are ongoing responsibilities but they may not be unremitting. Even the most chauvinistic husband might watch the baby while his wife runs to the supermarket; even those who believe housework is beneath them might take out the trash.

If women in married-couple households have daily responsibilities for housework and child care and are assisted somewhat by men in these activities, a body of data suggests that men spend substantial time in the pursuit of traditionally male tasks such as outdoor chores and repairs. This body of data further suggests that they receive less help from women

Table 1.5 Comparison of Housework Responsibilities of Married Men and Married Women

A. National Sample, 1995

Hours devoted to each group of housework activities	Married Women		Married Men		Difference	
	Time Diary	NSFH2*	Time Diary	NSFH2	Time Diary	NSFH2
Core housework (cooking meals, meal cleanup, housecleaning, laundry, and ironing)	15.8	27	3.7	7.5	12.1	19.5
Other housework (outdoor chores, repairs, garden and animal care, bills, and other financial)	3.7	3.5	6.7	7.7	-3	-4.2
Total number of hours devoted to housework	19.4	30.5	10.4	15.3	9	15.2

*National Survey of Families and Households.
Source: Suzanne M. Bianchi et al., "Is Anyone Doing the Housework?: Trends in the Gender Division of Household Labor," *Social Forces* 29, no. 1 (September 2000): 213.

B. Percent of Men and Women Who Routinely Participate in Home Care Activities, Vermont Sample, 1999*

Participation in Activities	All Married Couple Households (N = 156)	Married-Couple Households Without Children (N = 67)	Married-Couple Households with Children (N = 89)
Housework			
Men	48%	47%	49%
Women	94%	94%	94%
Child care			
Men	39%	does not apply	69%
Women	55%	does not apply	97%
Lawn work			
Men	90%	90%	89%
Women	64%	59%	65%
Car repair			
Men	68%	63%	71%
Women	10%	12%	8%

Source: Recalculated from Nelson and Smith, *Working Hard and Making Do* (Berkeley: Univ. of California Press, 1999).

for these activities than women receive from men for the traditionally female tasks. For example, Bianchi and her coauthors report that while men devoted on average approximately 7.5 hours (out of a total of 15.3 housework hours) to "women's work," women devoted but 3.5 hours (out of a total of 30.5 housework hours) to "other" tasks. Women thus act in a more "gendered" manner than do most men: Women devote but 11 percent of their total housework contributions to "male" activities while men devote almost half of their total housework contributions to "female" activities.[48] Among the married-couple households in Coolidge County that Joan Smith and I studied, the patterns were also highly gendered: As wives the women in these rural households were far less likely to participate in the male tasks of yard work and car maintenance than were the men in their households and they were far less likely to do men's work than men were to do women's work.[49]

Both sets of male contributions—engagement in core household tasks and participation in "other" (male) household activities—are lost to single mothers, even though the daily lives of these women have not necessarily changed so as to preclude the necessity for (at least most of) them. Single mothers who have not previously participated in these activities sometimes seek to acquire the skills necessary to manage traditional male tasks on their own and, when they do so, report considerable satisfaction. Sheila Davis, who had never before handled the wood stove, proudly claimed: "And I'm actually much more independent now and I want to be independent," even as she acknowledged, "I'd love to have somebody in my life that I didn't have to pay to help me do that little stuff because I'm not that great at it."

But whether or not the women can acquire some of these new capabilities, having to perform daily tasks without male assistance has several significant consequences. First, single mothers need to spend more of their time and energy locating help in completing the work for which they previously might have relied on a partner. When they find that help, they also find themselves dependent in new ways on others in their social world. Sheila Davis commented that she had originally had to "enlist a lot of friends to educate me how to take care of my house. Really dumb stuff that I should know." At the same time, she added that she did not want to "have to lean on people," because "they all have their own houses and their own families." Single mothers may also need, as Sheila Davis did, to rely more on their children for these activities; they thus shift the social dynamics within the household. In so doing, they may become enmeshed in ongoing struggles with those children and they may sometimes jeopardize their own desires to be able to allow their children to have what they consider to be an ideal childhood (see chapter 4). Sheila commented on this issue: "I try not to load Thomas up too much because I want him to do schoolwork and play." Finally, when single mothers purchase these goods and services in the market rather than supplying them from within the home, they face new and unexpected charges against budgets that are already strained; indeed, because they have altogether less money than do married-couple parents, they may be poorly positioned to make these purchases. Sheila noted that even though she had a steady income, the cost of purchasing needed services could disrupt her budget: "If I need something done I have to figure out a way to put some money aside to hire somebody to come and help me do some job around the house."

The tactics of doing work themselves, finding informal assistance, and asking children for help, can eat up considerable time and energy. As single mothers combine these new tasks with the traditional women's work of cleaning, cooking, and child care, they also experience a hidden poverty of leisure. These tactics also eat up goodwill on the part of one's social network: When a woman asks for help in one sphere, she might find that she cannot also ask for it in another. And, obviously, the tactic of purchasing essential services in a market eats up cash as well, without guaranteeing that the women will accomplish their targeted goals. Single mothers may find themselves not only experiencing hardship, but also suffering from feelings of inadequacy if they cannot keep their homes as presentable as do their peers.

The Vermont Policy Response to the Poverty of Single Mothers

As indicated above, a variety of state supports are available to help single mothers. None of these supports, however, responds to the two problems of limited time and limited energy. Nor do they address many simple jobs of household maintenance. Joan Meyer commented on the fact that the available help ignored her most pressing needs:

> The work around the house goes undone.... I've tried in different areas but there's no help there—"Don't have time"; "You need to get the supplies"; "You need to get this"—and I'm, like, going, "I don't have the supplies or the money to get the supplies." There's no agencies that will come in and do the skirting around my trailer; there's no agencies that can help you [repair] your steps or plow your driveway.

There are, however, a variety of cash-assistance programs, the most significant of which is welfare. As was the case in the rest of the country, Vermont engaged in welfare restructuring in the mid-1990s.

Indeed, Vermont's round of welfare restructuring was actually implemented in 1994 (two years before the Personal Responsibility and Work Opportunity Reconciliation Act), when the Vermont legislature passed Act 106, its Welfare Restructuring Project (WRP).[50] This particular version of restructuring continued until 2001 (and thus through the period during which the interviews for this research were conducted) and it was codified as permanent policy (called Reach Up) thereafter. Though often referred to as welfare "reform," the new combination of work requirements and time limits made life more, rather than less, difficult for many single mothers. I thus refer to this change as "restructuring" (as does the state itself) rather than grant it an accolade that suggests a more beneficial set of policies.

In several ways, Vermont's restructuring provisions were, and continue to be, more generous than those in other states. First, Vermont's basic welfare grants are relatively large. In 2004 Vermont's monthly cash assistance for a family of three (a mother and two children) was, at a paltry $629 a month, among the highest in the country; when compared to the median income, which is low relative to the country as a whole, Vermont's assistance has a higher ratio than is found in the vast majority of states.[51] In addition, Vermont offered child-care subsidies without any limit in months for families with earnings below 200 percent of the federal poverty level; the state also made available transitional Medicaid for thirty-six months.[52] Third, under its Welfare Restructuring Project, Vermont allowed welfare recipients to attend higher education programs as well as enroll in training to complete a high school diploma or a general equivalency diploma (GED).[53] Even more significant, Vermont also initially allowed a longer period of time (thirty months) before single-parent participants were required to engage in any work-related activities, at which time work was required of all recipients. Finally, although Vermont refers to its policies as the "first test of time limit," in actuality the state did not choose to terminate clients who failed to comply with the work requirement as was done in other states. Such recipients were instead subject to sanctions; the state took control of the monetary grant and used the money to pay the recipient' bills; and recipients were required to attend frequent meetings at the welfare office.[54]

Additional social policies in Vermont also ease the lives of its poorest citizens. The state has relatively generous provisions for health care coverage through its Medicaid extension program (VHAP), which offers insurance for medical care and pharmaceuticals to those with incomes less than 150 percent of the federal poverty level; as a result, a lower percentage of adults are uninsured in Vermont than is the case elsewhere (14% vs. a national average of 20%) and a higher proportion rely on Medicaid (12% vs. 8%). Children are especially well covered in Vermont because of the Medicaid extension Doctor Dynasaur Program, which extends health insurance to those families below 300 percent of the poverty level; as a result, few of Vermont's children are uninsured when compared to other states (5% vs. a national average of 12%) and more of them rely on Medicaid (40% vs. 27%).[55]

Other social welfare policies operate in Vermont much as they do elsewhere. Among the most significant of these, the Department of Agriculture's Food Stamp Program serves those with net monthly incomes at or below 100 percent of the poverty level and its Women, Infants, and Children (WIC) program provides food to pregnant women and women with children under five if their incomes are below 185 percent of the poverty level. Although rural areas are cited as places with low social welfare program use, Vermont levels of use actually exceed national averages with respect to some programs.[56] For example, almost three quarters of those eligible for Food Stamps in Vermont draw on them, compared with less than two thirds of the eligible population in the United States as a whole (73% vs. 59%).[57] On the other hand, fewer Vermont families take advantage of child care subsidies than is the case in the nation as a whole (14.9% of those eligible vs. 18.3% nationwide).[58]

THE IDEOLOGICAL WORLD

Vermont participated in welfare restructuring in a somewhat kinder and gentler manner than did the rest of the nation.[59] Even so, Vermonters were not insulated from the associated discourse that prevailed during the mid- to late-1990s, the period during which I conducted this research. This discourse, which Valerie Polakow, Therese Halskov, and Per Schultz Jorgensen termed a "social threat" discourse, identified single mothers as the "active agents in the creation of an underclass...that has little stake in the social order, is alienated from it, and hostile to it, and thus is a major source of crime, deviancy and social breakdown."[60] While the majority of the diatribes about single mothers were focused on those who were poor, implicitly (and sometimes explicitly) African-American, and welfare reliant, the condemnation spread more broadly. Two major themes in these broader discussions shape the ideological context within which single mothers make decisions about how to meet their daily needs. The first of these themes addresses the issues of independence and self-sufficiency, especially for women who cannot easily survive without assistance from the state; the second attaches to the moral and psychological adequacy of the single-parent family, whether or not that family relies on welfare.

Self-Sufficiency as a Social Ideal

Since the mid-1990s, discussions about welfare, what was called "dependence" on the state, has increasingly been regarded with contempt. And what was true in the nation as a whole was true in Vermont. As politicians and conservative commentators across the nation castigated welfare mothers for laziness (as well as for their supposed excessive fertility and cheating), the then-governor of Vermont made his own statement: "[Welfare] recipients don't have any self-esteem. If they did, they would be working."[61]

Such attitudes did not go unnoticed by the respondents in this study. One woman, who described how difficult it had been to rely on welfare for a brief period after she left her husband, referred directly to governor Howard Dean's comment as a source of her sense of shame:

> It was one of the most horrible things I've ever had to do.... Even Howard Dean, the way he runs his mouth on TV about how horrible it is. It's really—people shouldn't judge, because they never know where they're going to be in life—because he was born with a silver spoon in his mouth.

Silver spoon or not, under Governor Dean's leadership, Vermont passed the Welfare Restructuring Project (WRP), which clearly states the project's central goal of making dependence on state benefits short-term by requiring recipients to rely on their own employment earnings within two years. In so doing, the state does not promise that this new source of income will produce economic well-being. Rather, the reform was predicated on the notion that self-sufficiency—as proven through earnings—offers a better "quality" of life than is possible with dependence on the state. As the state itself explained:[62]

> WRP transforms ANFC from an income maintenance program that fosters dependency to a transitional assistance program that encourages, assists, and, when necessary, requires ANFC parents to support themselves and their children financially through work by establishing work requirements that reflect the labor market behavior of the vast majority of Vermont parents, both mothers and fathers.... The Department of Social Welfare is sending a **new message: we are here to offer transitional help and support toward achieving a better quality of life than dependence on welfare provides.** (Bold emphasis in original.)

In laying out employment as the route to well-being, the state calls on common practice to establish a moral norm. Indeed, this admonition to seek out employment may have had particular resonance in rural Vermont, where the labor force participation rates of both men and women have traditionally been higher than they are in the United States as a whole, and where the dual-earner couple has been found more frequently.[63] Thus, when Vermont's Department of Social Welfare insisted that the work requirements "reflect the labor market behavior of the vast majority of Vermont parents, both mothers and fathers," it did not overstate the fact, even though it implicitly overestimated the ease with which a single mother could support her family on her wages alone. In this context, it is not surprising that the women we interviewed take pride in their work-based efforts to provide for themselves and their children, but that they find the alternative of welfare reliance problematic.

As analysts Nancy Fraser and Linda Gordon have argued, although notions of dependence change over time, during the period preceding welfare "reform," not only was particular animus directed at dependence on the state, but dependence was viewed as being rooted within the individual who contained (and represented) a set of pathological, feminine traits. A woman's dependency was thus seen as "a behavioral disorder and the product of bad personal choices."[64] If welfare "reformers" targeted single mothers who were welfare reliant for particular disdain, the women in this study heard society's *broader* condemnation of dependence. They were quick to deny that they were dependent, whether they were describing their relationship with means-tested programs or their relationships with friends and family members. Indeed the welfare critique worked because it tapped into widespread social values.

Amy Phelps, who had difficulty sustaining her VHAP eligibility, was especially proud of not having been welfare reliant: "I do have to say through all of my down times...I never went on any kind of public service, only the health insurance, which is a form of Medicaid." When she spoke of dependence on her family she talked in positive terms and used active verbs to describe her behavior: "So that I guess that's really an *accomplishment* for me with just *accessing* support from families." In so doing, she suggested that reliance on her family did not constitute a passive dependency. She also suggested that social norms had quite possibly prevented her from getting the full range of supports that would have ensured her and her children's survival in the difficult period that followed her separation from her husband. She thus indicated that her social economy was configured to support her personal morality. When Karen Kelly, who *was* welfare reliant at the time of the interview, was asked about the specific financial arrangements on which she relied, she responded crisply: "*Rely*. See, that *rely* word isn't one that I do." She thereby sought to deny that her welfare reliance constituted a shameful dependence.

As they rejected dependence, the women interviewed for this study, like Sarah Stanley, quickly aligned themselves with the morally *approved* traits of self-sufficiency and independence: "I really try and anticipate things so I don't get to the point where I need support. I'm not the type—I like to do things on my own, I like to be self-sufficient"; "I'm real self-sufficient"; "I've always been pretty independent, and I did have to grow up kind of fast.... I guess I prided myself in being self-sufficient." These code words *self-sufficiency* and *independence* tap into deep values with widespread appeal and they become a theme in the lives of single mothers.[65] They resonate particularly well in a rural area where, as shown above, people often take care of a wide range of individual material needs and often link doing so to a local culture of self-reliance.[66] The need to demonstrate self-reliance, self-sufficiency, and independence, however, runs counter to the very real needs single mothers have: The material realities mean that they cannot get by without drawing on others for assistance with daily living and financial support and, occasionally, without drawing on the state. (Chapters 2 and 3 will turn directly to these issues as I examine how single mothers resolve the contradiction between their "economic" strategy of relying on others and their own adherence to these prevailing social norms.)

The "Defective" Single-Parent Family

The welfare debates of the 1990s were conjoined with moral statements about the significance of marriage both as "the foundation of a successful society" and as "an essential institution...which promotes the interest of children." As the sociologist Sharon Hays notes,

> Although the attention paid to state efforts at placing welfare recipients in jobs has led many to believe that work requirements are the centerpiece of this legislation, a reading of the Personal Responsibility Act makes it appear that the intent of lawmakers was to champion family values above all else.[67]

This emphasis on marriage was no more a passing fancy, here today and gone tomorrow, than was the emphasis on time limits and work requirements. Just as his administration's proposal for TANF reauthorization in 2003 recommended increased work requirements, so has president

George W. Bush repeatedly sought to reinforce the nation's moral commitment to marriage.[68]

Single mothers do not need either the PRWORA or Bush's marriage promotion policies to tell them that their family form is associated with poverty (and that they might well be better off—at least financially—if they were married); nor do they need the Heritage Foundation or the National Marriage Project to tell them theirs is not the preferred family form.[69] Most of the single mothers interviewed for this study had their own dreams of what they wanted for themselves and their children. Sarah Stanley believed that she had fallen from the "America apple pie dream," and she had struggled within herself to find a way to consider her diminished family "valid." Another woman also expressed a sense of failure and inadequacy: "I didn't get married and have children to create children of divorce, and the guilt that comes along with that." Moreover, these single mothers have their own daily experiences to remind them that, as women raising children on their own, they bear the burden of a discredited status, of difference, and of inadequacy. Recall that Sarah Stanley did not like to refer to herself as a "single parent" because she believed that there was an immense stigma attached to that status. Another woman heard this condemnation as well. Though she sought to differentiate her own circumstances from those she believed should be subject to social disdain, she also believed that the condemnation spread more broadly and that she was also (and unfairly in her view) subject to stigmatizing practices:

> I guess I'd have to say that in the communities and in this rural area, I guess, single parents are still looked upon very poorly as though we choose this life. . . . And no matter what the case is when you are looked upon as a single parent, you're looked down upon, and I don't feel that's right. There are cases where I agree that they should be looked down upon, but there are places where I feel they should not. It's very sad that there's not that differentiation. It's just as hard for a single parent [to survive] no matter [whether] it's a situation of choice or stupidity versus a situation of circumstance. But, if you have no control over that circumstance, then why should you be penalized?

In his classic work, *Stigma*, Erving Goffman describes how a "stigmatized individual is a person who can be approached by strangers at will" with questions about his or her condition.[70] While Goffman demonstrates the particular burdens and particular vulnerabilities associated with having *visible* stigmas, the fact that single mothers experience the same kind of "approach by strangers" suggests that they also bear the weight of a stigmatizing condition simply because their family form deviates from the norm. A young woman interviewed for this project told me that during the four years she was a single parent, people she barely knew asked questions about her relationship to the father of her child and about her daughter's adjustment to living without him: Were you ever married? Why did you and he separate? Where is the father? Does he ever visit his daughter? How does your daughter feel about her father? How is she doing in school?[71] Such questions assume that a single mother's private life is an appropriate subject of inquiry and an appropriate topic for casual conversation, simply because it is different.

These questions also assume that "difference" constitutes a problem. Though a term like *broken family* seems archaic, it is still used on occasion; *fatherless family* is even more commonplace in its use as are (opposing) terms like *intact family*, *traditional family*, and even *normal family*.[72] Much as women who are employed are referred to as *working women* (rather than *workers*) and mothers who are employed are identified as *working mothers* (rather than *mothers*), families headed by women are specially designated as *lone-parent families* and as *single-mother families* (rather than *families*).[73]

Without a doubt, social scientists bear a significant burden of responsibility for both the assumptions of deviance and inadequacy and the use of terminology that differentiates. Much research focuses on the negative effects of single parenting on children.[74] Even though many sophisticated analyses identify poverty as the primary culprit for these effects, even when holding income constant, these studies also find residual problems that suggest that single parenting itself has disturbing outcomes for children. Newspapers in turn pick up these conclusions with less sensitivity to nuance and subtlety than the tentative or cautious analyses would imply. In 2003 the headline on the front page of a regional Vermont newspaper announced "Kids of Single Parents Face Struggles: Mental Problems, Addiction Twice as Common, Study Says"; the same story appeared two days later in *The New York Times* with the headline "Children in Single-Parent Homes Found at Risk of Mental Illness."[75]

In this context, it is hardly surprising that teachers, social workers, and the general public tenaciously hold this set of assumptions about the inadequacy of single-parent families. As the sociologists Dorothy E. Smith and Alison Griffiths have shown, teachers read "back from a child's behavior in school to its cause in the family; and from a knowledge of family problems to an interpretation of the child's behavior in school."[76]

These processes do not just affect minority families or low-income households. Although they were white women *and* professionals, the two single mothers Smith and Griffiths found that their families "were viewed at school as defective families who produced defective children."[77]

Agencies explicitly designed to offer help and support to single mothers may also confirm notions that their life circumstances result from their own—bad—decisions. The sociologists Rita Rhodes and Miriam McNown Johnson, for example, report that social work students are able to "identify oppression as a factor in the lives of women" but that for the most part, "their perceptions of single parents underscored the belief that the life conditions of female-headed families are the consequence of individual choice, rather than of societal arrangements that have a disproportionately negative impact on women."[78] To be sure, there *is* choice involved in becoming a single parent: Women do *choose* divorce and they sometimes do so because the circumstances—alcoholism, mental illness, or violence—make the choice imperative. In a context in which this choice itself is defined as causing problems, women who make such a choice can hardly escape feelings of guilt or the burden of having to deal with the reproach of others.

Single mothers have to contend with other stereotypes as well, including the notions that they are both more predatory and more promiscuous than married women.[79] A thirty-three-year-old woman interviewed for this study said that when she started to date the man to whom she subsequently became engaged, his family warned him that she was more interested in finding a man to help her support her son than she was in having a "relationship," and they urged him to be especially suspicious of her "morals." Other women described how, when they became single mothers, their friends pulled back from them, fearful of the contamination of divorce and unwed parenting.

I do not mean to exaggerate the "stigma" associated with being a single parent. Recent surveys show widespread cultural acceptance for the "fact" of single parenthood—especially as a "lifestyle" choice on the part of women.[80] But it is hard to know just what the respondents of polls are thinking, or what qualifications they might impose to make this "choice" a morally or socially acceptable one. The prominent stories of public figures who have had children on their own may lead to the impression that most single mothers who opt for this as a "lifestyle" are rich.[81] The respondents of these polls might give very different responses if they have in mind an individual for whom having a child on her own would entail a stint of reliance on welfare, or a woman who "chooses" to leave her marriage in order to escape unsafe conditions.

Vermont as Conservative

In 2000, Vermont astonished the country by passing the nation's first Civil Union bill, which offered all the legal protections of marriage to gay and lesbian couples.[82] Such a progressive move might suggest that Vermont is especially hospitable to diversity in family structure. That assumption would not be entirely wrong: Vermont's largest city, Burlington, has been described as one of our country's "latte towns"—"liberal communities...that have become crucial gestation centers for America's new upscale culture."[83] But neither its civil unions nor its pretty centerpiece city captures the full measure of Vermont and its attitudes. The debates about civil unions unleashed a strong homophobic backlash represented by the slogan "Take Back Vermont," which had a twofold reference: to take Vermont back from the outsiders (called "flatlanders") who were bringing in novel, and unwelcome, ideas, and to take Vermont back to the way of life promised in the pristine postcard images.[84] And many "real" Vermonters think of Burlington—latte town or not—as the big and wicked city.

Furthermore, although single parenthood is growing more rapidly in Vermont than it is in the United States as a whole (and growing so much so that Vermont's rates are now equal to those in the rest of the country), the single-parent family retains its status as the new kid on the block. One woman made reference to this seeming novelty when describing her situation: "I was like the black sheep [in the family]—the first one to be divorced." Others also made reference to the conservative attitudes they encountered: "I guess I'd have to say that in the communities and in this rural area single parents are still looked upon very poorly as though we choose this life." One woman, recently transplanted from New York City, where she felt "it was very easy to be single," described coming to Vermont as entering "Noah's Ark land."[85]

This sense of isolation might be associated with the distinctive geography of Vermont. Single mothers are more dispersed in rural areas than they are in urban areas: In Vermont only 3 percent of children live in neighborhoods with a high rate of female-headed families (above 35.2%) compared with 17 percent of children nationwide.[86] This dispersal produces a particular kind of visibility, even if it is not as intense as that experienced by Sarah Stanley, who, now that she lives next door to her mother, often finds her waving from her kitchen window. Small-town life means that you are likely to see someone you know when you dash out to the drugstore or walk down a main street. You are likely as well to see someone you know while you are engaged in less frequent activities such as visiting a dentist or consulting with a lawyer. You are also likely to be visible at those moments when you least want to be: The local paper prints a police blotter (read assiduously by many) that indicates whom has been picked up for drunk driving and which street (if not which house) was the location of a rowdy party or a "domestic incident." And, as popular imagery would suggest, gossip is rampant. As Patsy Downey, a twenty-four-year-old, never-married mother of two, who has lived in the same community for most of her life, noted: "My God, [the members of my family are] the most nit-picking, into-everybody-else's-business people that I've ever met in my entire life. . . . I don't talk to them because it moves throughout the whole family [and] it gets changed like ten times before it gets back through to me."

CONCLUSION

A variety of current social trends make likely the possibility that a woman with children will spend at least some period of time as a single mother. When she does, both throughout the country and in a rural state like Vermont, she will face serious problems with making ends meet. Some of these problems result from the simple fact that a single mother has to support her family on but one income when the vast majority of jobs in Vermont—whether held by men or women—do not pay enough to support a family above the level of a living wage and, quite often, expose them to even more dire poverty.[87] In a family with two income earners, the adults not only have the option of combining resources (and therefore can accept less-well-paying jobs), but they are also better positioned to handle the ongoing demands that attend family life (housework as well as child care and transportation) and to save money by self-provisioning. In the absence of these resources, single mothers face not only a poverty of income, but also a poverty of time and energy.

During the 1990s, the growing number of single-parent families and the economic plight of that population became a subject of national discussion. Rather than instituting policies explicitly designed to support single mothers over the long term, however, the policy response—as represented in the PRWORA—relied less on the carrot than on the stick. Ignoring the realities of the difficulties inherent in women's attempts to make ends meet through waged work (and in the process devaluing the other work that women do in the home), the newly instituted policy required that all single mothers abandon dependence on the state and achieve self-sufficiency.

The social threat discourse that accompanied debates about changing policy "justified" the harsh treatment of welfare recipients, even as the resulting act made proclamations about the good person and the good society. The former was modeled after the ideal type of male worker: an individual who was able to support himself (and his family) on his own wages. The fact that some male workers were able to support a family on earnings because they could also draw on the waged—and unwaged— contributions of a spouse was overlooked, as *self-sufficiency, personal responsibility,* and *independence* became the code words for morally approved behavior. At the same time, the prevailing discourse declared marriage and the two-parent family as centerpieces of the good society. It thus held out for an individual single mother the choice of making it on her own or hitching up with a man, even as full moral approbation was reserved for the latter.

At the national level, the PRWORA was thus both policy and prescription, a set of rules for determining when the state would offer support to its neediest members and a set of guidelines for proper action on the part of individual citizens. The same is true in Vermont, where, although marriage is less prominently a stated goal, the WRP insists that employment offers "a better quality of life" than welfare reliance.[88] Though not all single mothers were *directly* affected by these new policies—at any given time the vast majority of single mothers are not welfare reliant even if many rely on some form of means-tested state services—the moral content had broader ramifications. Sarah Stanley believed that being a "single mother" placed her within a stigmatized group; her peers linked that stigma to the way the governor "ran his mouth" about welfare, and to a more general moral condemnation of single mothers.

As single mothers seek to make ends meet, they are pinched in the middle. The difficult job of trying to solve their economic problems is compounded by a morality that deems self-sufficiency an ideal while denigrating the single-parent family. I turn next to how these challenges give rise to a social economy, one element of which works within the framework of reciprocity while resting on a careful choice among competing sources of assistance.

2

NEGOTIATING RECIPROCITY[1]

When Sheila Davis, a relatively well-off woman who has been divorced for two years, does not have enough money in her savings account to cover the year's property taxes, she borrows from her parents and friends. Because she cannot (or does not want to) mow her own lawn or shovel her own driveway, she relies on the assistance of a neighbor. When she faces a scheduling conflict and cannot be there for her children at the end of the school day, Sheila asks one of her friends to drive them to their after-school activities.

Anne Davenport has been divorced from her husband for only a year, and she has an income that, as a combination of welfare, employment, and child support, is less than a quarter of Sheila's income from waged work ($9,300 vs. $42,000). Like Sheila, Anne draws extensively on others. She relies regularly on her parents (in whose backyard her own trailer home sits) for babysitting, grocery money, and the loan of a working car. In addition, she counts on assistance from her single-mother friends for help with child care, transportation, and emotional support.

If both Sheila and Anne create a social economy by turning to other people for a broad range of assistance, they do so with different frequency and different sentiments. Perhaps it is because she expects more of herself at age forty-one that Sheila Davis is humbled by this new experience of not being able to make the necessary adjustments to her diminished income and manage on her own. Her financial management skills actually compound this feeling of inadequacy: "I feel sort of embarrassed that I don't have it together. I make my living as an accountant so I should know how to do it. And I *do* know how to do it. It's just about lifestyle changes [since the divorce]." Anne shares Sheila's desire to be self-sufficient, but at age twenty-nine asking for help seems to come a little more easily to her: "If I run out of money for the week, I ask my mom."

Age (and personality) differences aside, the two women have different resources. Not only can Sheila purchase more help to respond to her needs, but outside of her work hours she has more time and energy to focus on meeting those needs, both because her children are no longer toddlers and because they spend almost half of their time with their father. Sheila also has many friends in the community in which she lives. And, although she lives some distance from them, members of her family are wealthy, and she remains in close contact. Anne, by contrast, has more "free" time outside of employment because she only works part-time. But both of her children are young and Anne cannot rely at all on *their* father, whose alcoholism prevents him from being a reliable caregiver to his sons. Without his help, Anne has both accepted and nurtured other significant assets. Not only does she live near her family, but she has also built up a large network of friends in the community. While neither her family members nor her friends are as affluent as Sheila's, both still serve as important resources.

Clearly, the different conditions under which these two women live significantly affect their experiences of single motherhood. This chapter is not focused on the impact of these differences, however, or even on the amount of support these two women receive. Instead my interest is on the question of how single mothers who rely heavily on others make sense of, justify, and enact that reliance in a world both where independence and self-sufficiency are enshrined as social values and where asking for help exposes them to the judgment that the single-parent family must be inadequate. I find the answer in the practical efforts single mothers make to choose among potential resources so as to evade scorn and stigma, as well as in their significant efforts to enact reciprocity.

Social exchange theory focuses our attention on a rational actor's attempts to benefit from social interaction. However, sociologist Karen V. Hansen draws on Alvin Gouldner's seminal "The Norm of Reciprocity: A Preliminary Statement" to remind us that reciprocity does not operate only to ensure benefits or even only to secure balance. Rather, reciprocity is also a *norm,* something that "holds that people should help those who help them."[2] And the normative imperative attached to reciprocity differs from the obligations attached to kin: The status duties of kinship "may require an almost unconditional compliance in the sense that they are incumbent on all those in a given status simply by virtue of its occupancy. In contrast, the generalized norm of reciprocity evokes obligations towards others on the basis of their *past* behavior."[3] Hence the norm of reciprocity requires not just assessments of future gain, but also the fulfillment of prior "debts."

With respect to their moral and practical commitment to these normative obligations, Sheila and Anne converge. When asked about those times when she drew on her friends, Sheila claimed that she fulfilled her obligation to give back as much as she received: "I make them dinner or I take care of their kids.... And that feels like it equals out." Later in the interview, she mused about the exchanges in which she was involved, and she insisted that valuing reciprocity carried considerable material costs of time and energy: "I lean on the side of doing too much for people, at my expense—like not sleeping or something.... Nobody is saying you should even it up, but I do that." Anne Davenport said that she, too, believed in the obligation of reciprocity, and that she also made efforts that enabled her to make returns for assistance received. Her explanation combined family ties and friendships in a way that showed that a similar broad norm applies to both sets of relationships: "I try really hard to reciprocate with friends. Same with my family. I always feel obligated to give back."

THE STUDY OF SOCIAL SUPPORT AND RECIPROCITY

For more than thirty years, Carol Stack's *All Our Kin* has shaped ideas about how the survival strategies of poor single mothers are rooted in relationships of exchange.[4] A central theme in that analysis is that the "give-and-take" in these relationships can be understood within the anthropological perspective of the gift: Giving carries with it the obligation to reciprocate, an obligation that carries "kin and community sanctions."[5] The idea that social networks operate on the basis of reciprocity is now a well-worn, if often underexamined, assumption.

The distinctiveness of the population, community, and even the time (of stable welfare) in which Stack undertook her research raises questions about the extent to which similar relationships of mutual support would be found in areas where single mothers are white, live in the small villages and towns of a rural state, have access to relationships with those who have greater resources, and cannot rely on welfare to undergird a long-term survival strategy. Single mothers who live exclusively in rural areas are less frequently the target of scholarly investigation than are those in urban communities; when the rural population *does* receive attention, their relationships of mutual support are frequently romanticized.[6] The "fictive kin" of Stack's research stands next to the barn raising as, if not a scholarly icon, a cultural one.

A substantial body of quantitative research offers more skepticism about the availability of support than either Stack's qualitative study or the fanciful imagery of rural life would suggest. For example, using a somewhat narrow definition of support networks—living in an extended family situation, receiving at least half of her income from someone other than her husband, or getting free child care—researchers Dennis P. Hogan, Lingxin Hao, and William L. Parish found that although the majority of single mothers participate in a support network, "substantial proportions of single mothers fall outside such informal support systems."[7] In a later study that was limited to intergenerational support, Hogan, with David J. Eggebeen and Clifford C. Clogg, further explored the differences between single and married mothers and found that while unmarried mothers more often receive support from their parents than do their married peers, less than half of the single mothers receive significant amounts of this support. Furthermore, the researchers found that "parents in poverty are significantly less likely than persons with higher incomes to be involved in either the giving or receiving of support."[8] Ann Roschelle similarly challenged research that claimed that social support, whether from family or friends, is prevalent and can mitigate the deleterious effects of poverty.[9]

If these (mostly quantitative) studies appropriately indicate that informal social support cannot be relied on to lift the poor out of poverty, they also suggest that some (albeit limited) support is present in the lives of most single mothers.[10] But most such studies do not count *small* exchanges (which can make the difference between buying food or not) or small favors (such as a ride to the grocery store to pick up that food); nor do they assess the frequency with which these loans or favors occur. Perhaps even more significantly for this argument, few studies assess the evidence of reciprocity. Roschelle, for example, acknowledges that her data do not allow her to determine whether or not "the individuals giving help to respondents are the same individuals who are also receiving that help."[11] And even those quantitative studies that do examine exchanges between partners in a relationship (and thus explore reciprocity to a limited extent) neither assess the quantity of goods given or received (but simply record presence or absence of giving or receiving) nor consider whether their definitions of reciprocity are shared by the actors.[12]

There are compelling substantive and theoretical reasons, however, to believe that individuals might view themselves as being in reciprocal relationships even when the available data suggest that they are net recipients. Three reasons for this stand out. First, quantitative data cannot get at the subtlety of exchange relationships. As is discussed further, and as theorists have noted, gratitude, dependence, loyalty, and deference might serve as items of reciprocation, and these are notoriously difficult to measure.[13] Second, the time span in most studies is quite limited: Many use reports of items given and received within the recent past. They are thus more likely to measure what Marshall Sahlins defines as "balanced reciprocity" where "relations between people are disrupted by a failure to reciprocate within limited time and equivalence leeways" than to measure what he calls "generalized reciprocity" where "the material flow is sustained by prevailing social relations" and the "expectation of reciprocity is indefinite."[14] Some of the single mothers who could be identified as net recipients in a particular study might understand their current receipt of goods and services as repayment for gifts offered in the past (or even of obligations they expect to fill some time in the future). They might also view themselves as net givers because the items they consider relevant to an exchange had not been measured in that study.[15] Finally, a body of research has shown that individuals often report giving more than they receive, and that "overreporting" may result from what British sociologist Raymond E. Pahl terms "the general concern of people not to appear too dependent on others."[16] Even among families, where Sahlins would argue that generalized reciprocity applies, Janet Finch and Jennifer Mason note that "people try to keep a balance between dependence and independence" in their relationships and that "some very fine calculations (which of course may not be successful) take place to try to ensure that no one becomes a net giver or net receiver, or is beholden to someone else."[17]

A "bias" toward reciprocity shows up in the comments of Sheila and Anne, as well as in those of other women. All voiced sentiments showing that they did not want to be only on the receiving end of exchanges. Megan Paige, a divorced mother of three children, explicitly drew on an analogy that made overt the careful assessments of the economic components in exchange while demonstrating her commitment to avoid "overbenefiting" from her relationships:[18]

> I've done a lot more asking since I've been single than I used to, but I don't lie awake feeling guilty that I have to ask people for help. And the way I [prevent myself from feeling guilty] is to feel like I'm always proactive about that in the sense that I'm always offering support to the people around me. I'm not waiting for them to ask me. . . . I'm always calling them and I'm saying, "Can I help you with that?" Sort of the "support thing" is like the checking account—first you put the money in and then you make the withdrawal and there's no problem. It's when you do it the other way around [that] there's red ink.

Janet Linden, a forty-nine-year-old mother of a daughter she adopted as a single woman, said that she prefers that her requests operate as "a two-way street" and that "if it turned out not to be after a couple of requests," because the other party did not ask her for equal gestures of support, she "would probably hesitate to request again." While theory might suggest that only compliance with the social norm of reciprocity motivates these statements, the interviews suggest that the commitment to this norm is tied to two other related sets of desires: to be, and to be perceived as being, independent and self-sufficient, and to protect oneself, and one's family structure, from being subject to negative appraisal.

Cathy Earl, a forty-one-year-old mother of three, for example, when questioned about what she believed it was appropriate to ask of her friends and family, responded, "I like to do things on my own, I like to be self-sufficient, so [asking for help is] not something that I do a lot." This response should come as no surprise. As noted above, self-sufficiency is not only a key term in the social discourse of welfare, but it is a valued norm within this community of Vermonters.[19] And Cathy has another goal at hand. She would prefer to make requests of people who "aren't going to judge me, look down on me," and who will be there "because they understand" the constraints in her life as a single mother.

Megan, Janet, and Cathy—like Anne and Sheila—thus find themselves in a bind. They have to ask for help but they neither want to jeopardize a stance of self-sufficiency nor expose their need or their failures to meet that need within the single-parent family structure. They also have limited time and energy with which to enact reciprocity. The solution to this dilemma is found in the way they divide their world of social support into three central groupings—others in the same boat, family and friends deemed to have superior resources, and those who are part of a broader community—and apply a different form of reciprocity to each set of relationships.[20]

A COMMUNITY OF NEED:
TRADING FAVORS WITH OTHER SINGLE MOTHERS

Most of the single mothers in this study spoke about their involvement in rich relationships of exchange with other single mothers. As was true of the women interviewed by Carol Stack in *All Our Kin*, the women in Coolidge County shared a variety of resources, including transportation, child care, and small sums of money; they also shared emotional support, advice, and conversation.[21]

As was also true of the women Stack studied, the women in this study used kinship terminology to represent the nature of the bonds they shared with other single mothers. In so doing, the women demonstrated that they differentiated between biological kin (i.e., individuals with a similar background but possibly different current circumstances) and individuals who acted as kin (i.e., those with similar circumstances who shared resources).

For example, when asked to comment on a network diagram she had drawn, Sheila Davis explained, "My immediate family is not in Vermont and what I realized is that all of these people [on my diagram] are my family; I mean not in that intimate kind of way, but they're definitely my support system." Anne Davenport similarly reversed causality to make explicit how "gifts make friends" and to explain how gift-making friends become "family":[22]

> It's always been clear to me that my friends [who are single mothers] are my family here, because I can count on them more than I can count on my own family often. I mean, I can call up and say, "Look, I need this or I need that," and they're available.

Anne also insisted that this form of mutual obligation trumps biology:

> I have a group of friends that are absolutely amazing as far as the sacrifices that we make for one another are huge. Easter was a really good example. I had lunch with my parents, which was the traditional lunch with my parents and our minister...and then I had dinner with my friends. Somebody asked me what I was doing for Easter and I said, "I'm having lunch with my parents and I'm having dinner with my real family."

A Shared Boat

If kinship terminology helps to bind individuals in trusting relationships, trust does not rely on the assertion of kinship alone. Perhaps even more important to the creation of trust (and the claiming of others as kin) is the assurance that those who live in similar circumstances will understand, and be sympathetic about, one's circumstances.[23] In drawing on this support from this group, single mothers can avoid the stigmas associated with both poverty and a "deviant" family structure. Forty-year-old Kara Lattrell, the mother of one daughter, described a variety of people on whom she depended. She subsequently spoke with particular warmth about her relationship with two of her friends. In accounting for why they helped one another, she referred to their common situation:

> You know, we're really kind of in the same boat. I mean all three of us are single parents and we all have one child. We were all older parents when we had our children....So I think there's a lot of

that common bond...you know, sort of a shared life situation. It kind of makes it easy to think about helping each other out.

Other respondents also referred to a "shared life situation" as the reason why other single mothers would understand the strains in their lives and be sympathetic about the *need* for support. Using precisely the same image as did Kara, Anne Davenport said of her friendship with Joan Meyer: "We talk four times a day....She's a single mom and I think we're both in the same boat....I can trust her that she's not going to judge me or look at me in any different way and [that she] respects me for me." And Megan Paige listed a variety of reasons for wanting to shift her friendship circles when she became divorced. She put first the practical needs that motivated her creation of new friendships:

When I became single, I went out and I sought other single women friends....I realized that I particularly needed to be friends with other single parents because they were going to be the people that would be most receptive to having a network of helping each other out.

She also added that she believed single mothers would provide significant information and ongoing support for complex moral decisions:

A second benefit of [having a network] was just being able to talk: "What do you do about...." Like right now [my son] is riding his bike home. [I worry if this is] really a safe thing for him to do. And if something were to happen I would feel like I would have to defend that decision...I would have to defend that all on my own....And you make two thousand of those [moral decisions] a day as a parent...so you need to just [bounce] those things off other people....So I did seek people out to get certain kinds of support I didn't need before I was a single parent.

Though most of the women identified as "kin" those whose circumstances were very similar to their own, they also included within that framework other individuals who were perceived as having comparable, if not identical, needs, as well as individuals perceived as being in a similar position of social marginality. These people, the women insisted, could also be relied on to understand, and be sympathetic about, the problems single mothers face. Cathy Earl indicated that she had arrived at her preference of relying on those in similar situations after repeated negative experiences with asking her biological kin for help. In discussing her brothers she explained that although they had a shared background, they did not understand her current situation and that a biological connection alone did not make them sympathetic supporters or make her feel comfortable asking them for needed financial assistance:

Interviewer: Has there ever been a time you've needed [financial assistance] and haven't asked?

Cathy Earl: Oh, all the time.

Interviewer: And why don't you ask?

Cathy Earl: Because…you don't want them to think, "Here's Cathy again, she needs help again," you know, "She just can't make it." [My brothers] don't have any idea what it's like to be poor, to not have savings to fall back on. They've never been in that position. So there's a tendency to judge; even though they do help, they kind of feel like, you know, "What's wrong with her? Why can't she make it?" They don't have any idea what it's like to be single, to be a woman, to have three kids to support.

She then described the relationship of mutual support she has established with an older woman friend. Cathy believes that this friend will provide nonjudgmental assistance because of her own history:

You are either going to be seen as somebody who just can't make it, or [who is] always needy, and I think that is the real drawback in asking for help—except for my friends who are in similar situations, like other single mothers. I don't hesitate at all to ask them for help because they know what it's like. And same with Dorothy, an older woman, who lives on a fixed income, who raised her kids on welfare, and knew what it was like to be a single parent. Those are the people who I know that I can go to. They aren't going to judge me, look down on me. They're going to be there because they understand.

Cathy's belief that Dorothy is in a similar situation is, as she said, based on Dorothy's experience of living on a fixed income and raising her children on welfare, as well as her knowledge of what it meant to be a single parent. The circumstances need not be quite so precisely comparable as Cathy and Dorothy's, however, for a single mother to find in another person an affinity of marginality. Even so, the single mothers rarely include within their networks those who differ radically in terms of social class. And the most intense network bonds are often found among those who not only share class status, but also are of a similar age and educational background (see Table 2.1).

Table 2.1 Friendship Groups Among Respondents

Name	Age	Marital Status	Adopted a Child	Total Household Income	Welfare Reliance	Current Employment	Number of Children	Age of Oldest Child	Age of Youngest Child	Current Educational Activity	Highest Level of Education Completed
						Group 1					
Polly King	20	Never married	No	$7,884	Recent	Children's librarian	1	1.5	1.5	College	High school
Julie Marshall	23	Never married	No	$11,590	Current	Unemployed	1	1.5	1.5	College	High school
Rose Bishop	21	Never married	No	$10,760	Current	Service worker (fast-food restaurant)	1	1.5	1.5	College	High school
Group Average	21.3			$10,078			1	1.5	1.5		
						Group 2					
Leah Goodman	43	Never married	No	$8,700	Never	Unemployed (previously worked as medical technician; now disabled)	1	16	16	None	BA
Hannah Warner	44	Divorced	No	$19,251	Never	Administrative assistant	1	19	19	None	BA
Group Average	43.5			$13,976			1	17.5	17.5		

Name	Age	Marital Status	Adopted a Child	Total Household Income	Welfare Reliance	Current Employment	Number of Children	Age of Oldest Child	Age of Youngest Child	Current Educational Activity	Highest Level of Education Completed
Group 3											
Karen Kelly	39	Divorced	No	$9,504	Current	Unemployed (in school)	2	10	7	Graduate school	BA
Kate Harrington	36	Never married	No	$14,148	Current	Unemployed (in school)	1	0.5	0.5	Graduate school	BA
Barbara Quesnel	37	Divorced	No	$16,840	Never	Licensed practical nurse	1	6	6	Nursing training program	AA
Emily Quesnel	40	Divorced	No	$18,450	No	Bartender	2	8	4		AA
Group Average	38			$14,735			1.5	6.1	4.4		
Group 4											
Mary Farmer	40	Divorced	No	$36,656	No	Elementary-school teacher	3	11	5	None	BA
Stephanie Miller	40	Divorced	No	$30,334	No	Preschool teacher/after-school teacher	3	11	5	None	BA
Group Average	40			$30,334			3	11	5		
Group 5											
Grace Jordan	43	Never married	Yes	[no data]	No	Unemployed (previously worked as a teacher)	1	5	5	None	MA
Valerie Ramsey	46	Divorced	Yes	$49,000	No	social worker	1	5	5	None	MA
Group Average	44.5			$49,000			1	5	5		

Creating and Sustaining Close Networks

The commonalities within friendship and "kinship" groups among the single mothers in this study supply one piece of evidence that these networks do not arise by chance: They are not naturally existing communities to which the women gain entrance simply by virtue of being single mothers, but rather they represent careful creations comprised of those with shared demographic characteristics. Single mothers put considerable effort into establishing a social economy that includes within it like-minded individuals in similar circumstances. This effort encompasses the work of evaluating potential network members and choosing from among them, of traveling to be with those selected for inclusion in a network, and of creating opportunities for congeniality even in the midst of the pressing demands of daily life. Indeed, in the rural community in which this research was conducted, access to other single mothers requires this effort; rural dispersion means that neighborhoods do not necessarily supply a ready-made set of individuals for a network. As Megan Paige said, she actively "sought" other single mothers to become her friends. And recall how Sarah Stanley noted that her friends were located "all over the place," that she might have to "drive half an hour out of [her] way and drop [the children] at someone's house," and that she "worked really hard to make these friends." Sarah insisted as well that even though she found it hard to find the time to be with her friends, she considered doing so a priority because otherwise she would miss out on both the congeniality and the vital material support offered through friendship:

> It's hard to take the time to even be with friends sometimes, but I always make time—I always make a lot of time for friends. I have friends over; I do a lot of entertaining. Because friends are like our mainstay. We have a great time together and also we know that we're going to be there for one another. So there you go.

All of these efforts constitute significant costs of the social economy of single mothers, even as they lay the groundwork for significant benefits.

Negotiating Rules

If Sarah focused on the efforts that went into creating and making use of her network, other women made it clear that as participants in intimate relationships of support they had to learn to abide by implicit rules.[24]

The members of these networks might make exceptions for extraordinary needs, but by and large they operate on the basis of a fairly balanced exchange of equivalencies within a limited time span, even though the language of more generalized reciprocity—"what goes 'round comes 'round"—prevails. When asked whether she had needed help with child care during the past six months, Joan Meyer described how during routine times the friendship network operated on a loose formula of "switch-offs": "My friends and I do switch-offs [for child care]....The other switch-off that I do, is switch-off with rides....We try to schedule appointments around the same time frame." Similarly, Kara Lattrell described how her relationship with her mother had involved personal "banking services" to cover everyday needs: "When my mother was still alive we used to borrow back and forth a lot....For some reason, she might need twenty bucks, and I'd just have it on hand, and just whip it out, and loan her twenty, and I'd need ten, or fifty, or something, so she'd loan me, or she'd pay a bill, or I'd pay one of her bills, or something." Even though her relationships within her network of single mothers do not involve similar financial exchanges, as one of the few women who lived in close proximity to other single mothers, Kara described a constant flow of goods and services:

> We're sort of like the old, across-the-fence kind of neighbors. We trade back and forth, you know? The odd roll of toilet paper goes back and forth from house to house...and the cup of sugar, that kind of thing. We've traded child care a little bit, and [Mary] gives me rides sometimes now because she has a car.

Kara explained that it was "easy to think about helping" out Mary because she could assume that what went 'round would, indeed, come 'round. She approached her relationship with Claudia, another single mother, in the same way. Indeed, she described a support "triangle" among the three women: "If it's me, it means that sooner or later I'll help her and sooner or later Claudia will help me and then I'll help Mary and then Claudia will help Mary, and you know...."

As the women are questioned more fully about the details of these relationships, it becomes clear that notwithstanding the loose language of sharing, a balanced exchange of equivalencies *is* expected. On the one hand, Cathy Earl, like Kara, said she did not operate on a strict basis of immediate tit for tat. When asked by the interviewer, "Do you try and keep track, for example, with your friends? If you've asked one at one point do you try and ask someone else another time?" Cathy responded, "No, not with my friends, I don't." On the other hand, she also suggested that she kept a mental balance sheet of who had loaned, and of who was owed, as well as of their awareness of her reliability in paying back her debts. Furthermore, she reiterated that the sharing was acceptable because—as "true" kin—they would understand both how her need emerged and how it felt to experience that need.

Interviewer: If you needed money, for example, what do you think you would do?
Cathy Earl: Actually, Sarah has loaned me money before, so I could probably ask her, and Dorothy, for small amounts.... I feel okay about that. I always pay them back and I've done the same for them. Like I say, they know what it's like so it feels okay.

Anne Davenport indicated that the requirement of reciprocity was motivated by her awareness of the distinctive pattern of needs among women living close to the margin. Indeed, she believed she had special obligations to the single mothers in her network:

Because my group of support involves single women, single parents, moms...I want to make sure that it's reciprocal. [All that] comes into the decision: When have I last called them? Are they able to handle this right now? What can I do for them in exchange? Is there something I could do this week to help them out? I mean, you're always thinking about that.

Though Anne regards the fact that the other members of her network are single mothers with urgent needs as a reason to be especially careful about reciprocity, others make clear that issues of shared need and of shared vulnerability underlie the commitment to material balance in relationships with a broader range of individuals. Sheila Davis, for example, holds herself to a tight standard of balanced reciprocity with her elderly neighbors: "And then my neighbors, my elderly neighbors, I do their tax return and do dinner for them, and they mow my lawn." Recall that Sheila spoke in general terms when asked about her sense of obligation in relationships in which people offered material assistance ("Nobody is saying you should even it up but I do that"). But she isolated this relationship as one in which she wanted to make certain of an especially tidy balance sheet: "I don't want to take advantage of them at all."

As Anne's comment above suggests, the rules for survival in these relationships extend beyond maintaining balance. Anne believed it was her responsibility to be sensitive to whether or not someone was able to "handle" a request at a given time. And, as Anne continued her discussion of implicit rules, she explained that her network expected its members to avoid taking advantage of momentary vulnerability:

I think everybody—community, friends, family—has different things to offer and I think you need to be mindful that this one friend may be on overload and you cannot ask them for any more. [When Joan was in a car accident], for example, I knew she was tired, I knew she was in pain.... It wasn't like I was going to call her up and say, "Hey, want two more kids?" Even though I had a need I wasn't going to make her life miserable because of it. Being mindful of that and paying attention to what is available and making sure that you're not asking too much—keeping an eye on that [is important].

A Failed Relationship

The rules may be held in abeyance for a given moment. In the long run, however, failure to abide by them can result in being thrust out of a sustaining network. Kate Harrington, a new mother at age thirty-six (about whom more will be written below), described how a violation of these norms had broken up her circle of support. In her description she vacillated between taking responsibility for the dissolution of her community and expressing a sense of grievance at being abandoned, suggesting that she was still trying to figure out the rules for a new set of circumstances.

Kate Harrington: I've needed a lot of emotional support.
Interviewer: And where does that come from?
Kate Harrington: Well, it's not [coming] right now, because my community is kind of dissolving.... I'm in transition trying to create a new one.... I just had two people really kind of back off of me, and my feeling was I was asking for too much, although, realistically, I don't believe that I was, but I think that that's what they were feeling, so they backed off. So I just lost two of my support people.

Without privileging either voice, it is worth noting that one of the two lost members of her network—another single mother—believed that Kate had violated the norms of this kind of relationship. According to thirty-seven-year-old Barbara Quesnel, who has been divorced for two years and is the mother of one six-year-old daughter, Kate took more than she gave and was not sensitive to availability.

Interviewer: And Kate is a friend?
Barbara Quesnel: Yes. (*In an exasperated tone of voice, she laughs.*)
Interviewer: Oh! (*Laughs.*) And what's given and received in that [relationship]?

Barbara Quesnel: I actually do more giving than she does. She's a taker....[I give her] babysitting, emotional support, listening to her victimized life.

Interviewer: So how do you negotiate that relationship?

Barbara Quesnel: I met her in the crisis of my life. And she was very, very emotionally supportive; I was very vulnerable....She's constantly asking things of me, and I have a tendency to say yes, when inside myself it's not really what I want to do.

As this example of a failing relationship suggests, the work of getting support does not cease simply because a community has been created. Maintaining these support networks requires enormous efforts. Recall how Cathy Earl included an older woman, Dorothy, in her close network because she thought Dorothy could empathize with her needs. But Cathy insisted that this relationship requires a lot of daily maintenance and is not simply there for the asking:

> She can consume a lot of my time, she's quite needy, and some-times I get frustrated with her because she gets kind of possessive of my time, but she's always been there for me.... We have fights. You know, she'll get annoyed at me because I didn't call her....I have to kind of keep constant contact with her, so it's kind of a high-maintenance relationship. If I don't call her every few days her nose gets a little bent out of joint.

To be sure, biological families and biological kin also require this kind of work, and women frequently assume responsibility for it. As anthropologist Micaela di Leonardo shows, it is often women who send cards and remember birthdays.[25] Similarly, the sociologist Marjorie DeVault demonstrates that it is women who prepare the meals that enable individuals to enact family life.[26] And whether relationships are high maintenance (as Cathy described hers with Dorothy) or low maintenance, their sustenance depends not only on material gestures of support but also on the emotion work of listening and caring.

RECIPROCITY WITH FAMILY AND FRIENDS IN A MORE FORTUNATE WORLD

While single mothers appear to find comfort in, and rely heavily on, equitable and balanced exchanges in their relationships with other single mothers (as well as with others who are perceived to be in similar circumstances), these close networks cannot fulfill all their needs. Single mothers thus also reach out to other members of their social worlds as they strive to meet the demands that caregiving, employment, and the everyday activities of housework make on their time and energy.

Family members can become especially important as sources to draw on for assistance; this is especially likely when they are perceived as being more fortunate than the single mothers themselves. However, it is also the case that these arrangements of support from kin are often fraught with difficulty, as is indicated by the above comments and as will be discussed further below. Friends who are not single mothers can also be drawn into relationships of support. Like the single-mother friends, these others, both family and friends, offer a wide range of goods and services to the respondents, including emotional support, limited financial support, and help with the tasks of daily survival (e.g., transportation and babysitting). However, these "other" individuals are more likely than are single-mother friends to offer substantial financial support, which is a form of assistance unavailable from those who have little extra themselves.[27] If the elements of what the single mothers receive from these other individuals are otherwise the same, the understanding of the relationships is quite different. Indeed, the women are far more likely to acknowledge imbalance in the material content of these relationships than they are in their relationships with those considered to be in "the same boat," even as they proclaim their commitment to reciprocity.

Some "Balanced" Reciprocity

That said, it is also the case that relationships with those more privileged (economically or in life circumstances) do not necessarily lack *elements* of a balanced exchange of material goods and services. When possible, single mothers try to sustain the exchange of equivalencies. Joan Meyer, for example, listed her mother (in addition to her friends Anne and Martha) as someone with whom she had a "switch-off": "My mom helps out quite a bit, which is a godsend, and with her the switch-off is that . . . when they go away, I have to go watch their house and feed their dogs and take care of their birds and do that kind of thing." But Joan also admitted that she could not always return equivalencies, even to her mother, because although her mother provides child care while Joan house-sits, her mother has also in the past provided Joan with substantial financial support. When Mary Farmer, the thirty-eight-year-old mother of two young sons, described her network, she depicted help from her family as a "humongous arrow" *toward her.* She acknowledged that she had not only accepted that inequality, but that she had also allowed a large debt to accumulate in a broad friendship circle:

> I get out of work a little bit later than my youngest one gets out of kindergarten, so I have various friends helping me out—they take care of him for about forty-five minutes... until I get there to pick him up.... I kind of feel like I need to reciprocate but on the other hand I can't really do that.... We kind of have a babysitting co-op... and I'm like ninety hours in the hole.

The failure to be able to reciprocate in kind is not surprising. Recall that the single mothers *do* have acute and unpredictable needs, and for the most part, limited material resources, time, and energy with which to make exchanges. This is not to imply that the women readily accepted unmitigated dependence. In order to accept substantial assistance without admitting to dependence, Joan and Mary, like the other single mothers interviewed, did the "cultural work" of coming up with strategic explanations for how their behavior could be conceived of as fitting within the norm of reciprocity. They also, like the other mothers, made whatever concrete gestures they could to enable them to accept help without incurring debt.[28]

Material Imbalance

Reciprocity Through Gratitude, Emotion Work, and Loyalty

Much theoretical writing about reciprocity would suggest that exchange relationships can be balanced by repaying material goods with gratitude, emotion work, and loyalty. What is striking, however, is that it is only with respect to those identified as being more fortunate than themselves, that single mothers define gratitude, emotion work, and loyalty not merely as vital elements of repayment for goods and services received, but sometimes as the sole repayment. In asserting that these are sufficient items of exchange in some, but not all, of their relationships, the single mothers distinguish among sets of relationships; they also accept the costly burden of engaging in actions that can undermine their position as social equals, even as they claim reciprocity as a way to fulfill the obligations incumbent on an adult in our society.[29]

A straightforward economy of gratitude operates in some cases.[30] Phoebe Stark, a forty-one-year-old mother of twin sons, first asserted that her relationships with others were "all pretty reciprocal" and she noted that she preferred it that way because she didn't want to "be obligated to people." Yet she also acknowledged that she was the recipient of gifts for which she incurred debts fulfilled by simply offering thanks: "People are always giving [Christmas presents] to my kids and... I don't give gifts anymore, except for my immediate family.... We make sure that [people who give presents are] thanked and we are grateful." Indeed, the women view an understanding of the requirement of showing gratitude as part of a growing maturity, even if fulfilling that requirement places them in a subordinate position. Twenty-one-year-old Rose Bishop explained, "I definitely feel an obligation to let [people] know how appreciative I am.... I used to always forget to say 'thank you.'" Alexis Smith, now age thirty-four, described a similar personal shift: "As I get older I'm more aware of the balancing. I think when I was younger I just tended to take it for granted, like someone would always be there, always, always, always. And it's just not like that."

Phoebe Stark added as well that in relationships with those more fortunate she viewed "emotion work" as a valuable item of exchange: "I might give in other ways. I have a tendency to give in other ways to people, not in material ways—by being there or calling and, you know, checking on people and friends and talking."[31] Similarly, Kara Lattrell suggested that she recognized a debt to her brother and sister-in-law because, "they're supportive of me in my situation.... They take my daughter and provide me time to rest and sort of recharge my body." And she suggested that she paid off a portion of this perceived debt by sharing her intuition and knowledge: "I give them support in different ways. I mean, sometimes we'll talk about a problem and then we'll just discuss it. And I'll listen to them. I guess sometimes they appreciate my insight into things."

Jackie Ferland, who relies regularly on her mother to babysit for her three boys, talks about creating balance by calling and checking up on her mother at times when she is *not* in need, thereby putting "money into the bank" in advance. However, unlike Megan Paige, who made concrete gestures of assistance to her single-mother friends as a hedge against emergencies, Jackie is exchanging loyalty (rather than practical assistance) for her mother's regular response to her child care needs: "[I reciprocate by] just calling her. I hate it when I have to call her to ask her to do something and I'll find myself thinking sometimes, even during the day, 'I need to call Mom because I *don't* need anything from her.' I want to call and let her know that I do [call] sometimes *not* needing something."

For the most part, these reciprocal gestures include concrete actions—thanking, listening, and remaining in contact with visits and calls—which cut into leisure time and emotional energy. But, given their great needs and their limited resources, it may not be surprising to learn that some single mothers believe they are fulfilling the demands of reciprocity simply by *not* acting. Barbara Quesnel was hospitalized for depression in the months immediately after her husband left. She suggested that she repaid her mother for support by not revealing the intensity of her anguish: "Right after I came out of the hospital I knew that it was very, very difficult for [my parents] to see me because I've always been very, very strong and I...did not want to hurt them so I pulled away." (Although Barbara stresses not wanting to "hurt" her parents, she might well have been protecting herself from humiliation, as she hid the pain and distress that attended the breakup of her marriage.) In short, some women are so conscious of the many times they do *not* call a parent or friend, despite their striking and significant needs, that they come to see that withholding as a "gift." Of course, as they do this, they also deny themselves necessary support and might strain their relationships with those hurt by the lack of contact, even as they defend themselves against the intrusiveness of those who might question their actions.

Affiliation with Themselves and Their Children

In addition to gratitude, emotion work, and loyalty, single mothers view affiliation with their children, and in some cases affiliation with themselves, as resources that meet the demands of reciprocity. If the quid pro quo is so attenuated here as to seem to vanish, in context the women make it clear that they embed affiliation within their notion of the obligations of reciprocal exchange.

Indeed, children frequently become "pawns" in the strategy of giving and receiving. Betsy Black, a thirty-eight-year-old mother of two sons, simultaneously asserted her rights as a single mother with ongoing needs to have care provided by her own mother *and* suggested that she was not left in debt because her mother derived pleasure simply from being with the grandchildren: "Because I'm a single mom I ask [my mother] to spend time with the kids.... And it's a really good experience for the kids and she loves it of course." She also said that she rarely repaid her friends in kind because their children so loved having her children visit, it made their parenting easier: "And then my kids go for sleepovers because their kids like having them there." When Kara Lattrell was asked "what's given and received" in her relationship with her brother and sister-in-law, she responded, "Well, let's see. I probably get more from them than I give, but I give them my kid! That's a lot!" And although Anne Davenport refers to her friends as her "real family," she has, indeed, been very dependent on her flesh-and-blood parents. She has not paid them rent in years or reimbursed them for paying her fuel bill during the previous winter. In addition, she uses their car and they regularly babysit her children. While it is not always easy for her to dispel her sense of dependence, she balances the account sheet by pointing to the satisfaction they derive from ensuring that their grandchildren are cared for well: "I know my parents and know them well enough to know that they would not be happy if they didn't feel like they were doing something and making sure that their grandchildren were taken care of."

Satisfying the Giver's Expectations

A different, but closely related, gesture of reciprocity involves drawing on evidence that a mother has satisfied the giver's expectations and desires. Most simply, the women point to their own survival and the survival of their children, as meeting the perceived desire of friends and relatives to ensure the livelihood of those they love. In doing so, single mothers often highlight the positive outcomes of divorce or separation.

Respondents suggest, for example, that relatives and friends who have watched them suffer emotional pain and even physical violence in their prior relationships are "reimbursed" when they see the women escape. As one woman said, "It was very clear that it was no strings attached and [my father and brothers] didn't want [the money] paid back at all. They were really proud that I had gotten out of a bad situation and they wanted to help me out and make sure it worked."

In some exchanges, single mothers understand well that satisfaction on the part of the giver is linked not just to their "survival" or to their getting out of a bad situation, but also to the expectation of other kinds of *specific* actions on their part. In the next chapter I consider how single mothers prove "worthiness" when they receive support from the state. Difficult as that might be, single mothers do receive relatively clear directions about appropriate behavior, and a clear determination of what is "owed," in their relationships with social-welfare caseworkers. In their relationships with family and friends, however, the means for demonstrating that they are sufficiently worthy to be helped are not clearly spelled out, and the nature of the debt is left undefined. In both sets of relationships single mothers might be compelled to act in ways that contradict their own desires. In their relationships with the state, the failure to meet that obligation can have immediate monetary repercussions. In their relationships with family and friends, there is more room for negotiation. Even so, a failure to meet an obligation—whether or not it is clearly stated—can result in residual guilt.

As will be shown, Betsy Black suggested that her father had learned that it was enjoyable to give. She also understood that her father's pleasure was tied to the fact that she was pursuing a goal *he* valued: "My dad's helping me out.... I know he thinks it's really important. He's very excited that I'm going back [to school]." Alexis Smith makes a similar claim. During the interview she itemized some of the help she had recently received, and for which she was grateful, from members of her family:

My father recently [helped when]...I just had a whole bunch of car trouble, car insurance, all that stuff....My family has been very good and when they know I'm in trouble, they help. They're very generous. My mother on her own decided that she would write me a check every month for a hundred dollars to help with the rent, for example. Or when we go visit my brother he'll pay for both the kids' tickets and he'll pay for mine.

When asked whether she believed any "obligation" stemmed from these gestures of support, Alexis responded affirmatively, amplifying her response by noting that she felt that obligation as a persistent pressure tied closely to her family's expectations of her. Though she tried to dismiss the full weight of these expectations with reference to the members of her family being happy if she were happy, she also acknowledged that they weighed heavily on her:

Oh yes, that's the kicker. I pressure myself a lot about [that]. Bottom line—they really would love to see me get a BA, an MA, a PhD and really, really just shine the way they see shine. But I also know that they're cool and they'll be happy if I'm happy. If I get to the place where I'm happy and I'm really loving what I do and taking care of myself the way I want to take care of myself, they are there and they are willing to help me get there. So, the money thing, they don't really hold it over my head too much. It's really inside my head. It's constant though. It's constant.

When probed to explain further how she managed this constant pressure, she responded: "I just try to get better and better at my life and get happy....I guess the way to fulfill an obligation is just to show them that I am living well and doing well by my kids."

While it is not surprising to find discussions of exchanges with parents and siblings that rest on the recipient's assumption that the giver will be satisfied by ensuring her survival (and that of her children), some single mothers used the same logic in their relationships with friends. Joanna Darling, a forty-five-year-old mother of five children, was asked directly, "When things are done for you or given to you, do you feel obligated to do something in return?" She responded in the affirmative but immediately added that the balance was "complicated." To illustrate what she meant, she described her relationship with a friend, Jon, who had not charged for the chiropractic work he had done on her back:

There's a part of me that is like, "Oh, God, what can I give back to him!" You know? And I've struggled with it and I've said, "Jon, please charge me!" And at one point I realized that I didn't need to do anything [for Jon] other than just love myself.

The Giver Is Satisfied by Giving

Scholars have pointed to the ways in which employers may hire domestic helpers or child-care workers and redefine these employees in ways that minimize their efforts. In so doing, the employer implicitly minimizes her *own* obligations.[32] For example, mothers who rely on family day-care providers describe them in ways that make giving love and daily care part of the individual's personality rather than a service requiring financial reimbursement. As one mother explained, when describing her day-care provider, "[She] is just a special person with little kids—it's a mothering, nurturing thing that doesn't stop with her own."[33]

In relationships where the shoe is on the other foot and where the *less* powerful person (by virtue of circumstance) is in the position of receiving more assistance than she is able or willing to repay, these same techniques are used to evade responsibility for making an equivalent return. In this new equation, the recipient describes how the giver derives pleasure from an act of generosity and argues that this pleasure is sufficient to expunge any further obligation. One mother said that she was not sure what she offered in her relationship with a downstairs neighbor ("I guess to some extent some emotional support"), but that in a sense, returning something of equivalent value didn't matter because that convenient neighbor was "an incredibly giving person." Alexis Smith similarly could accept presents from her brother because he was "sweet, very sweet" to think of buying her sheets for her new household, and she could accept clothing from her mother because her "mom tends to like to buy my daughter a dress or something." And Betsy Black could accept help from her father not only because she was meeting his expectations, but also because "he's learned that it's delightful to be able to give support."

Residual Conflict

Single mothers strive to find ways to reconcile dependence with independence and the need to expose insufficiency with the possibility of scorn for that insufficiency. When they fail to reconcile the competing needs—when they believe they have become too dependent or too exposed to contempt—the single mothers sometimes break off relationships with individuals from whom they may very well need support. Recall that Cathy Earl preferred to borrow small sums of money from her friends rather than from her brothers because she could not stand being seen as "as somebody who just can't make it." Cathy indicated that this calculated decision to privilege her pride over their disdain meant forgoing vital support, and that sometimes she had to make the opposite choice. Even then, however, she chose carefully from within her network:

> If it's something financial, something I just can't swing, I would call my brother Kenneth. He would be first on the list. My brother Michael, he's second because he's not quite as understanding. For small things, a ride somewhere, or could you help me pick up the kids or something like that, I have Dorothy, I have my friend Sarah, I have a couple of other friends that are nearby here that I would rely on.

Cathy also suggested that she tried to avoid a man who had previously been her boyfriend, because he humiliated her with his constant reminders that she might have been better off staying with him:

> He's the type who would pitch in and help, but there's a price there. You know, the price is, you have to listen to him say, "See, you couldn't make it on your own, could you, Cathy." And so he rubs it in, so even though he's willing to do a lot for me...but he'd go, "Hey Kid, you really need me, don't you, after all. You couldn't make it on your own." And so, as much as I need him, or it would be nice [to have his help], you have to put up with that attitude, and so I really try not to [ask him].

Ultimately, women who cannot accept the price of "gifts"—or who cannot find any explanation for their failure to repay gifts received in the past—may withdraw from and even terminate relationships with those to whom they perceive themselves as being in debt.

> I haven't called [my friend Peter] for a long time because...I really want to pay [back the money I owe him] and I hate not being able. And he says, I mean, he says over and over and over again, "I know you'll pay it when you can." It's very hard for me. And so I have withdrawn....I haven't talked to him in almost six months.

STRETCHING AND RESISTING RECIPROCITY

Generalized Reciprocity in an Ideal Community

As the women we interviewed discuss their relationships with the broader community in which they live, reciprocity emerges in a new guise. At one level, the women sound as if they believe the world should operate on the basis of an easy flow of generalized reciprocity over time. When asked what it is appropriate to ask of the community in which she lived, twenty-year-old Polly King responded, "I feel it's appropriate to ask as little as you can get away with, give as much as you can, and somewhere along the line everybody gets what they need." Liz Miles, who is considerably older than Polly, also described a world of generalized reciprocity:

> I believe if there are balances other places, that it doesn't necessarily have to be between two people, in the sense of somebody may give me something and I may give someone else something. But when it doesn't feel balanced to me is when I feel like I can't give to anyone else, when people are giving to me and I can't give to anyone else.

At another level, if these two women do accept the requirement to make returns for gifts received, they acknowledge that the constraints are much looser than those that apply in their more intimate relationships: Liz may give to one person today and assume that person will pass on the favor, and Polly needs only to give what she can.

As Polly and Liz shift their attention to the flow of goods and services throughout a community, they rely on an idealized vision of human nature in which individuals readily hold themselves responsible for, and eagerly respond to, the needs of others. The embodiment of this kind of human nature may well be an especially expected feature of the "tight" community Sarah Stanley hoped she would find when she moved to Vermont. The language women employ when they describe that "hope" also rests, at least in part, on the imagery of a traditional, rural community in which everyone knows everyone else, where needs and wants are public concerns. Addressing this issue more directly, Sarah said, "I would like to see communities where neighbors are there for one another, to help out in the middle of the night if there's like a crisis or a flood. I believe in giving and receiving and helping, helping one another. That makes sense."

Resisting Claims

If Polly, Liz, and Sarah believe in generalized reciprocity, they also resist the notion that the obligation to give falls equally on everyone's shoulders at any given point in time. Although Sarah said she believed "in giving and receiving and helping," she rejected the notion that there was a "should" attached to this ideal: "Some people have more time, more money. They're not overwhelmed in their daily lives and they have the time and the energy to devote to the communities." Sarah thus excluded herself—and others in similar circumstances—from the obligation to give during periods of acute distress. Similarly, when Rose Bishop says that she believes "people are pretty understanding right now [that] I can't offer a whole lot," she acknowledges that she is not now in a position to engage in reciprocal behavior (though she anticipates that there may be a time when she will be able to play a different kind of role in the chain of generalized reciprocity). We could recall as well Mary Farmer, who now owes ninety hours to her babysitting pool. When asked to discuss her feelings about this, she said, "I don't feel like I reciprocate as much as I'd like to, but a lot of times it's because [the others] don't really have the same needs that I do in terms of child care." Grace Jordan, a fifty-one-year-old, never-married mother of one adopted daughter, provided yet another, subtle variation on this theme. While she originally accepted the obligation to reciprocate to a friend who had done much for her over the years, ultimately she rejected that obligation because she deemed her friend's needs excessive and even trivial when compared to her own:

> I never figured out how to reciprocate with her except this one time. I said, "Let me! Tell me what I can do." And so when she asks me, she says, "I'm flying to California and David can't take me to the airport, could you take me?" She's finally asking me for a very concrete way I can help her. And I said, "I can't do it on that day, I'm really sorry!" And she said, "Well, David can't either and I don't know what I'm supposed to do." And I said, "I've got to tell you something. No one ever drives me to the airport. I drive myself and leave my car in the long-term parking lot." It's not a big deal; that was my subtext.

Hating to Ask

When single mothers rely on others for assistance to get by, they do so through practices that enable them to believe in their own independence, avoid scorn and humiliation, and sustain commitment to the ideal of a "tight" community. Thus they simultaneously solve practical problems of daily life and the moral problem of conceiving of themselves as *worthy* citizens. In doing so, they not only have to work to develop appropriate networks, but they also must overcome their own resistance to asking for help, and develop the fine art of asking.

Many women said that it had been difficult for them to ask for help because doing so changed their own self-image; some even described the act as leading to feelings of resentment about having to ask at all.

Kara Lattrell believed that sometimes she should simply be the recipient of "pure" generosity and that she should not have to ask for needed assistance. In explaining how she arrived at this position, she told a story about having yelled at her child in public, which led to her being the object of a neighbor's gossip. She examined her anger with her neighbor and found its roots in the neighbor's failure to make extra efforts to meet the needs of single parents:

> It kind of sunk in that the reason why I was angry at her was not because she was talking about it, or not because she noticed it, or not because she was concerned about it, but because what the hell had she ever done to prevent it?...And [I want to tell her] that the thing to really look at is not how awful I was that I yelled at my kid, but how, if she doesn't want to be part of the problem, she needs to be part of the solution. And part of the solution means that...she has a responsibility to the kids, and having a responsibility [means] really going to a parent and saying, "Hey, you know, I noticed you're a single parent. I'll bet that's pretty stressful." And it's like, "Gee, I guess I could have your little Billy or little Susie come over to my house and play with my kid, like, you know, once a week for a couple of hours." And how would that be? That would really help you out. God! If somebody did that to me I'd feel like I was in seventh heaven.

Amy Phelps, the divorced mother of two daughters, expressed the same sentiment in a less ferocious way:

> I just did [my own snow shoveling and plowing] and then eventually [a neighbor offered] to plow and that was nice. I think there's still some people out there that will see that it's just her and her two kids and maybe I can help out. There still are a few nice people like that. And that's happened to me a couple of times so that's been great....Sometimes I feel kind of weird—like you think I can't do this—and then sometimes, I guess it depends on the day, it's like, "Oh, thank you." Most of the time I don't refuse them. I say, "Thanks so much."

In short, while the single mothers want to see themselves as equal participants in a world where generous giving prevails, they also believe that their current situation of need entitles them, at least temporarily, to be on the receiving end of that generosity; they thus introduce a notion of noblesse oblige (even as they reject its associated costs of deference).

In so doing they retain their social status as citizens who have (eventual) obligations to a community and they locate the help they receive within the moral framework of what decent people do for others. By insisting that decent people respond to need without being asked, they shift the burden of responsibility from their shoulders to the shoulders of others.

Learning to Ask for Help

If they resent having to ask for help, the women know that they often have no choice; they have to accept the fact that they cannot manage on their own. As this acceptance seeps in, they come to regard their acquisition of the skill of seeking out assistance, as a concrete achievement emerging from their changed circumstances. As one woman described it, she had never had to ask for help before, but she believed that in learning to do so she had acquired an important new set of skills:

> Well, I really think that [asking for help is] something I never did before and I just, as a single parent, I've realized that I have to ask for the support I need. So I've learned to do that. And it may have been hard at first, but I really, at this point, I feel like okay, they can say no, you know. And the financial part—that's just a small, small piece of the whole picture. Mostly what I need is support with the kids. And I do ask for help. . . . I've just gotten a lot better at [asking for help] than I was before. . . . It's easier because I've been practicing.

Moreover, those who have mastered the fine art of asking suggest that they have also acquired the challenging skill of judging who is available, competent, and appropriate for a given need. Janet Linden explained, "It's really hard to trace my thought processes because there's just an image that comes up and when I feel like I need someone to talk to, a face appears, and that's who I call, and I would be real hesitant myself to try to trace what has happened." Alexis Smith spoke similarly about an elaborate process of determining whom she could ask for assistance with each of the different tasks of daily survival:

> So I decide by—I try to decide by checking in and seeing what I need. And if it's a financial thing I call my dad—or my mom. And if it's an issue of like an immediate thing or an immediate crisis or decision, I would call a friend; but also, if it's something I feel like my mom just wouldn't get it, I just wouldn't call her. . . . I guess

it's pretty intricate. . . . Because then you're thinking about what is this person's relationship to you? And I guess different parts of me are out there with different people.

Kate Harrington, the woman whose network was dissolving, spoke eloquently about not yet having acquired the necessary skills during this "unsettled" period in her life.[34] While her focus in the quote below is on learning how to be a single mother—what she calls this "24-7, just me"—her comments also made clear that she had not yet learned about how being a single mother had changed her needs, and with them her relationships with those in her circle of friends. The comments also suggest that she is still learning how to balance her own needs with what she can offer to others in return for their assistance. As she considered this issue, she both assessed her own gifts and acknowledged the limits of her energy and understanding:

> Well, you know, this is kind of new. You know, before [my daughter was born], friendships were friendships and I didn't have as many needs. Since then, you know, it's just kind of like trial and error. There's a lot I can do. I'm really good at giving emotional support. You know, I'm good at that. But there's a lot of other things I can do too that people—like my one friend didn't accept my offers to help her move. . . . I have to be careful because I don't have a lot to give right now. So I have to be careful about how much I ask for because I don't have a lot. I mean everything is pretty much going into learning how to be a single mother and handling this like 24-7, just me. So I don't have a whole lot to give out.

CONCLUSION

This chapter has shown that when single mothers rely on others they distinguish among different groups of people in their social worlds, and they operate within the constraints of a broadly defined reciprocity even as the enactment of that norm shifts with the perceived situation of the giver. The analysis in this chapter has also shown that maintaining relationships of support, balanced or not, is challenging work. In some ways the dispersed rural setting of Vermont intensifies the work of community: Because they live in relative geographical isolation from others in similar situations, single mothers have to work especially hard to make exchanges with, or to do favors for, others who share their circumstances of need. In contrast to the women interviewed by Carol Stack, for example, these mothers cannot simply run next door for assistance; nor can they assume that neighbors will notice their need, and if they do notice, either be available to help out or be sympathetic to the situation.[35]

At the same time, the dispersion means that these women are not segregated into tightly bounded or segregated ghettos of poverty where no one has much to give. As Kathryn Edin and Laura Lein note in *Making Ends Meet*, single mothers living in very poor neighborhoods receive less cash assistance from family and friends than do those who live in somewhat better or more varied surroundings.[36] The latter women, like those in this study, are more likely to be in contact with individuals who possess greater resources, even as they are more likely to be exposed to direct scorn from those whose lives differ from their own.

It might also be the case that the rural context helps to support an idealized vision of community where pure generosity prevails. In fact, as I discuss in the Conclusion, in the thinking single mothers do about a desirable social policy, this idealized community looms large. The actual dealings single mothers have with local agencies that formally represent community, however, differ significantly from that ideal.

3

ACCOUNTING FOR WELFARE[1]

As was noted in chapter 1, during the debates about what has euphemistically come to be called "welfare reform," much attention was focused on the issue of "dependency." The conservative goal, built into the Personal Responsibility and Work Opportunity Reconciliation Act (PRWORA) of 1996, was to bring individuals to a state of economic self-sufficiency—defined more or less as independence from public welfare programs. All able-bodied adults, unless independently wealthy, were to be engaged in work for wages.[2]

This goal of self-sufficiency rested on the simple notion that poverty and dependence were one and the same phenomenon. Some thought that both ultimately derived from the character flaws and bad values encouraged by existing social welfare provisions: The causal analysis suggested that a reliance on social welfare led to dysfunctional subcultures (replete with fatherless families), which, in turn, engendered inadequate personality traits, which, to complete the cycle, resulted in further reliance on social welfare. Charles Murray, one of the most outspoken early critics of welfare, for example, viewed the existence of welfare programs as creating "moral hazards"; once these programs were provided, individuals were encouraged to choose them over work and thus became trapped in a cycle of dependency.[3]

Although Murray illustrated the moral hazards of welfare dependency with the hypothetical couple of Harold and Phyllis (who used a cost-benefit analysis to choose welfare over employment), single mothers—the chief recipients of what was then called Aid to Families with Dependent Children (AFDC)—became the specific focus of much of his critique, and that of the broader population. In the social threat discourse so prevalent during the 1990s, the growing number of single-mother families was used as evidence of the moral breakdown of the society as a whole.[4] Indeed, single motherhood itself came to represent a host of wrong "choices"—to live without men, to raise children without fathers, and often, given the demographics of the population, to be black or Hispanic rather than white. Single mothers who "chose" welfare reliance over waged employment were viewed as representing a particularly dangerous set of character flaws: They were lazy, unmotivated, likely to cheat, and, in the worst case scenario, had children simply to lengthen the period, while increasing the monetary value, of their benefits.[5]

A substantial body of literature demonstrates that these stereotypes, and the myths of middle-class independence on which they rest, are accepted not only by the general public but also by welfare recipients themselves. A 1966 study by Scott Briar found that black, white, and Mexican-American women receiving AFDC never spoke of "us" but instead used the word "them" to refer to others who shared their structural position, thereby creating an illusion of distance between themselves and the "typical" recipient of public aid.[6] Later studies showed a more overt self-criticism. In 1976, Harold R. Kerbo found that some welfare mothers internalized the stigma of being recipients and believed that people are poor because they are lazy and irresponsible about work.[7] Nancy Goodban's 1985 study also found that many women blamed themselves for their situation and were ashamed of relying on welfare.[8]

Three more recent studies confirm the basic findings of these analyses. In 1996 Liane Davis and Jan Hagan reported "some striking similarities between [their] findings" and those of earlier studies:[9]

> Like Briar's participants, these women clearly differentiated themselves from the stereotype of the welfare cheat.... One of the ways the women dealt with the stigma of welfare was to externalize the reasons for their entry into the system.

Karen Seccombe, Delores James, and Kimberly Walters found in 1999 that while welfare recipients attributed "their own reliance on welfare to structural factors, to fate, or to the idiosyncrasies of the welfare system itself," they attributed "welfare use by other women to laziness, personal shortcomings, or other inadequacies."[10] One year later, Ann Tickamyer and her coauthors, drawing on data collected in four focus-group discussions among welfare recipients, found that the women made "strong distinctions between deserving versus undeserving recipients that mirror(ed) the views of the larger culture."[11]

Like these studies, this chapter examines how welfare-reliant women deal with the stigma associated with their status. I first turn my attention to data showing the extensive use of means-tested programs among single mothers. I then turn to the issue of how single mothers view their own use of these programs. I show that, in contrast to the strategy discussed in the previous chapter of emphasizing commonality with others in the same boat, women who are welfare reliant differentiate their use from that of others in the same category, and they maintain social networks that develop from similarities in age and educational background rather than from shared reliance on welfare alone. I also demonstrate that welfare recipients argue that their own reliance on welfare expresses both a long-standing commitment to self-sufficiency and an equally fervent interest in providing for the physical care of their children.

In the third section of the chapter I investigate the changes in recipients' attitudes that occurred in conjunction with Vermont's Welfare Restructuring Plan (WRP). Contrasting the views of women who were welfare reliant before the 1994 restructuring with those who were welfare reliant in the postrestructuring period, I show how a claim of worthiness shifted from evidence of nurturing their children well to evidence of progress toward individual self-reliance. I also show that this shift had its roots in the public debates about welfare "reform" and in the administration of welfare itself. I thus demonstrate that assertions of moral worth for actions within a social economy build on, and reflect, the institutionalized discourse.

Finally, I discuss how the new, and more intrusive, administration resulted in altered relationships with welfare personnel. Recipients during the prerestructuring era viewed themselves as having a right to public money. Because the state essentially left them alone, they maintained ownership of, and personal pride in, the accomplishments of self-improvement during the period they were welfare reliant. When the state made welfare contingent on evidence of "progress," individuals came to view their achievements as part of a contract with the state. Instead of envisioning state support as a right available to all, they come to see it as an individual reward for moral worth.

THE FREQUENT USE OF SOCIAL WELFARE

Single mothers and their children frequently rely on welfare and they constitute the vast majority of all welfare recipients. In Vermont, for example, approximately one quarter of all single mothers with children under age eighteen rely on welfare. Sixty-seven percent of the state's families relying on Temporary Assistance for Needy Families (TANF) today are headed by a single parent.[12] These figures are explained by both the widespread poverty of single-mother families and the social policy that gives priority to single-parent families.

But even these statistics are deceptively low. Because there is considerable mobility on and off the welfare rolls, the number of single mothers who have *ever* relied on welfare is considerably larger than the one-quarter statistic suggests. Among the women in this study, for example, only one quarter were welfare reliant when we spoke with them, but an additional one third of the women had relied on welfare some time in the previous decade. Scholarship that examines welfare-reliant women separately from wage-reliant women overlooks both this mobility and the fact that the two groups of women have a range of experiences in common. One of these commonalities is likely to be reliance on other stigmatized programs. Although welfare is subject to particular disdain in our society, many other social programs also expose participants to public condemnation, and the individuals who rely on these programs far outnumber those who ever become welfare recipients. In the early 2000s, for example, when a total of 12,494 adults and children were receiving cash assistance from Vermont's TANF program, 16,290 children alone were enrolled in the food stamp program and 15,903 women and children were enrolled in the Women, Infants and Children program (WIC).[13] (Among the women in this study, on top of those who were welfare reliant at the time of the interview, an additional four were receiving food stamps and an additional seven were receiving WIC food supplements; many more had relied on these benefits at previous times in their lives.)

THE AWARENESS OF, AND RESPONSE TO, SOCIAL DENIGRATION

Recognizing Stigma

As was noted in the previous chapter, when women sought help from friends and family, they chose carefully from among the available resources and they created particularly tight relationships with those in similar situations. They did so to avoid being the objects of scorn of those they believed would be unsympathetic to their need or their family structure. Reliance on the state for welfare can also subject one to *private* occasions of humiliation. Some women reported that individuals within their social worlds (often the fathers of their children, ironically), reminded them of the stigma attached to this practice:

There are so many people out there that say, "Welfare moms: All they do is pop out kids; they're lazy. They're just using the system," or whatever. Sometimes I have a really hard time with that, especially because [my son's] dad thinks that. His dad says that to me a lot.

Even for the women who lived in a more forgiving personal world, the use of food stamps—a highly visible marker of poverty—had the potential to expose them to both imagined and very real denigration:

The toughest piece of it was using food stamps.... I was so embarrassed at first that I wouldn't even use them. I would get so nervous, I couldn't even read the numbers on the food stamps. It was just awful for me.... I'm standing in line, I have my fruits in my hands, and I'm using food stamps to pay for strawberries, and the person next to me starts yelling at me...how can I buy strawberries with my food stamps? They thought that was, like, a luxury.

But the women did not need these external reminders of denigration. The women had absorbed their society's attitudes and they could speak quite vividly about the imagined "welfare queen." Drawing on images that have been deeply linked to racism in our society, the women applied them to the welfare recipients they knew, even though the women to whom they referred were, like themselves, white women in rural Vermont: "The woman I was talking about before... it was going around for a while that she kept having more kids to stay on welfare, and she has twelve or thirteen kids now."[14] Indeed, the women even applied these images to themselves. One woman, when asked about how she regarded people on welfare reiterated the accusation of insufficient productivity: "They're lazy. That's my take. I don't know. I got a stereotype for them too and I'm one of them."

Responding to Stigma

With social condemnation so prevalent, it is hardly surprising to learn that the women who include the state as a "partner" in their own social economy make efforts to distinguish themselves from others who do the same. When it is available to them, the women draw on social class as an indicator of difference. They also refer to temporary circumstances and the motivation to respond to the needs of their children to justify their reliance on welfare.

The Uses of Class

Perhaps it is not surprising to learn that their claims to difference emphatically make reference to their membership in the class of those who are perceived to be "productive" members of society. Social class becomes a marker of distinction.

Julie Marshall explained that she had come from "a middle-class family" and had expectations of working to support herself. In her reference to her sister's achievements, she indicated the path she was "meant" to follow and provided evidence that she had definite notions about her appropriate place in the world:

> The first time I ever went to welfare, and the first time I went to my Reach Up appointments, it was really, really scary because you never know what people are going to think, and there's such a stigma to welfare.... And especially for me, coming from a middle-class family and not thinking that I would ever be on welfare, thinking that things would always be provided, and that I would be working, ultimately, I mean. My older sister's twenty-five. When she was [my age] she had a really good job in Boston, she was living in an apartment, you know, [and] she was probably making more money than my mother even. If you listened to me, that's where I thought I'd be. So to even be in this place is definitely strange and it takes some getting used to.

Similarly, Doris Douglas, when recounting how she came to rely on ANFC when she was thirty-two (for a five-year period beginning soon after she separated from her husband), insisted that she had previously known nothing about these programs. Clearly, we cannot take literally Doris's claim to ignorance: She "knew" that these programs existed. What she did not "know" is that they would ever have relevance in *her* life.

> A while after I got divorced I was on ANFC and food stamps. I didn't even know what they were. I mean, I'd never even grown up with any [of those services]. I didn't even know any people [who used them]. I didn't even know what the food stamp system or the grant system was.

Women also noted that their backgrounds had prepared them to expect they would support themselves through employment, and they express commitment to this ideal. One woman said, "We were an upper-middle-class family.... I was just raised for [work], and I still strongly believe that you're supposed to work. You're supposed to work for what you need." Another commented, "I come from a working-class family. My family are farmers...so I was very used to having work be my life and my life being my work." In telling us that they are not "like that," the women make claims about their own characters and distance themselves from others in the same situation.

The Uses of Special Circumstances

A number of the women we interviewed explained that special circumstances made it impossible for them to seek employment for the short, or in some cases the relatively long, term. These circumstances, they argued, explained and justified their reliance on welfare.

Although she was no longer relying on welfare when we spoke with her, Diana Spender commented that during the brief period immediately preceding her child's birth, as a single woman without a partner, she had no alternative:

> [When you are pregnant] your whole body just kind of changes and slows down, and I just...couldn't get the work, and after I was eight to nine months pregnant I was substitute teaching too, for extra money...and that just sort of slowed down as well. So being on state aid was a last resort.

Diana explained her stint of welfare reliance as a last, and a short-term, resort. Joan Meyer's reliance was likely to be for a longer period. She wanted us to understand that her status was beyond her control: "I was not a teenager. I did not go out and get pregnant just out of stupidity. I was married. I had children in wedlock. And he got to walk out." She also wanted us to understand that she could not possibly seek employment outside the home, "because for me at minimum wage with three kids it's not possible [to support myself through employment] until they are all in school full-time, which is another three years." Karen Kelly, who had so adamantly insisted that *rely* was not a word in her vocabulary, recounted a harrowing story about the circumstances that led her to move to Vermont:

> My daughter was violently molested on Cape Cod, and the perpetrator was not removed, and continued to try and harm her and kill my other daughter and our cat. And it went on for a year. And in the process we lost my job, our home, everything. I had a choice. I could stay there, and continue to fight the fight, or I could get my daughter safe.

For the Children

Perhaps most commonly, the women say that they rely on welfare to fulfill what they perceive as being their obligation to meet their children's material needs. Welfare use is thus incorporated into, and justified by, being a good mother.[15] Anne Davenport, who had said that welfare was embarrassing because of what she termed a "middle-class" background, stated that welfare would not be her choice, but that in the absence of child support from her ex-husband, she had no alternative if she was going to take care of her children:

> If it was me and I needed money I would be very hard-pressed to apply to the state, but because I have children I really don't have a choice and I really hate it. Believe me, I really hate it. But I don't have a choice, especially having no support from their father.

Jackie Porter shared Anne's sentiments:

> You know, people can look down on me, and people can talk and say, "Oh, she's on welfare," or "Oh, she's getting food from the food shelf." But you know what? I don't care. I have a child and if she needs to eat, I'm going to get food. I'm going to get beans if I have to!

Elizabeth Vincent no longer relies on welfare. When we asked her if it had been a hard decision to turn to ANFC six years before, she responded, "No, because I had to feed my kids and I couldn't do it anymore....I was working full-time and couldn't do it."

I will discuss further how welfare restructuring changed the understanding of what the state should do to enable a mother to care for her children. For now, it is sufficient to note that both earlier and more recent recipients want to meet their children's material needs and they believe that welfare should be there to help them do so, even if only as a last resort. And among both groups of women a certain dissociation occurs. In *Working Hard and Making Do*, Joan Smith and I observed that married men often talked about social-welfare programs like WIC and food stamps as serving the needs of their wives and children rather than being vital supports on which they also relied. Single mothers similarly talk about welfare as serving the needs of their children, rather than their own needs.[16] The stigma associated with means-tested programs gives rise to, and may even require, this kind of distancing, whereby some individuals insist that those for whom they are responsible (the "truly dependent") rely on aid while they take active steps to provide for them in whatever way they can.

Reconciling Welfare with Self-Sufficiency

Indeed, as welfare-reliant women draw on stigmatized sources of social support to keep their children alive, they do not entirely abandon claims to self-sufficiency. Weighing the cost of dependence on family and friends against the cost of dependence on the state, some women come to find the former more easily reconciled with a sense of themselves as independent agents in the world. Amy Phelps, a thirty-four-year-old mother of two girls, has relied on both her own and her fiancé's families for help in her daily life. Recall that Amy believed that getting by in this manner demonstrated more strength of character than relying on agencies: "I do have to say through all of my down times and transitional periods...I never went on any kind of public service—only the health insurance which is a form of Medicaid. So I guess that's really an accomplishment for me with just accessing support from families."

Other women, however, came to precisely the opposite conclusion. Barbara Quesnel, who was hospitalized for depression after she and her husband separated, is now employed in a nursing home part-time while attending a community college. She never relied on ANFC itself, but she did draw on food stamps, Medicaid, and subsidies for child care. These supports, she suggested, were preferable to informal support. She explained her reasoning in a way that merged pride in her own accomplishments with hesitation about disclosing need to intimates. On balance, she found impersonal support easier to endure: "It's always been very important to me to be able to take care of myself. I would feel like a failure around my friends as opposed to an agency." Although Sarah Stanley was more concerned about avoiding her father's control than she was with the threat to dignity that would come from revealing need, she also opted for state reliance: "Even though my dad agreed to pay—continue paying for health care—I don't have to ask him. I just went and made my own arrangement."

No single demographic variable (such as family background, age, or marital status) can explain why some women find state assistance compatible with a sense of autonomy while others do not. It is likely that these decisions rest on quite complex interrelations of material resources, age, background, and, of course, personality. As was demonstrated in chapter 2, the determination to follow one strategy rather than the other may also rest on the degree of disdain expressed by friends and by the members of one's own family. (When Cathy Earl needed help, for example, she preferred to call on her friend Dorothy or her other single-mother friends; if she did need to rely on her family, she approached her brother Kenneth before turning to her brother Michael because the latter was "not quite as understanding.")

While this question awaits further research, it is important to reiterate that those who do rely on state support do not view this practice as being incompatible with the exercise of independent agency in a tough situation. That is, while not holding themselves responsible for the circumstances in which they find themselves, the women express pride in the fact that they have actively sought to alleviate those circumstances. In so doing, they insist that "dependence" on the state does not come at the expense of independence.

Kitty Thompson is a twenty-four-year-old mother of one child born outside of marriage. When her daughter was younger, Kitty relied on ANFC; now that she is employed full-time as a production worker at a craft factory, she has reduced her reliance on the state. Yet she still receives a subsidy for her housing, assistance in meeting the expenses of child care, commodities from WIC, and Medicaid. Even so, Kitty argues, she has never been dependent, because she has been proactive in the search for resources. Likening that search to doing her homework, she suggests that she has met the moral obligation to take care of herself:

> When I first moved here, what I did was I called up every department of social services in the two counties. I called up every resource possible. They give you out these sheets with all these different numbers. And I basically did all my homework, and called everything I could possibly think of that might be able to help me. So I haven't really needed help, just because I've investigated everything possible.

Erin Newton, a never-married mother of a five-year-old daughter, relied on ANFC in the past but at the moment she only receives food stamps and Medicaid. Erin spoke much the same way as did Kitty insofar as she defined active assistance-seeking work as evidence of self-reliance: "I'm very independent when it comes to, you know, trying to find a way to make ends meet. I'm good at that. If this person doesn't work, I'll call [another] person. I just wasn't finding a job [when I went on welfare]." Like Kitty and Erin, Elizabeth Vincent was willing to risk the condemnation attached to food stamps because she believed they enabled her to ensure her children's survival. She spoke proudly of her efforts to keep her family alive: "And I started thinking to myself, 'Hey I'm doing this for the kids.' So I'm proud of it, because I'm using my skills to find the resources that I need to get where I want to go for my family and I."

In short, when the social economy of single mothers includes reliance on stigmatized social welfare programs, women engage in the "cultural work" necessary to claim self-worth. They also make efforts to align that claim with the institutionalized discourse that privileges independence and self-reliance. In doing so they maneuver within a similar set of constraints and contradictions as do those who eschew state support and instead rely on those they know. What the state has deemed independence also requires dependence—albeit on friends and family. Indeed, all forms of "self-sufficiency" are really both more or less than that. But the particularly American notion that some ideal form of self-sufficiency is possible allows that to become the standard against which individual women (and couples) measure themselves.[17] Ironically, they participate in that very process of myth making as they insist that their *own* claims to worthiness that depend on that standard.

Claiming the Right to State Resources

This myth of self-reliance is modified when the single mothers imagine an idealized community in a rural state. In that imagining they invoke notions of generalized reciprocity to justify the occasions when they receive help without making immediate reimbursements. Community members, the women argue, *should* take care of one another. If, as single mothers, they are not now in a position to be on the giving end of pure generosity, they can anticipate a time when they will be, and they can point to occasions when they have helped others. Receiving this kind of help requires little moral justification: Anyone can experience a momentary need; those who help do so, at best, out of a purely generous human nature and, at worst (from a recipient perspective), out of sentiments of noblesse oblige.

In the United States, the real "community" of the state operates on different principles. Individuals must demonstrate need according to strict criteria and they must demonstrate that they are sufficiently worthy to be helped. Although the demonstration of need has been a constant in U.S. policy of aid to the poor, the grounds for demonstrating worthiness have changed over time (as have the groups eligible for these services).[18] The shift from AFDC to TANF is but the most recent of these policy changes. It was accompanied by a newly emphatic discourse that involved a large-scale attack on the moral worth of welfare mothers and heralded a new age in which preparation for self-sufficiency (rather than the demands of caregiving) would constitute the only legitimate reason for welfare reliance.

This shift in discourse had a practical component insofar as it was accompanied by concrete changes in the administration of welfare itself.

Welfare restructuring put in place a system whereby progress toward self-sufficiency would be assessed on a regular basis through individualized client plans for self-development and through close contact with a caseworker who would monitor those plans. And, of course, welfare restructuring also put in place time limits on both temporary and lifetime use of welfare.

All of these shifts resonate in the voices of the women we interviewed. Women who had relied on welfare before the new rules were put into effect (more than a decade ago in Vermont) viewed it as a public right, access to which was justified by caring for one's own child for as long as that care was needed. The fact that welfare sometimes also enabled them to meet individual goals of self-improvement was considered as a bonus, but not something intrinsic to their reasons or justifications for that status. The women thereby effectively maintained ownership of those achievements. Within the context of the new social discourse a personal interest in one's own children no longer justifies welfare reliance. Welfare becomes contingent (rather than being a right) and short-term. And its justification rests on progress toward self-sufficiency (a progress viewed, at best, as a partnership with the state, and, at worst, as an obligation to it). Thus there are now new and different moral costs associated with including the state in one's social economy.

BEFORE THE WELFARE RESTRUCTURING PROJECT

Nine of the women we interviewed had been welfare reliant before the Welfare Restructuring Project was implemented in Vermont. They were, on average, considerably older than the more recent recipients at the time we spoke with them (though not necessarily at the time they initiated their own welfare reliance). Our discussions thus drew on memories and, in some cases, an acute awareness of the personal distance they had traveled since being the recipients of state services. These factors might account for some of the differences between the interpretations they had of welfare reliance and the interpretations of current recipients.[19] Even so, the differences are striking. Unlike the women subject to the new regulations of the WRP, these prior welfare recipients indicate that they have not bought into the new rhetoric to supply themselves with a retrospective rationale for welfare reliance. That is, although there would have been room to do so, they do not locate their behavior in the context of claims to worthiness *because* of actions taken to improve self-sufficiency. Rather, they claim that they were entitled to welfare because they had both the obligation *and the right* to meet their children's emotional and physical needs. Motherhood—not the personal responsibility, independence, or self-reliance central to today's welfare ideology—resonates profoundly in their moral claims.

Mothering My Own Children

Most significant, the earlier ANFC recipients speak about having relied on welfare in order to care for their children. In doing so, they extend the notion of care beyond meeting children's *material* needs to *raising* their children, and this broader notion becomes the justification for welfare reliance. In their minds (as in the minds of many who supported welfare in the past), welfare reliance was, above all, a mechanism for ensuring that mothers could both provide for and nurture their children. They thus elevate maternal care to the status of a meaningful, and valued, activity:

> It was a long time ago. I went on welfare...with my first [child]. I didn't want to work [because] *I wanted to raise him myself....* (Emphasis added.)

> When I was pregnant I made the decision that I was going to have [the child]. Then I knew that I would have to—not support her in the way of money-wise—but I knew that I was the one who was going to *raise her and I was going be the major influence in her life.* And I knew I was going to have to do it on welfare, because I was working minimum-wage jobs, you know, seasonal jobs, being laid off, being fired, being whatever. I knew that I could not count on a paying job *to keep me stable to raise her.* (Emphasis added.)

Private Achievements

These women also often refer to other personal achievements completed during their period of welfare reliance. That is, they point with pride to the fact that during that period in their lives they enhanced their own human capital: Several talked about completing high school or receiving degrees in higher education; others talked about involvement in job training, locating meaningful employment, and individual activities of "self-improvement." But, in a striking contrast to those women subject to the new welfare regime, these women adamantly insist that they regarded (and continue to regard) these activities as their own, quite private concerns. In their view, these activities neither constituted grounds for an external judgment of worthiness nor represented an obligation to the state. As Kara Lattrell says of her college degree, "It represents to me a really, really long, hard road to get something that *I* really wanted. And in the end, I did really well." Because the state was not regarded as having a role in these accomplishments, it did not figure so centrally in the depiction of an individual's social economy, and was even sometimes utterly dismissed. In fact, the women occasionally suggest that they achieved certain successes in spite of, rather than because of, the state's intervention. Elizabeth Vincent was proud that she took advantage of her time of welfare reliance to resolve her issues with alcohol. But she is insistent about her belief that the state had no role in this achievement: "I was dead drunk at every single welfare review for years. No one ever told me about [Alcoholics Anonymous]."

Administration in a Minor Key

To the extent that the state is present in Elizabeth's account, it is at best a negligent partner who ignores overt signs of acute distress. In fact, Elizabeth explicitly drew an analogy between the state and a husband, an analogy that has prevailed in past feminist analyses of women's reliance on the state:[20] "And yes, there's bitterness there, and yes, it's called accountability. And yes, I hold it against this government for being such a poor husband to me." Another woman shared Elizabeth's sentiment regarding the state's negligence. She said that because the state failed to provide regular help with the concrete activities of her daily life, she relied extensively on the less formal components of her social economy:

> I had known a friend who had been, you know, sort of on the system before. And she had told me about … Section 8 [housing], and so I had sort of heard about that from her. … But never once did I go to welfare for any of that. In fact, I hardly ever went to welfare for anything! Because they were *so* unhelpful! (*Laughs.*)

Other women raised additional concerns about their dealings with the state. They explained that the people who administered welfare were "picky" in their application of eligibility criteria, they complained that some workers held negative attitudes about clients, and they mocked the size of the grants they received. Indeed, some openly acknowledged that "paltry" stipends resulted in casual abuses of the system: "Asking a family of three to live on $550 a month is ridiculous, and it's asking people to lie, and to cheat, and to steal." Missing in these stories was any mention of deep attachments to, or intimate relationships with, individual case workers.

The Right to Long-Term Support

Some of the women who were welfare reliant prior to the implementation of Vermont's WRP indicated that they were conscious of, and adamantly opposed to, the reforms that limited the period of welfare support and made its receipt contingent on progress toward self-sufficiency. These women spoke of welfare as a "right" that rested solely on their status as mothers in need of support. Public monies were there, they argued, to enable them to meet an important goal. By and large, the women voiced a firm opposition to the newly instituted time limits. They insisted that individuals, and not the state, should determine when a child is ready for its mother to seek employment: "They were going to tell me that I had to go to work, and I had to leave my daughter. And it's like, uh, uh, uh. It's like, it's not your choice, that's *my* choice." And, in their minds, welfare is no different from other needed policies the society should implement to ensure the survival of its citizens: "I also believe . . . everybody should be guaranteed an income. You know, because there's gonna be somebody who's out of work. You know, because we don't have 100 percent employment in this country."

AFTER WELFARE RESTRUCTURING

These claims disappeared in the mid-1990s. The disappearance reflects the changing moral basis for welfare receipt as codified in the Welfare Restructuring Project, which says self-sufficiency will "offer a better quality of life" than dependence on the state allows. The disappearance reflects as well the changing administration of welfare delivery, with its more intensive engagement with individual clients working toward self-sufficiency within a two-year time limit.

Mothering All Our Children

Women who are welfare reliant under the terms of the WRP do not speak about wanting to care for their children as providing sufficient justification for ongoing support from the state. While the women do express real interest in being available to, and spending time with, their children (and find in their children's material needs a *motivation* for welfare reliance), they do not draw on the rhetoric of motherhood to provide the moral basis for sustained welfare reliance.[21] Thus, for example, in sharp contrast to the woman who justified her welfare reliance by her desire to be the "major influence" in her child's life, and in sharp contrast to the woman who thought it was her right to decide when to "leave" her daughter, Julie Marshall (a twenty-three-year-old, never-married mother of a toddler) does not claim that she has any personal rights or personal responsibilities with respect to her child. In her contradictory use of the concept of "deservedness" and in her switch from the personal *I* to the impersonal *they,* she disregards her own distinctive connection to her child and locates this mother–child pair within a broader social context. She is just one of the many people "trying to make it the best" for all children—her own included:

> I don't feel like I deserve [support], but I feel like [my son] deserves it. I feel like, of course, our society should want to take care of our children. We should want our children to get the best. And if you see people who are trying to make it the best, I think that they deserve support in any way that they can.

She thus gives up rights that hinge on both *being an individual child's mother* and doing the carework associated with mothering, for a universalistic obligation shared by all citizens.

Achievements Owed to the State

A second shift accompanies the changing terms of welfare discourse. Not only has Julie given up her "right" as a mother to care for her own child, but she has also given up her right to welfare regardless of whether or not she demonstrates achievement during the years she draws on this resource. In so doing, she eventually cedes her personal achievements to the state as part of her ongoing obligation to it.

As we have seen, Julie invokes a state interest in her child. She also defines the state's interest in her as being contingent on making progress while accepting its funds: "I'm using this to better myself, so that makes it okay [to rely on welfare]." In fact, Julie likens the state's interest in her to the economic terms of investment, where initial outlays are paid with larger returns: "I think I am an investment opportunity for the state of Vermont because I want to stay here. I want to be in the state of Vermont, and I can contribute to the state of Vermont." Julie thus surrenders ownership of her achievements as a worker, as she did the right to support as a mother: She becomes an "investment opportunity" for a state that takes an interest in her accomplishments.

Other women used a term other than *investment.* Most commonly they spoke about the state offering *incentives.* Here too the notion of contingency emerges, as welfare support comes to be viewed as *encouraging* progress toward self-sufficiency:

> I really approve of the welfare system the way it is set up in the state right now.... I think that it is important to motivate people to go back to work. And if you have to do that by saying you're not going to be paid [through welfare] until you go to work, I think that's important that they do that.

In a circular fashion, when the state provides these "incentives" or makes these "investments," it strengthens the moral grounding for welfare use itself. Julie Marshall believed she could claim two years (as the time limit allowed) for her own use, so long as that use fell within the state's mandate. That is, the fact that the state offered her two years meant that she had the right to take those two years, provided that she engaged in activities that would ensure subsequent self-sufficiency ("I'm using this to better myself, so that makes it okay [to rely on welfare]"). Indeed, in suggesting that there is a "right" and a "wrong" way to use welfare, and in insisting that she falls into the former camp, Julie actually gives welfare use itself a greater legitimacy than it would have if these competing alternatives (of right and wrong) and the accompanying time limits were not available:

> In a way I think that [the time limits are] really good because people that are on welfare to use it for what it's meant to be used for aren't going to care that there's a time limit because they're going to understand that there's goals that they have to meet in that time limit in order to make it so that they don't ever have to be on welfare again. So I think somebody that's really in the system to use it for what it's for isn't going to complain about a time limit. The people that are going to complain about a time limit are going to be the ones that are, like, not doing anything.

Julie's good friend Rose Bishop is in much the same position. Both women rely on welfare as they take community college courses, and both care for young children. Rose, like Julie, insisted that she was "using [welfare] for a good reason." As she assessed her own behavior, she included Julie in a positive, personal evaluation. Both of them, she insisted, were appropriately relying on welfare to support their education that would, she hoped, ensure their *self*-reliance down the road: "Both of us, both going to school [are] trying to make it so we won't be on welfare forever."

These attitudes about a right and a wrong way to use welfare within the newly stringent framework are in line with the state's definition of welfare as "a transitional assistance program." They presuppose a quite different meaning from that ascribed to welfare by women who had relied on the program *before* restructuring who, as shown above, talked about welfare as a secure (albeit denigrated) safety net. But, if the earlier recipients understood welfare as offering a long-term safety net under ANFC, and the current recipients have accepted the new meaning of "welfare" as temporary assistance under TANF, the latter have not forgone the notion of security altogether. Indeed there is evidence that they impose their own meaning on time limits to create at least *temporary* security. Rather than seeing time limits as constraining, they interpret them as enclosing that period during which welfare reliance (provided one is using it in the "right" way) is morally acceptable. That is, time limits, by circumscribing a period of time, offer permission to rely on welfare for that period of time, after which, recipients hope they will, indeed, achieve "a better quality of life than dependence on welfare provides."[22] Thus, the circle that precludes this survival tactic also licenses it.

Administration in a Major Key

Welfare recipients did not make these shifts in interpretation on their own. In a 1998 study, the Manpower Demonstration Research Corporation (MDRC) reported on the responses to the implementation of WRP in Vermont by two staff groups—the eligibility specialists who are the frontline officers making decisions about whether clients can receive benefits, and the case managers who engage clients in activities designed to lead to "self-sufficiency" through the program called Reach Up.[23] MDRC found that the eligibility specialists, in general, had become more fully engaged in "client assistance," that their relations with clients were more "involved" and "intense," and that they were doing more "social work."[24] MDRC also found that Reach Up was "highly individualized," that the program placed a strong emphasis on intensive case management (with caseloads capped at sixty per worker as mandated by state law), and that the centerpiece of that case management was the creation of a Family Development Plan that outlined the manner in which a client would prepare for self-sufficiency.[25] Each caseworker thus "helps the Reach Up participant to carry out the [Family Development Plan] and monitors his or her progress throughout the service delivery phase, modifying the plan as necessary."[26] In short, with intensified case management and carefully drawn Family Development Plans, welfare recipients in Vermont (as elsewhere) were now subject to a new form of surveillance. As such they had to learn to present themselves as worthy within the terms of the new institutionalized discourse.[27]

Some commentators assume that this surveillance produces a new sense of stigma and a new passivity. A close observer of welfare restructuring, Sanford Schram, for example, writes that the text of "personal responsibility" "risks reinforcing the tendencies already built into welfare to stigmatize, demonize, and even criminalize poor single mothers" and that the administration of welfare reliance will ensure that clients are acquiescent.[28] Schram's analysis, however, draws its conclusions from studying the texts alone. Actual observations of welfare offices and actual discussions with welfare recipients allow for a more nuanced understanding of the consequences of the new administration.

In *Flat Broke with Children*, the sociologist Sharon Hays draws a distinction between what she terms the "work plan" and what she terms the "family plan."[29] The former, she argues, is designed "to instill the commitment to work that welfare recipients are presumed to lack" and it contains within it an essential contradiction "between demanding individual autonomy and exercising social control."[30] The family plan (which is in itself in contradiction to the work plan), Hays argues, is enforced "in the welfare office [as] an image of the proper behavior of mothers." Its enactment often takes place within the context of highly personalized relationships with caseworkers who operate on the basis of both "caring maternalism" and a high degree of "caseworker discretion." Moreover, she argues that this new regime has its positive aspects insofar as it "has once again made it possible for welfare workers to *act* on [care and concern for the lives of welfare families] by defining the mentoring process and determining what kind of support is needed on a case-by-case basis."[31]

In the reports of Vermont's welfare clients, a less sharp distinction is made between the work and family aspects of welfare reform. Still, a distinction is echoed in the division clients make between eligibility specialists and individual case managers. Welfare clients often complain bitterly about the former, referring to them as "the state," and as the bureaucratic embodiment of rules and regulations, but by and large express fondness for their caseworkers. In their accounts of interactions with the latter, I hear, like Hays, evidence that they perceived their caseworkers as offering both "discretion" and "maternalism."

As examples of their caseworkers' discretion, several women spoke of times when the rules were bent on their behalf. Jackie Porter, a divorced twenty-six-year-old woman, explained that when she needed additional money to repair her transmission, she presented her case to her Reach Up counselor who subsequently called to say that "she called some head of this district or something" for Jackie. And Julie Marshall suggested that her caseworker had helped her find a way to circumvent written policies:

The food stamps I didn't get until later on, and they actually help a lot, and it was because of my social worker that I got them. She said, "You know, I know you're living with your mom, but why don't you just say that you're eating separately, and that way you can contribute more to the household." So, she definitely helped me in that way.

Respondents also mentioned their caseworkers' caring "maternalism." Julie spoke of a close relationship and personal interest: "She's like my counselor too. I mean, when I was having a lot of trouble with my family this summer because my sister was really, really sick, she totally listened to me and was there for me in that way too." Julie appreciates as well the caseworker's interest in her as an individual client and her attentiveness to opportunities that will enable Julie to meet her goals of getting a good education:[32] "She sent me a brochure on a pair of educators' conferences that happened last week.... And she was like, 'I really think you should go. You might be able to get credit for it.'"

In her analysis of the effects of PRWORA, Sharon Hays argues that there are intrinsic difficulties with *both* discretion and maternalism:[33]

> Discretion assumes the superior judgment of middle class caseworkers, allowing these workers to impose personal standards of behavior on poor mothers. Like the bureaucracy, this system can also perpetuate the problem of treating welfare mothers as childlike dependents.

And I would agree. Both deference to the judgment of caseworkers and childlike dependence on them can be heard as the women describe how they engage in negotiation for support. Julie values her caseworker's opinion and relies on it to guide her choices: "And she's looking at me, and she's saying, 'You know, you're making the right choice to sacrifice not having a job and only going to school for three classes so that you can be with [your son] at this time in his life.'" Jackie Porter described her own infantilization in her explanation of how she got additional money from Reach Up when her car broke down:

> And I called them up and I begged and pleaded and was just saying, "You know, I feel really, you guys have helped me so much, I think I can swing $300 and even more if I have to." I'm like, "I'll pay whatever I have to but I need something."

Pushing at the Edges

As these examples suggest, Julie and Jackie ask for more than the rules allow. But, because these claims are made in the context of a relationship with a discrete individual, are contingent on appropriate behavior, and in their dependent and pleading tone resemble the requests a child makes, they cannot readily be transformed into rights. Indeed, getting that "more" depends on buying into the system, and on attending to a given two-year limit in which to make progress. And, rather than engendering a collective politics, maternalism and discretion might even encourage "sibling rivalry" with other clients as women struggle for scarce resources and for what they perceive as being equally scarce approval.

This is not to suggest that the women are not often critical of the limits of what is offered. Julie, for example, believes that she deserves more than the state's promise of two years of support and assistance toward a degree from a community college. Perhaps because she has sisters who have been able to attend liberal arts colleges and achieve more substantial progress toward self-sufficiency, she knows that the state's offerings are too meager. She does not believe that she should have lost the opportunity of attending a four-year college (and receiving financial aid from it) because she had a child out of wedlock before completing her education. Welfare reliance has not erased all her class-based feelings of entitlement:

> Even now the things that they're offering, like, yes, I'm going to school, but if I didn't have a kid and I was going for my master's, there would be a college that I could apply for a grant that would set me up with a stipend and set me with everything I would need. And [the state doesn't] do that. There's kind of like limits as to what they're setting you up with.[34]

TRANSITIONING OFF WELFARE: A DISAPPOINTING REALITY

If Julie is beginning to understand that the benefits she receives will not adequately prepare her for real self-sufficiency, women who have actually reached their time limits experience that inadequacy as an everyday reality.

Women in Transition

I have already noted that the distinction between women who rely on welfare and those who do not ignores change: Many of the latter were in the position of receiving aid at an earlier time in their lives and they may well be in that position again. I note now that the distinction also ignores the fact that many recipients are in transition from full grants to partial ones.[35] While total income theoretically rises with increased hours of employment, during this transition women are more likely to note the reduction in grant size (and in related benefits) and to feel a pinch as their work-related expenses (both financial *and* emotional) also rise.[36]

Kara Lattrell, who relied on welfare both before and after the 1994 restructuring, insisted that although her welfare payments had *always* been inadequate, they had the virtue of total reliability. Welfare was something to count on:

> One of the things about welfare is, you don't get a lot of money. I mean, you get barely enough to survive.... It's like a lousy, meager, paltry handout. But there's a mentality that is incredibly strong that at least you know it's there. You know it's coming. There's not a rug [that can be pulled out from under you]—there's no rug under that check because it's always going to come on the first, and it's always going to come on the sixteenth. You can always plan on that. There's, you know, birth, death, taxes, and welfare payments. And you know the money is there. And as long as you don't work, you know what you have. You can make do. You can cope somehow.

By way of contrast, Kara explained that she had found her first glimpse of life after welfare very scary:[37]

> When you go to work, suddenly you're in a state of panic all the time because you're never quite sure [what's going to happen]. Are they going to do the right paper? Is the check going to come at the right time? Are they going to lose the paperwork? Did I earn too much this month in my job and now next month I'm going to get less in my welfare? My food stamps are up, then they're down, then they're over here.

As they cope with this uncertainty, women more pointedly assess the promise of welfare restructuring to help them achieve self-sufficiency and they more insistently ask questions about whether the state is fulfilling its end of the bargain. If they welcome the opportunity to work their way "off welfare" and take pride in their increased earnings, they are distressed by diminished support. Not surprisingly, they find that the combination can entail an even greater gap between what they have and what they need. They begin to wonder whether the incentives were more "stick" than "carrot."

I return in the Conclusion to the social policy ideas that emerge when welfare is taken into account. For now it is pertinent to note that the welfare discourse itself might have set single mothers up to believe that their material needs could be met, initially through a combination of transitional state support and wages, and eventually through wages alone. When single mothers find that even the first stage is more dream than reality, they express a sense of betrayal.

As an example, consider Polly King, who has almost completed her transition off welfare. Now that she works full-time she has seen her grant drop down to $17 each month. Polly believes the state should be supporting her more fully because she is doing precisely what it required of her in exchange for her welfare grant; she has fulfilled her end of the bargain but, as many forecasters predicted, she is still not making it. By her estimates, she is short almost $70 each month when calculating her *gross* income against her fixed monthly expenses. Polly directs some of her anger at the welfare system for being what she believes to be more generous toward another woman, Rose Bishop, than it is toward her; she thus buys into a competitive stance vis-à-vis other recipients. But Polly's anger is also rooted in her realization that the state ceases its benefits once you begin to be employed and in her belief that the state *should* continue its support if need remains. She argues that if it offers incentives to encourage people to seek employment, it should provide the backup support that makes that employment feasible. Polly thus dreams of a state that underwrites the survival of any individual whose earned income does not bring her up to the level of a *real* living wage:

> And I also think that they should offer more help if you're working, and you have a job, than if you don't. Because Rose—I mean, she gets like five or six hundred bucks a month, and she doesn't work. She doesn't have to, because she gets that money. She's better off than I am, and I'm working my ass off! I get $17 a month! I think they should give me more help, because I'm out doing something, and not less because you're out doing something. I think that's a little backwards. I know that it has come a long way, as far as the incentives of trying to get you to go back to work, but I kind of think they're not going about it the right way, as far as, you know, like not offering people who are working more support, some backup to some level, if they're working as hard as they

can, as much as they can. And maybe they don't consider me to be working as much as I can, but I think I'm working more than I should!

Case Closed

Women who were recently "terminated," either because they reached their time limits or because they began to earn "too much," also expressed a bewildered outrage about the disappearance of their grants. Kitty Thompson is both indignant and confused. She has bought into the notion of time limits and she is committed to getting "off" welfare. Even so, she now finds that enacting the vaunted personal responsibility means that the state sends you packing:

> Well, I think they shouldn't have a program where you can stay on it forever and not have any consequences. I think that the other programs that they have are good incentives to get you off of it. But I also think that they should be able to help you. If you're working full-time, and you're trying to make ends meet, why would they drop you, versus, if you're working part-time, help you out immensely?

As she bemoans the loss of the Reach Up supplements that are no longer available to her, she itemizes the daily troubles she faces. She wonders in retrospect whether it was wise for her to buy into the morality that underwrote a system of support designed to disappear the moment she fulfilled its stated expectations:

> I don't even receive any Reach Up help because I'm working. That was a major bummer for me. Because, I figure, I can do without the ANFC. . . . I would like to have food stamps but I can do without them, but Reach Up, you know—my car insurance is due, oh my God . . . or I got a flat tire, I need a new tire, what am I going to do? So, I think they really should help out people working even though they are working full-time. . . . The way I'm struggling from day to day, I make just as little as I do in my employment as I would on ANFC. So I can see a lot of people, why they just give up, and say, "Fine, you're going to pay my way, anyway."

Almost as problematic for Kitty is the loss of the relationship with her Reach Up counselor. As she said mournfully, "I'm done. I'm closed. I'm not getting any more. My last Reach Up session was like two weeks ago, and my file is closed. It's really sad because you kind of build a relationship with your worker."

If Kitty Thompson sounds, as critics like Charles Murray and Lawrence Mead would predict, like someone who has become dangerously dependent on the system, and if, as their models suggest, she is making a strictly economic calculus to determine whether employment constitutes a "rational choice," she is also turning both the dependency reproach and the economic calculus *on their heads* and demonstrating that she operates within a richer and more complex social economy.[38] Kitty fully accepts the notion that she should be working. Indeed, she is proud of her job and its attached benefits: "I receive my first raise in December, on my anniversary. But I've already taken my paid vacation. It's great. I never thought I'd ever see the day that I'd have one!" She values the "new paternalism" not because it *made* her work, but because it *allowed* her to do so. She also believes that if the state were truly upholding its end of the bargain (as promised in the institutionalized discourse of the welfare program itself), it would subsidize employment (or at least such legitimate expenses of employment as owning a car) so as to make it genuinely more advantageous than welfare reliance. That is, having bought into the notion that the state was preparing her for self-sufficiency, having observed that the state actually made an investment in that preparation, and having contributed her own time and energy toward that goal, she now wonders just how she is supposed to be self-sufficient on the wages she earns.

Drawing on the new experiences of employment in low-wage work (in the absence of significant state benefits), those who were no longer "in transition" when we spoke with them were even more explicit about what they viewed as the deficits of the current program and as the failure of the state to carry through on *its* promises about what work would provide. One woman, for example, suggested that although the state "promised" to help you achieve self-sufficiency, its rules and regulations made it difficult to take advantage of the full range of opportunities:

> They weren't set up for you to succeed. They aren't saying, "Let's help you while you do this so that you're able to support yourself. Let us give you this." [Instead they say], "You can't work, you can't do this, you're only eligible to do this."

Moreover, although clients like Julie Marshall could envision needing more time or training than is allowed within the current limits, those who have completed a stint on welfare *know* that the limits are often unreasonable. They plead for more flexibility, especially because they understand that human capital development can intersect with macro-structural changes in problematic ways:

> I think that [the five-year lifetime limit is] a bit extreme.... What happens if you're on [welfare] for a year or two and you get a job and then Bush becomes president and there aren't any jobs in that economy, and you're on it again for three more years, and then you get another job, and twenty years later you'll lose it and then where will you be?

CONCLUSION

The social economy of single mothers often stretches to embrace the state. When this is the case, single mothers are exposed to the stigma that accompanies reliance on social welfare programs. The shift from AFDC to TANF (or, as it is known in Vermont, the shift from ANFC to Reach Up) has not altered the interest welfare-reliant women have in finding a way to locate themselves outside of that denigration. Nor has it fundamentally altered some of the strategies they employ to do so: Both the earlier welfare recipients and the more recent ones point to a family history of hard work, explain welfare reliance as emerging from special circumstances, and regard taking aid as the expression of a sincere interest in meeting their children's material needs. Both groups of women also link welfare reliance itself to the significant efforts they make on their own behalf and thus as evidence of a willingness to work hard.

But much has changed with the new welfare regime introduced in the mid-1990s. Those who were welfare reliant *before* those changes valued their work of nurturance as well as the activities directed toward meeting their children's physical needs. They also maintained complete psychological ownership of their achievements and took *personal* pride in them. Because welfare was not negotiated with a "caring" individual and did not carry time limits, it was more easily seen as an economic and social right. But even, and perhaps *especially,* in a relatively benign state like Vermont, the combination of the new discourse and the new intrusive administration of time-limited welfare created a new set of social justifications for welfare reliance. In the new world of the Welfare Restructuring Project, women eschew a discourse that makes the work of mothering central to their moral self-definition. The individual achievements of preparation for employment are transformed into a set of obligations to a state that invests in its citizens and offers incentives to strive for self-sufficiency. Rather than being extra and thus legitimating pride, these hard-won gains are now merely what mothers *owe.* The discretion and maternalism through which state power is exercised encourages negotiation for special favors in a wheedling voice, even as it discourages an assertion of rights for which a given individual can fight with, rather than against, others "in the same boat." "Sibling rivalry," rather than collective action, emerges as each woman tries to define herself as exceptional and more worthy than her peers.

Welfare receipt, then, occurs both in an ideological context and as a social relationship with a given individual who manifests both discretion and maternalism. Although in *Flat Broke with Children*, Sharon Hays states her concerns about these stances, she also leaves room for optimism, at least with respect to the issue of maternalism:[39]

> Arguably, this caring ethos is nearly as important as the more tangible supportive services in engendering the genuine expressions of hope that I so frequently heard from welfare mothers as well as caseworkers. The practices of mothering and care also provide a visual and practical reference for thinking about commitment to others. They reiterate the stories about how "independence" is achieved only in the context of human relationships and connection. And, in an important way, these practices speak to just how difficult (and how unfortunate) it would be to completely bury the logic of nurturing under the routines of bureaucracies or the pressure for absolute self-sufficiency.

But if the women who are welfare reliant express "hope" and enjoy evidence of "commitment," they soon learn that a system of time limits brings both their hope and that commitment to a sudden end. Clients who fulfill their end of the new bargain—as they come to understand it—often find that its enactment means that they are now personally responsible for the poverty that is the almost inevitable result of trying to raise children on meager salaries in the absence of substantial state support. These former clients find that life after welfare can be lonely and hard and that they do not experience real "self-sufficiency." As do other single mothers, they continue to draw on personal networks of resources. After welfare, however, they no longer have the option of trading off the support that comes from their personal networks for more impersonal support, should they prefer to do so. Thus, they may experience *less* autonomy and *less* control than they did when they had retained the option of state support. Indeed, autonomy and control were precisely what Sarah Stanley sought to achieve when she rejected the conditions her father set out before he would continue to pay for her children's health insurance.

In addition, single mothers might actually find the state's judgments about what constitutes moral behavior easier to define and easier to meet than the diffuse expectations that come from family and friends in return for the support they offer. Julie Marshall discussed this difference, noting that it was simple to understand what formal institutions expected of her: "With welfare and Reach Up and the college [I attend] and stuff, there are definite things that are required of me. Those things [are] clearly outlined and it's right there." By way of contrast, she explained she found it difficult to know how to interpret her mother's often contradictory expectations for her. Later in the interview Julie mocked the notion that she was supposed to be "self-sufficient" when she was still living in a house with her mother, and thus reduced to a childlike dependency in her relationship with her. Yet, even in that situation Julie was not "just" dependent. Her caseworker might have been finding a way to stretch the rules when she suggested that Julie pretend she was eating separately from her mother. But stretching or not, the state support enabled Julie to make substantial financial contributions to her mother's household. And because Julie was not working a forty-hour week, she had time to help out at home with the routine tasks this complex household required.

In short, although reliance on the state is often depicted as dependency, it does give women room to maneuver. When the state remains a source of benefits, single mothers can exercise options. When that support erodes, single mothers become more, not less, dependent on individuals within their social networks. And although this dependence counts as "personal responsibility" within the framework of the welfare discourse, single mothers experience it differently.

The welfare recipients we interviewed took literally the promise that employment would offer "a better quality of life than dependence on welfare provides." It is hardly surprising that they did not find the time to read the fine print in which the agency responsible for the Welfare Restructuring Project offered its disclaimers and denied that it ever promised a rose garden: "All families, including working families, have problems. We cannot solve all of a family's problems before expecting the adult in that family to work.... [The Department of Prevention, Assistance, Transition and Health] alone cannot help families go to work and stay employed."

It also comes as no surprise to those studying the aftermath of welfare "reform" that the system cannot transform welfare recipients into fully self-sufficient citizens or even ensure a "better way of life."[40] While respondents in Vermont (as elsewhere) repeatedly say that they value employment and enjoy great pride in earning wages to sustain themselves and their children, they also report extreme difficulty in making ends meet.[41] As former (and transitional) welfare recipients struggle, they believe it unfair that the state turned out to be such a poor partner in their social economies. And they say that they feel betrayed by a state that requires personal responsibility of them but is unwilling to fulfill its side of the bargain. It neither rewards them for that show of initiative nor enables them to enact that personal responsibility (as they understand it) by becoming fully reciprocal members of the networks they turn to in the absence of state support. But, of course, by the time they realize all this, it is too late.

4

BUILDING AND REBUILDING THE FAMILY

Whether single mothers rely primarily on employment or welfare for income, material constraints remain a significant feature of daily life as the women seek to provide for themselves and their children. The vast majority of single mothers are in no position to purchase substitutes for their own efforts on behalf of their families. Many do rely on paid child-care providers during the hours they are employed, but most do not have the resources to hire full-time caregivers in the form of nannies or au pairs. And most cannot look to the market for those ready-made goods and services (such as prepared dinners or house cleaners) that would relieve the burden on their time and energy.[1] Although many single mothers get some support from other people for at least some of these activities, the bulk of the routine work associated with maintaining a family falls squarely on their shoulders alone.

The poverty of single motherhood intensifies these burdens. When women rely on social welfare for supplements to their incomes they have to negotiate with complex bureaucracies. When their equipment is old or lacking, routine tasks—such as laundry and lawn mowing—take more time.[2] And the range of resources on which single mothers rely, as well as the unpredictability of at least some of these resources, also intensifies these burdens: When their husbands miss child support payments, they have to negotiate with them, even as they make do with temporary deficits and shuffle more bills; when they lose jobs they may experience delays before they can sign on to essential means-tested programs.

Limited resources and their associated difficulties do not, however, free women from either internal or external expectations that they will conform to social standards of good mothering. Numerous studies have alerted us to the fact that, rather than resting on any determinative, scientific evidence, these standards shift with political and cultural norms.[3] Some of these shifts appear, in retrospect, merely convenient, as we abandon bulky carriages for agile strollers or even Snuglis. Others impinge more on the physical health and well-being of our children: Generations of mothers who put their children on their stomachs so they wouldn't choke in their sleep now know they were risking sudden infant death syndrome. Still other shifts in standards are tied into broader political and cultural trends, as parents abandoned the tight schedules of the 1930s and early 1940s for the child-centered responsiveness preached by Benjamin Spock.

Regardless of the specific "rules" that make up guidelines for "good" parental behavior at a particular moment, and regardless of the specific manner in which a parent interprets these "rules," mothers in all social classes "share a set of fundamental assumptions about the importance of putting their children's needs first and dedicating themselves to providing what is best for their kids, as they understand it."[4] Among middle-class mothers, this set of assumptions stretches to include the notion that the mother should lavish "copious amounts of time, energy, and material resources" on what sociologist Viviana Zelizer has called a "priceless child."[5] Taken as a whole, these beliefs, which Sharon Hays calls "intensive mothering," also maintain the privacy of the family and position the mother, whether she gets assistance from outside or not, as the central caregiver.[6]

In the first section of this chapter, I suggest that as a direct response to the pinch between material demands and a desire to be "good" mothers, the single women I interviewed developed a strategy that I call "practical motherhood." This strategy acknowledges limits to children's needs and makes visible the concrete efforts associated with maintaining a family; it thus provides the foundation for educating children into a teamwork model of family life whereby some responsibilities are shifted onto children.

In the second and third sections of the chapter I turn to issues that emerge as single mothers draw on the resources of the members of other households—whether by choice or not. Most prominently, of course, single mothers are linked to the fathers of their children. In much academic research and popular accounts, all single-mother families are lumped together as if there are no differences among them with respect to the role played by a nonresidential father. In addition, paternal involvement is almost invariably presented as a social "good." By way of contrast with these approaches, I demonstrate that single mothers vary in their perceptions of the father's role in his children's lives, which means that not all mothers view that role as positive; having done so, I explore how the social economy of a single mother shifts in response to her perceptions of the father's influence. Finally, I look at the issues that arise when other individuals are integrated into the social economy of family life, whether through residential arrangements or through more episodic participation in the care of children. I demonstrate that these other individuals can create additional burdens, even as they help with the daily activities of family life.

MODIFYING INTENSIVE MOTHERING

Practical Mothering

Vanessa Menard provides a good initial example of the manner in which a single mother adopts a stance that modifies, but does not directly challenge, the norm of "intensive mothering." A recently divorced mother of a six-year-old daughter, Vanessa is employed full-time as a graphic designer. During our conversation she offered the following account of what happens at the end of most days:

> I'm sorry for the fact that I have to accomplish tasks and chores when I get home from work, even when [my daughter] needs to talk to me. I try to really change my focus to her, even though sometimes I have really got to get something done.... I think that I could be better in trying to involve her in some of the chores that I need to do. And one of the aspects of my personality is that I'm not good at delegating. My mother was always saying, "If you want something done right, just do it yourself." And that's the way I am at work, and that's the way I am at raising Rachel. And I know that that's not serving her very well, so when I can, I try to see that I'm doing it, and change it.

To be sure, this is a rich comment, both in what it articulates plainly and in what it hints at. Vanessa openly acknowledges an inadequacy she regrets. She expresses the belief that to be a "good" mother she should be available to talk to her daughter, and she worries that she is "not serving her very well" when she is distracted by "tasks and chores."

Yet Vanessa also suggests that not all of a child's desires must be met. If there are occasions when her daughter "needs to talk" to her, there must also be occasions when her child's interest in talk can be ignored. And even as Vanessa is apologetic about her inability to respond to her daughter's (actual) need for her attention, that apology is framed by her account of the competing demands characterizing her daily life.

Vanessa's admission that she might be inadequate, when measured against a standard of "intensive" motherhood, is thus balanced by her emphasis on her own very real *need* for scurrying: "I have to accomplish tasks and chores"; "I have really got to get something done"; "[there are] chores that I need to do." (Indeed, Vanessa suggests that this need for scurrying might even, perhaps legitimately, prevent her from being aware of the problems that arise: "so when I can, I try to see that I'm doing it.") Moreover, Vanessa acknowledges that there might be a solution to the problem she faces (a point I develop more fully below): If her own mother has misled her into a strategy of not delegating work, Vanessa could adopt a new strategy that would "involve [Rachel] in some of the chores" that await at the end of the day.

Other women emphasize similar conflicts between their desires to respond to their children's "needs," on the one hand, and the efforts required by the routine responsibilities of daily survival, on the other. These mothers also on occasion blur the line between children's needs and children's desires.

Sarah Stanley was not employed outside the home when she described her life as a single mother to Carol. Even so, she explained that she constantly had to race, simply to keep up with what she perceived to be her ongoing responsibilities:

> Sometimes I just will run. But I think a hard thing is when you've got to make dinner, do laundry, there's all these things that you have to do and the kids just want to play with you all the time. And sometimes they want to play outside and be free and I'll have to run in and get the phone or check that the rice isn't boiling dry. There are times when you know they're outside for three minutes alone and that's very, very stressful. Like yesterday I [had to handle some financial affairs and I] had to pick up phone calls and get e-mails and faxes and my kids were playing outside and the pool is out there. And I literally had to run in and check my e-mail and that was very, very stressful for me. Because, you know, this all happens spur of the moment; I didn't have time to call anyone. I couldn't be there for my kids a hundred percent, I couldn't be.

Just as Vanessa implied that some requests a child might make did not rise to the occasion of "need," Sarah elevates some of her children's wants and diminishes others. She does not question the charge on her to protect their safety: The pool is outside; if she turns her back she takes a risk. Yet even as she suggests that she really does want to be there "a hundred percent," her curious phrasing—"and kids just want to play with you all the time"—whispers of limits to the requirement of responsiveness. Who can possibly *play* all the time? Moreover, Sarah insists that e-mail, the fax, the phone, and the boiling rice also constitute legitimate demands on her time.

Two other mothers introduce additional sources of conflict that impinge on and sometimes impede their efforts to be what they define as good mothers. Tiffany Morrow, a widow, reminds the interviewer that "intensive mothering" directed toward one child might prevent her from enacting the same relationship with another, a particular challenge for her as the mother of a child with special needs. Like Sarah, Tiffany highlights the fact that she does respond to the *other* demands on her time, and especially to those occasioned by the need to coordinate, and travel to, her children's vital appointments.

> I wish there were two of me, one for each of my children, because no matter what I do, it feels like one is being neglected....And that's one of my regrets...I haven't always been there for Becca because I've had to make sure to keep Jonathan, and his stuff, on an even keel....It's been difficult with a special-needs child. It's been difficult being a single parent having to be only the one person to transport to dentist, orthodontist, doctor, parent-teacher conferences, and child care—stuff like that....I would like to put on the record that *it's a very difficult job being a single parent.* (Emphasis added.)

Another single mother, Liz Miles, focuses less on the stress of responding to competing pressures within the family. She concentrates instead on how striving to keep poverty at bay has cut into the time available to respond to her children's full range of needs as well as to her own ambitions. She thus situates herself as an individual entitled to have needs of her own:

> I see the cost [to my children] when I can't emotionally be there for them because I'm so tired of, you know, other things. I see the cost when I can't financially do what I need to do. You know, it has a big effect on them....I have long felt very, very frustrated about being a single parent trying to support a family. I felt very frustrated about what it's meant to my children....I mean, I feel like 60 percent of my time is taken up with survival, you know, and that has had a real devastating effect on my family, on my kids, on myself, on my work, on my dreams.

These four women each make reference to a different aspect of the conflict between meeting a child's "needs" and doing the material work that goes into sustaining family life. Even so, Vanessa's repetition of the reasons for scurrying, Sarah's enumeration of the demands she faced the day before the interview, Tiffany's desire to put her efforts "on the record," and Liz's assertion of frustration are all of a piece. Each woman makes central to her account of mothering the efforts that go into simply keeping her children alive and safe. Each woman also highlights the extra challenge incurred because of limited human and financial resources. As they do, the women acknowledge that their efforts might compete with, and occasionally cause them to diminish the range of, what they believe their children deserve.[7] In calling the resulting stance "practical motherhood," I purposefully draw out a contradiction similar to the one embraced in the notion of a social economy itself. The prevailing discourse idealizes motherhood as something beyond the *merely* practical. All mothers know otherwise. They know that they love their children, but they cannot always act on that love; they know that love itself requires the effort of "emotion work"; and they know that they cannot take care of their children without engaging in routine and burdensome chores. Single mothers make all of this knowledge explicit.

To be sure, as the quotes above indicate, each of the women also admits to uneasiness. This uneasiness is sometimes played out in solitude as the women review their days and evaluate their relationships with their children. Grace Jordan talked about feeling guilty when she was unable to respond with what she viewed as an appropriate set of rituals for the daughter she had adopted as a single mother. As she did, she mixed past and present to show that an old anxiety was still very much alive: "At night I felt so badly, when Miriam was much younger. It was all I could do to get her in bed—much less give her a fuzzy ritual and read her a whole bunch of books. I just don't have the strength. And I feel terrible for her."

The uneasiness the women feel about these painful compromises may well stand behind occasional shifts in their priorities.[8] Megan Paige, for example, said that although she generally had to put her material needs first (including her need to remain self-sufficient), sometimes she indulged her children with gifts that were more lavish than she could easily afford. When she did so, she justified her actions by elevating desires to the status of needs:

> I obviously do the bills that you can't get away with not paying first. And to make things happen for my kids, I have borrowed money. My daughter *had to have* this pony and I looked at it and I

said, what the heck, she's twelve once, she's not ever twelve again, she doesn't need a pony then, *she needs it now*. And right now I don't have the money. Well, too bad. I'll pay it and I'll be in debt or I'll have to work another five years. That seems less important than being twelve once. (Emphasis added.)

Overall, however, the women enact a more cautious, even practical approach. The effort and pain entailed in having to ignore desires, and sometimes even needs, and in having to balance both needs and desires against competing demands, are placed "on the record" during the interview.

Educating Children for Teamwork

This approach to family life, with its associated pain, is not just put on the record. More significant, single mothers transmit this articulated approach to parenting to their children in an effort to engage their participation in household chores, and even, perhaps, to engage their willingness to accept limits. The social economy of family life has both material and moral roots and both material and moral consequences.

When Grace Jordan acknowledged her guilt about failing to provide Miriam with "fuzzy rituals" at the end of the day, she embedded that statement in a broader expression of concern about the manner in which she handled the conflict between responsiveness to her child and practical demands. And she worried about whether or not she had spoken to her daughter too plainly and too often about the latter:

> But mostly I feel badly for Miriam when I'm so short on everything. She shouldn't have to—she's a child, it's her only childhood—she shouldn't have to have a parent that gets exasperated, and relays things. I'll say, "Miriam, you have to know I'm just [venting] here. You really shouldn't take this stuff seriously. But I do have to [do this and that]." I blabber on about things that she shouldn't have to hear. I've said, "Look, do you see anyone else here helping me? I'm sorry, but I've got to do this now. I can't play with you."

Grace's sense of guilt about imposing her own burdens on her daughter's "childhood" is shared by many of the single mothers in this study. At the same time, many of these same women insist that guilt coexists with, and may even be tempered by, an awareness that in educating their children about real difficulties, they are not only taking a pragmatic step toward getting their children to help relieve those burdens, but they are taking an ethical step as well. That is, as the women educate their children, they also lay the groundwork for a model of family life in which children become active members of a "team." They insist that as a consequence of adopting that new model they are producing children who will be better citizens and more responsible adults. This is a central moral consequence of the social economy of single motherhood as it is played out within the family.

For some women, this education involves simply (and sometimes painfully) making children aware of a mother's needs. Perhaps because they ritualized the practice of claiming their own space, two women suggested that teaching their children to be sensitive involved less pain than was the case for Grace Jordan. In fact, Sheila Davis spoke proudly of the fact that she had found a technique for dealing with the difficult transition from work to home. Noting that she could no longer rely on "someone else" to give her time to unwind, she said she had taught her children to respect her need for that time. Having learned that lesson, her children were able to take the additional step of insisting that she take that time rather than be short-tempered with them:

> One of the things that has become more difficult is that—when I'm tired or stressed out from work and I come home and the kids have a lot of homework or they're tired and they really need my attention—I can't say to someone else, "I need to go upstairs and chill out, can you hang out with the kids? Can you help with the homework?" Although now, if I have a hard day, I let the kids know as soon as I walk through the door [that] it's been a hard day and I need ten minutes or fifteen minutes to myself and they're old enough to understand and accept that. And, if I don't do that, they call me [on it].

Marlene Haynes's daughter is burdened with a serious physical disability and, at age four, she is considerably younger than Sheila's two children, who are nine and twelve. Even so, Marlene suggests that she has not only taught her daughter the same lesson that Sheila taught her children, but that she has done so as part of a mutual practice in which her needs and those of her daughter are placed on a relatively equal playing field: "You know, she knows Mommy, and Mommy knows her. She knows if Mommy is having a good day or a bad day, and Mommy knows if she's having a good day or a bad day, and we're respectful of each other's space—most of the time."

Some of the women not only express pride in having educated their children in this way, but they also suggest that this new understanding makes their children better people. Phoebe Stark separated from her husband when her twin sons, now twelve, were only two years old. She acknowledges her difficulty in maintaining a tidy house. She says that cooking has long been a catch-as-catch-can affair in her house, and that she let housework slide so much that in February, she still had not finished cleaning up from Christmas. But Phoebe did not hold herself solely responsible for this state of affairs. Rather, she suggested that she and her children had agreed about their priorities: "We're not into, like, the three-meals-a-day kind of thing. If [the boys are] around, they eat lunch if they're hungry.... Nobody likes to cook. We eat a lot of [take-out] pizza.... About once a month we vacuum. You see our Christmas tree is still up." Phoebe also claims, however, that her children have other responsibilities that began when they were quite young. They have "made their own breakfast since they were two or three," and now that they are older, they have an increasing role to play in family life: "They take initiative—they wash all their own clothes, they make their own beds [and] that kind of stuff." In addition, Phoebe says that her sons often earn money for themselves: One of the boys is an accomplished juggler and performs at children's parties; the other works part-time for a local carpenter. Sometimes, when Phoebe finds herself short of cash, she borrows from their earnings. Phoebe acknowledges that it is emotionally difficult for her to have to rely on her children in that way. But Phoebe also insists that the practice is embedded in a subtle "trade-off." When asked what she meant, she responded:

> You know, like, there's a lot of stuff that I feel that they don't necessarily have to have and I give at a sacrifice, so that they can have it. So, I feel like a lot of the money that they've so-called "earned" or been given was coming from me anyway (*laughter*) kind of thing. I'm honest with them about what's going on financially, in hopes that when they're older that they'll have a different reality, [a different] perspective of what it means to go—not to go without; but what it means that it's a shared [responsibility].... It's not that it's my kids' responsibility, it's not...but it *is*—there's a shared responsibility in having a family. They'll say, "Well, we did the dishes." And I'm like, "You know, nobody gave me a gold star for getting out of bed. That's just part of your responsibility of living in a family." And they're pretty appreciative of what they have, but they also know in some terms what it means to earn it or to have it.

Even as she stumbles over her words, Phoebe makes significant claims. As do other women, Phoebe distinguishes between what children "have to have" and what they want to have. She also insists that she be acknowledged for the efforts she put into the groundwork that allows her sons to make their way in the world free to have the occasion to earn their own money. She made "sacrifices" so that they could develop their skills as a juggler and a carpenter; she got out of bed each morning to prepare breakfast and get them ready for the day's activities. Phoebe wants her children to understand that a family requires a sharing of responsibility (and thus to recognize that it is a social unit); she also believes that this understanding produces better people who are both more realistic and more responsible. Not only do her two sons have the direct lesson of earning their own money to meet their own needs and especially to satisfy their own desires, but they also understand the effort that goes into the resources Phoebe has always provided for them.

Megan Paige makes similar claims when she explains why she believed she had actually become a better parent when she taught her children to understand how hard she struggled:

> I also feel... that I'm a better parent as a single parent than I was, that my kids respond better, that they're easier to parent than they were when I had a partner who wasn't really a partner.... I was trying to explain that to my friends one time and I came up with a metaphor. It was kind of like, you know, if you're riding in a car with kids and they're making noise and they won't behave and they won't pay attention or be quiet, and all of a sudden a deer runs in front and it's [*makes a screeching noise like skidding tires*], they're silent, not a peep, they're all sitting in the backseat like this [*sits upright*]. And a little... sense of danger goes a long way to having them pay attention to you. And when all the things happened in our lives, especially the divorce and stuff, they realized—most kids go through life without realizing, without valuing what parenting is to them. [Parents are] just taken for granted. But, although my kids lapse into that plenty of the time, they really know [that] when the chips are down you have to have someone there for you and that's important. And they know—they know because I tell them all the time—how hard it is for me and how hard I work and what our bottom line is and what the struggles are, and so they're more [willing to do their share]. We're a team. It used to be I was the horse pulling the cart and they were riding in it. Now they realize the hill's too big, we're not going to make it if they sit there, they're pushing, they're doing whatever they

can do to make us get there instead of dragging their feet.... So they've been easier to parent somehow because they're on board with it more.

Megan's account includes an explicit, albeit muted, comparison with her ex-husband: He was a partner but not "really" a partner. She maintains that she has taken on the major responsibility of raising her children. And rather than encourage her children to see both parents as being equally significant to their well-being, she would prefer that they understand that she is the "someone there for you and that's important." In order to enlist her children's cooperation, Megan makes them aware of her efforts on their behalf and she lets them know about her financial constraints. Megan is very explicit about the model of family life she has developed. Being "there" for her children does not mean that she has to be the "horse pulling the cart." Instead, the internal family dynamics of her social economy require that her children get out from time to time and help push.

A century or so ago, Phoebe and Megan might not have had to stumble over their words or reach for a metaphor to describe a pattern of family life in which children made active contributions rather than being the passive recipients of parental efforts. During the twentieth century, however, children's economic contributions to the household gradually disappeared and children became increasingly free from assuming responsibility for survival.[9] To be sure, the rate of adoption of this pattern varied by ethnicity, social class, and parental occupation. Even today, children in working-class and poor families take far more responsibility for themselves and for their siblings than do children in middle-class families; they also appear to understand better than do the latter the significance of limited material resources.[10] Both Phoebe and Megan are, by occupation and heritage, middle-class, even if their current circumstances leave them impoverished. When they proclaim teamwork as a family pattern, they may do so in an especially self-conscious manner because they are aware that they are violating norms adopted by their social (if not economic) peers.[11]

Sheila Davis found that the model of child rearing she had inherited from her own mother proved to be a bigger stumbling block than a comparison with her peers. Yet, when asked whether her children had responsibilities around the house, Sheila said that she was gradually and, she believed, appropriately shifting her priorities in response to a new mix of her own compelling needs and the emerging capabilities of her children:

What they have to do around my house is minimal and part of that has to do with how I was raised—my mom didn't want us to do any household chores when we were kids. She thought we should be kids and should be outside playing. And so I have sort of carried that belief forward in my own life. But I'm starting to expect more of them—and as a single mother I actually need [my son's] help.... Thomas helps with Ellie a lot; he helps her with her homework, he plays with her, which I consider help; he'll help me move furniture, bring the wood in, mow the lawn, things like that. I try not to load him up too much because I want him to do schoolwork and play.... As they get older I will expect more out of them.

Recall as well that Vanessa Menard had seen her failure to include Rachel in her end-of-the-day scurrying as a personality "flaw" transmitted from her mother to herself. Vanessa was coming to the realization that she would be better off adopting a new model to replace one "that's not serving her very well."

As the women talk about the teamwork ideal they also indicate that its enactment creates its own difficulties. When children in middle-class two-parent families are free from responsibility for housework and the care of younger siblings, the children in a single-parent family can come to believe that they are being treated unfairly when they are asked to assume those responsibilities. Excruciating conflict ensues. Sometimes Liz Miles needed to have her daughter babysit for her much younger brother. When she made that arrangement, she worried about the quality of care her daughter provided:

I'll have made plans for her to babysit and then she's just really being obnoxious to him, and almost to the point where I feel it's not safe, that she's going to really be abusive to him.... Usually she's fine. I mean, there have been a couple of times where she has hit him when she's not supposed to hit him.

Liz also worried about the integrity of her own relationship with her daughter. She was concerned that she had become too dependent on her daughter and that her daughter had too much leverage in their relationship:

I resent that I'm in that position where I have to ask her. I resent that she has the power to babysit. I feel like I could say to her, you cannot babysit unless you can be right with him. Then she would treat him better. But she sort of knows a little bit that I'm stuck.

Indeed, some single mothers suggested that struggles over doing chores, combined with struggles over how those chores were done, compounded rather than relieved their burdens; some women conceded that they had withdrawn from these struggles. In short, if teamwork has a practical motivation, it might ultimately prove impracticable.

SOCIABLE MOTHERING IN THE CONTEXT OF THE "MISSING" FATHER

When single mothers use "practical mothering" to pave the way for the model of teamwork, they are shifting child-rearing styles to accommodate to the new reality of raising children on their own. As they face this reality, single mothers also direct their attention outside of the family and develop some aspects of their maternal roles in response to the roles nonresidential fathers play. As was mentioned, most families headed by a single mother share conditions of impoverishment and limited human resources, but they do not have in common similar relationships between fathers and children. Hence more variability exists in the roles women adopt in response to fathers; these different responses, in turn, require different approaches to their children.

Three general patterns can be identified. When the father is viewed as destructive or even dangerous, single mothers emphasize their roles as protectors of their children. When the father is seen as being inadequate, the mothers emphasize the efforts they make to compensate for a father's failures; they may also assume responsibility for guiding that father toward more reliable parenting. Finally, when the father is perceived as acting appropriately, mothers enlarge the childcare team to include him and, on occasion, other members of his current family; the team then stretches across two households.

Before describing these patterns in greater detail, it is necessary to make a number of points that recognize their complexities. First, the patterns describe styles of relationships and not people; a single woman might experience more than one of these patterns (with respect to more than one father–child pair) and she might also find that her pattern changes over time.

Second, in describing these patterns, I am not claiming that the women necessarily offer accurate descriptions of the men's behavior as fathers; rather I am interested in outlining styles of mothering that emerge in response to what the women themselves perceive to be the father's role. I am looking at only one side of a ruptured relationship and I am aware that fathers might have very different assessments of the roles they play in their children's lives, and of why they are, or are not, involved in those lives through visitation and financial support.[12]

Third, the literature on the effects of single parenting generally treats all varieties of father absence as one phenomenon. For example, Sara McLanahan and Gary Sandefur's classic study *Growing up with a Single Parent: What Hurts, What Helps,* explores the achievements and attitudes of children in single-parent homes as compared with those in two-parent homes. For the most part, however, it does not distinguish among different kinds of single-parent families.[13] Thus, children living in situations characterized by the active involvement of a father, and children who have never had any contact whatsoever with a father, are combined into a single group for much of that analysis, even though the two sets of children are likely to have very different experiences of "fathering." The evidence in this study cannot rectify this large-scale omission; it does, however, suggest that how the mother conceives of *her* role (and how she behaves in response to her conceptions) might vary dramatically with her perceptions of the father's degree of engagement.

Fourth, these patterns intersect in complex ways with a set of relationships that revolve around the father's financial contributions. They reflect different aspects of the social economy as it is constructed in relation to these men. A mother might appreciate the financial support of the same man from whom she wants to protect her children. The pattern of compensatory parent, supplemented by that of guide to good parenting, can coexist with, and without, financial support. The same is true of the last pattern of expanded teamwork. In all cases, mothers have to balance carefully their own material needs with other interpersonal concerns: having a child sustain, or avoid, a relationship with an absent father, and having her own tolerable, or even any, relationship with him. Women who believe that by asking for child support they jeopardize one or both of the latter sets of relationships may opt to reduce their own expectations for a financial contribution, even if they thereby jeopardize their own material well-being.

Finally, it should be noted that single mothers do not construct these patterns on their own. The state has a large voice in issues of visitation, custody, and child support; as a result the mother's interest may conflict directly with the state's dictates. The state is thus a key player in the social economy of parenting as it is constructed in relation to an "absent" father.

Mothers as Preservers and Protectors

Slightly more than two fifths of the women in this sample viewed the father as being a very real threat or danger to his child.[14] Women who define the situation in this way claimed protection of their children *from the father* as a significant component of mothering.[15] In some instances, the perceived danger actually preceded the child's life in that the father urged abortion. Diana Spender, for example, conceived her child while she was in a relationship with a man who had recently been divorced and was, as she put it, in a "bad state of mind." Although he did not want her to continue with the pregnancy, Diana viewed herself as having risen above the issue of economics to assume the responsibility of ensuring the life of her unborn child:[16]

> When I became pregnant, it was fine with me, and it was not fine with him. He said that he did not want me to go through with the pregnancy—for financial reasons. He was paying a lot for his divorce and for his other kids, and he couldn't financially do it. Also he wasn't in any shape to be committed to another person. So it was my choice to have Georgia alone.

As Diana sees her daughter flourish, her earlier decision is affirmed, and she takes pride in the fact that she is the "preserving" parent. Indeed, as do many of the other women interviewed, when Diana is asked about her greatest source of pride, she names her child. But Diana puts "having" Georgia first, only secondarily mentioning her child's developing personality: "I'm proud of having Georgia, and then I'm proud of her because she's really something." She thus highlights her role as the protecting mother.

Protection is a different issue for those women who have raised children in the context of violent or abusive relationships. After separation from their partners, these women engage in ongoing acts of protection, sometimes at the risk to their own financial and emotional well-being. They thus demonstrate well that a single strand of the social economy can engender contradictory impulses. Ultimately, many of these women redefine the single-parent family—and their capacity for mothering within that situation—as a marked improvement over the two-parent family of their earlier experience. Monica Starr, for example, talked about how hard it had been to leave a relationship that included in its cycle what she called the "honeymoon phase after the beating."[17] She also indicated that once she came to realize that she was putting her child at risk, she believed it was her "responsibility to get my son out of that situation." Another woman similarly said that although she found it exceedingly difficult to separate from a boyfriend she loved, she was motivated by the fear that her son would adopt his father's model of violence as a solution to frustration; she was insistent that she "didn't want my son to grow up to be anything like him." Even if outright violence had not become a feature of daily life, some women said that they thought conflict between parents could leave its own scars. One woman said that hard as it was to be a single parent at age twenty-one, raising a two-year-old on her own, "there definitely isn't any fighting going on, which is a good thing."

When the women identified the destructive patterns of incautious spending, drinking, and drug use associated with "hard living" as a cause for the breakup of their relationships, they emphasized again the role of protection and they celebrated the disappearance of those behaviors from their households.[18] Anne Davenport ended her marriage when her husband's drinking spiraled out of control. In answer to our questions about the transition to single parenthood, she responded without hesitation that it was a relief to have "one less child in the house" and "a lot of reduction in stress level." Anne also noted that once she no longer had to cope with the consequences of her husband's alcoholism, she could take new pleasure in her children's antics:

> I used to put the kids to bed early because I couldn't deal with them because I had so much other stress going on. And I realized that after, little things that they would do, which are just kid things, which before would annoy the shit out of me because they were creating more work, now I can sit and laugh at them.... For a long time survival was my main goal. That was as much as I could work on at once—just getting through the day. Now it's different. Now we can actually live life and enjoy it. And [I can] enjoy them without being so stressed out.

Some research comparing the lives of children raised in single-parent families with the lives of children raised in married-couple families concludes that the purported "benefits" of marriage depend on the quality of the family life it provides.[19] The single mothers whose previous families harbored discord, abuse, violence, and hard-living men, understand well the reality of suffering behind those abstract findings. They define themselves as good mothers not in spite of the fact that they are raising children on their own, but because of it. A good mother preserves her child's life and protects that child from danger.

These actions can come at enormous cost. Some women moved great distances to get away from dangerous men. In the process they lost other valuable resources on which their social economies depended, including friendships and familiarity with the agencies in a community. Other women opted to forgo child support in order to avoid contact altogether with men they regarded as threats. But even if they are willing to absorb these costs, not all women can successfully or fully enact this role of protector of their children. Women who are welfare reliant have to name the father of their children as one of the conditions imposed on receiving state aid. In so doing, they can put both themselves and their children at risk.

When courts decree that visitation must be allowed between a violent man and his children, a mother also experiences distinct limits to her capacity to protect her children. Monica Starr took the steps she could to remove her child from the daily presence of her abusive ex-husband. However, Monica has not been able to challenge the court order giving him the right to have his son make regular visits. Monica has to facilitate those visits. When her son becomes "clingy and panicky," she takes personally her failure to protect him.

Compensating for Inadequate Fathers

Single mothers assume a different set of roles when fathers remain active in their children's lives and are less disruptive or threatening than simply inadequate. This is the case for two fifths of the women in this sample. These women believe they have been left with a new set of burdens that include evaluating a father's effects on his children, compensating for his failings, and guiding him toward better parenting.

April Yeaton described her ex-husband's inconsistent dealings with their son, Rick: "It's usually every other weekend [that his father comes to visit]. There's times when it'll go a month or so, or a month and a half without seeing him." She also indicated that she took on the responsibility of assessing the effects of these visits: "And I've weighed the [pros and cons]. You know, is it good for him to see him? Is it not good?" Ultimately, April decided to opt for regular visits: "And just by Rick's behavior I think he needs to see [his father] and he needs to see him consistently. It needs to be so that Rick can look forward to when it's going to be, because it seems to make Rick feel worse when he doesn't see him." April is willing to take on the burden of communicating with a man who was violent during their marriage—and who stalked her after she left it—for the modest goal of not having Rick "feel worse."

Now that she is separated from her partner, Marlene Haynes appreciates his reliable child support payments: "He's good about that." She is less appreciative of the way he handles his daughter's regular visits. Marlene believes that Peter is incapable of providing the discipline, creative interactions, and boundaries their daughter needs:

> She gets bored [when she is at her father's house]. And he's good to her, but he just doesn't have a clue. He doesn't know how a three-

year-old's mind works, and she gets bored, and she doesn't have
the security with him.... She never asks to go and see Daddy. Except in discipline, she'll say she wants Daddy because Daddy will
give in. Daddy doesn't give her the structure and the boundaries
that she gets at home. And kids need that. They may not like that
all the time, or think they like that, but she really does need it.

Marlene draws on general knowledge of children ("kids need that") and
the particular knowledge she has acquired over the years ("she really
does need it") to assess the impact of her daughter's visits with Peter.
She believes she counterbalances that impact by offering appropriate
routines and appropriate discipline in her home. Marlene takes on yet
another task, as she encourages her daughter's father to be a better parent. Fortunately for Marlene, this task is less burdensome for her than
the same task was for April Yeaton. As Marlene said, her ex-partner and
she have achieved an easier relationship than they had when they lived
together, and he now encourages her input: "Our communication, his
and mine, is much better now that we're not together. He actually listens
to me now. And he will ask me for advice."

An Enlarged Team

When fathers remain actively involved in their children's lives and are
assessed to be providing appropriate care, a single mother sometimes
reconfigures her role to include within it the activities involved in creating
and sustaining membership in an enlarged team. Women who characterized the fathers of their children in this positive manner described
calling an ex-partner with concerns about the children, consulting him
before making decisions having to do with discipline, and sharing plea-
sures in a child's developmental achievements. I do not mean to imply
here that this kind of cooperation is either easy or comfortable. Single
mothers must make enormous efforts to maintain sociability, and they
may have to put aside their own anger and grief. This explains, perhaps,
this pattern's infrequency—such collaboration takes place among only
one fifth of the women in this study.

Sheila Davis is one of these few women. On the one hand, she spoke
bitterly about her husband's affair that ended their marriage. On the
other hand, she admitted that although they had been "bad marriage
material," they had always been congenial as parents, and their divorce
had not disrupted that pattern: "And so I ended up marrying someone
whose values about raising kids were somewhat similar and we continue raising our kids in, I think, a wonderful way." If Sheila implies

a comfortable resolution, she also made explicit the effort on which it rested. Sheila worked through her anger to achieve cooperation. She also sacrificed her financial well-being when she chose to forgo child support "because of the animosity it creates." In response to a growing concern about her children's emotional needs, Sheila recently chose to change her employment. This choice has put a new strain on her financial situation. Reluctantly she has broached the idea of child support with her ex-husband, but she worries that doing so will jeopardize a hard-earned congeniality:

> A couple of months ago I [told my ex-husband], "I'm going to be taking a pay cut and I think I'm going to need your help supporting the kids." I just wanted to work it out between us. And I don't know how this is going to play out. But I don't want to *not* take the job because he isn't willing to support us.

Sheila thus weighs the different aspects of her social economy, even as they shift and change. Her social economy, like that of others, is a work in progress and not a completed project.

Joanna Darling has been even "luckier" than Sheila in that she has a broader group of men from which to draw support. Her five children were fathered by three different men and one of those men, along with his current wife, has taken over considerable child-rearing responsibilities for his own biological daughter as well as for one of his stepchildren. When that other daughter started acting out as a teenager, Joanna appreciated the intense engagement of several different adults all working together:

> Mikayla lived with [Keith and his new wife, Caroline] for a year and she was very difficult for a while . . . and we often got together as a unit, including Caroline, to talk about what was going on. . . . And sometimes that was me supporting Keith, sometimes it was me supporting Caroline, sometimes it was one or the other or both of them supporting me. . . . That worked really well. And Caroline and I became really good friends during that time.

As Sheila did, Joanna spoke about a parenting relationship that survived separation: "We give each other support as parents because both of us see each other as the parent combination—you know, the mom and the dad—in his family and my family in combination." In discussing how she now considers Keith and Caroline to be part of her family unit, Joanna implies that she is creating the "postmodern" family structure sociologist Judith Stacey describes as a possible, and perhaps even a common, outcome of divorce.[20]

If there are positive consequences to coparenting from two separate households, these arrangements are also often replete with problems of teamwork occurring between individuals with different priorities and concerns. The congeniality on which the social economy of sustained joint parenting rests requires careful coordination and sometimes painful compromise. Sheila Davis believes that she and her ex-husband work well together on major issues, but she does not like the fact that her children watch television when they visit him. Drawing on a notion of diversity, she learns to surrender control for the benefit of balance among competing approaches:

> It takes two people to have a kid and I feel like I don't always offer the balance I want to offer them in my house. We offer the balance externally, and it's fascinating to me—we're really different people in terms of our lifestyle. There's no television in my house. We either play games or we talk to each other. There's sort of the opposite scenario in their dad's house. I can't stand it but I remember that's just balance to what goes on in my house.

As Sheila explains more fully how she has learned to accept balance, she talks of the intervention of a counselor who taught this couple how to survive separation so as to "continue raising our kids in . . . a wonderful way":

> [We did] attend ten weeks with a counselor doing coparenting . . . and that's what kind of helped us to the place we are now. . . . We really worked at negotiating kid time and holidays and it works for us. It's a lot of work. It's exhausting.

By including a counselor in their negotiations, Sheila and her husband transformed the private family into a public unit; by emphasizing the effort that went into creating a good relationship, Sheila makes visible the work of family life, rather than treating it as a natural, effortless phenomenon.

A Variety of Men

When Joanna Darling married Keith she was fortunate to find a man who was willing to take responsibility for his nonbiological children, even though he lived with them for only a short period of time. Other women are not quite so fortunate in their choices, and the work of creating a social economy stretches to include the work of having to explain to siblings why they are treated differently from one another. Dan, the father of Liz Miles's son Mark, had never developed a strong relationship with Janette, Liz's daughter from a previous marriage. Now that Liz and Dan live apart, Dan likes to have Mark visit regularly, but he entirely ignores Janette. Unfortunately, Janette's father has also disappeared from her life. Liz suggests that at least part of Janette's anger at her brother (and abusive tendencies during those times she babysits for him), has its roots in her daughter's perception that life is "better" for Mark and that he has "more people who love him." In such cases the work of parenting can require developing different modes of response to her children—not just in response to their personalities, as is the case for all mothers of more than one child—but also in response to the treatment they receive from individuals who stand outside the current family.

EXPANDING THE BOUNDARIES OF FAMILY LIFE

A child's nonresidential father is but one of many outside influences on the relationship between a mother and her children. Both by necessity and by choice, some single mothers live with others and many ask others to help care for their children. These arrangements address needs for support and create opportunities for conflict.

Residential Arrangements

The majority of single mothers (in this study as elsewhere) live in a household alone with their children.[21] But many single mothers live for some time with other (nonpartner) adults; they are especially likely to do so in the period immediately following divorce or separation when they have to contend with newly acute financial and emotional needs.[22]

No matter what the mother's specific motivation for living with others, these occasions of coresidence may have the unexpected benefit of engaged emotional support of additional adults in her children's lives. Indeed, single mothers often express enormous satisfaction with, and appreciation for, this effect. In explaining why she would want her son to live with his grandmother if something should happen to her, Kelly Nye cited both his comfort with his grandmother (stemming from the years he and Kelly have shared her home) and that grandmother's ongoing concern:

[I would want him to live with her] because she knows him. I mean, he's been here, mostly, ever since he's been born. He's used to living with her. And he's happy with her and stuff. And I know that she'd be good to him.

This intense engagement between children and other adults may last well into the period when single mothers move into their own homes. Although Amy Phelps and her daughters lived with her parents for only a few months, she believed that her parents remained deeply involved with and concerned about their grandchildren. She also wanted to foster and acknowledge that connection. When asked who, besides herself, was the most important person in her daughters' lives, she gave an internally contradictory answer. On the one hand, Amy wants to dismiss her ex-husband's role because she believes he is unreliable (even though she believes her children take that unreliability in stride). On the other hand, she wants to privilege the more reliable caregiving offered by her parents and although she says her daughters are very "close" to their grandparents, she provides no evidence that the grandparents are more important to them than the father:

> I would have to say their father [is the most important person to them] but I do have some reservations about that because he's in and out. And they seem to be totally fine with his totally—I'm in your relationship this week and I'm out of your life next week. I would have to say my mom is [most important]. They're very close to my mother. She's been around and supported them through lots of issues, especially when I went through the divorce. She was there for them and whatever they needed.

Close as relationships between children and grandparents or other residential caregivers become, and much as women might want to value them, single mothers do not necessarily view child rearing as a shared venture (as they do with "involved" fathers).[23] When the social economy includes deep reliance on the members of one's extended family, women are relieved of the burden of some practical work, but they have to find their way among new hassles of competing attachments, outsiders' assessments of their child-rearing style, and disputes about lines of authority. In the essentially uncharted world of semishared parenting, these hassles constitute their own form of work.[24]

Julie Marshall readily acknowledged significant practical advantages stemming from her coresidence with her mother: "The advantages really [are] just a lot of financial ones, and babysitting." She also acknowledged significant disadvantages. Not only did she become jealous of her mother's important role in her son's life, but she also felt the sting of those occasions when her "new" parenting skills were held up to multigenerational examination. She believed she had to protect her choices from the judgments of others:

> And then the disadvantages [include] me dealing with her becoming such a big role as caregiver in Max's life. [My mom] has so much advice to give about what I should be doing with my son.... I try to listen with an open heart because I understand that she's just trying to pass along some wisdom, because my grandmother is the same way, you know. His great-grandmother, she comes [and she says], "You should do this; you should do that."

An incident that occurred during Kelly Nye's interview revealed underlying tensions in her household, in spite of Kelly's trust in her mother as a caregiver. Kelly described how she fed her son and, as she did, excited his immediate interest in the topic.

Kelly Nye: Usually he just wants a peanut butter and fluff sandwich or cereal or something.
Declan: I want a peanut butter and fluff sandwich! I want a peanut butter and fluff sandwich! I want one!

When Kelly and the interviewer ignored Declan's request, Kelly's mother chose to intervene:

Mother: Kelly, do you have a problem with me making him a sandwich?
Kelly Nye: No, go ahead. [*Turns to the interviewer.*] She doesn't usually ask me that. No, she probably would. I don't know.

The mother's intervention, combined with Kelly's self-contradictory response, prompts an awareness of ongoing battles in this household over who is really in charge and who should take responsibility for caregiving.

Patsy Downey did not live with her mother after she separated from her abusive partner, but she did live in close proximity to her, and for several years her mother had been a key player in Patsy's social economy. She had a practical role in child care (i.e., she included her grandchildren in her registered family day-care business) and she had formed strong emotional bonds with Patsy's two children. Now that Patsy is cohabiting with a new partner, she is trying to reclaim her children and include them in a more "traditional" family structure. When asked who, besides herself, was most important to her children, Patsy paused for a long time before answering and then emphasized the present moment. In the pause and the emphasis alike, Patsy acknowledged shifts in the membership of her social economy and shifts in the roles played by ongoing members: "I'd have to say my boyfriend at this point. We've only been living together for seven months at this point...." She then immediately (and as part of the same sentence) turned to a discussion of her mother's role in her children's lives. As she did, Patsy offered examples of conflict about child-rearing styles and used them as justification for seeking to remove her children from her mother's care:

> Because my mother's great and she lives next door, and she keeps them while I'm at work. But we've been like butting heads and butting heads and butting heads. Because I know how I was raised, I would never have dared to talk back to my mom. You just did it because your mom told you to. But it seems to be okay with her if *my* kids don't listen.... [I had to] tell my mom to back off because I felt like I was fighting her to get them to listen. I could never repay her enough for caring for them when I was at school and stuff, because I couldn't have done it without her, I'm not saying that at all, but I'm saying that she didn't raise *me* that way...and so it didn't make any sense. Why would you want your grandchildren to act like little animals? *It was like the best and the hardest.* It was trying to get her to back off. And we still have some problems. (Emphasis added.)

Patsy's examples of her mother's inadequacy are not entirely convincing and they are embedded in, and enmeshed with, a continued acknowledgment of the significant role her mother played during the first several years of her children's lives. Patsy appears to question implicitly her morality of recasting her mother's help (the "best") as now constituting a problem (the "hardest").

Later in the interview, as she discussed the relationship with her fiancé (a topic to which I turn more fully in the next chapter), Patsy indicated that she was willing to share the right to make decisions within her *new* family. Indeed, drawing on an image of shared parenting, she has enlisted her partner in her struggle with her mother and she has agreed to back up the actions he takes as a father, even in those cases where she believes they are wrong. In this new configuration, parental solidarity is a more significant goal than is the moral certainty attached to any particular child-rearing decision:

He was really supportive about me, like really standing up to my mom...and reining [the children] back in.... He's really supportive as far as decisions I made about the kids and how I want them to act, and now he has like an equal input into that as far as the rules that they follow and the way that we are choosing to teach them.... We definitely don't always agree about everything. But we've made an agreement: You don't discuss the kids in front of the kids. Even if he tells them to do something, even if I don't agree with it, we're not going to talk about it then because I don't want us to undermine each other in front of them.

Amy Phelps was also living with a new partner at the time of the interview, and like Patsy she was both observing the new household dynamics and trying to encourage her children to transfer their affections for their "real" father to her fiancé: "I'm getting married in August and my fiancé adores my children and it's a stepparent thing, it's an up and down relationship, and one minute my kids love him right to death and the next minute it's, 'You're not my daddy and you're not going to tell me what to do.' So it's kind of like that rocky-road relationship." But Amy had yet another issue to resolve. Although she had previously wanted her mother to have legal responsibility for her children if something were to happen to her (and had identified her mother as being preferable to the "real" father), Amy now considered privileging her fiancé's role over that of their grandmother: "Right now I have them listed with my mother [as their guardian] and I've been really torn with what should I do—should I change that [to my fiancé]? Should I give it a few years? I'm still struggling with that."

In short, when single mothers enlist cohabitants in the daily activities of caring for their children, they often value the intense affection that exists between their children and these other caregivers. While these relationships clearly have benefits, they also have drawbacks, beginning with jealousy and extending to a reluctant acceptance of differences in style. Most of these mothers do not cede authority altogether, and as both Amy's and Patsy's statements made clear, they do not always view these more social patterns as permanent. Single mothers want to retain their parental rights; they also want to be able to shift their children's affections in the direction of their own new attachments; and they appear to reserve a vision of shared parenting for a more "traditional" family structure.[25]

Nonresidential Arrangements

Whether or not they live with other adults, the women I interviewed actively seek to include a broad group of extended family members, paid caregivers, and friends in the venture of child rearing. Although these affiliations often emerge from straightforward material reasons, the women indicate that they are also consciously looking to ensure that their children are surrounded by people who love them, to provide variety in their children's lives, and to fill roles that they believe they cannot accomplish on their own. As Sarah Stanley said, "I feel good about [the variety] because I believe that that's healthy, especially in a single-parent family. I think it's healthy for them to be close to other loving people of all different ages."

In creating these opportunities, women carefully assess their own capabilities. After April Yeaton fled from her violent husband, she suffered from acute anxiety and a loss of self-esteem. Recognizing that neither she nor her ex-husband were being helpful to her son at that point, she enlisted her father to spend time with his grandson: "My father has played a big part in Rick's life. My father's, like, seventy-eight now, but when [the marriage broke up] Rick would go and see him quite often because he wasn't seeing his father.... So he needed somebody that he could be with." April was also pleased that her boss (who is the soccer coach at the high school where she works as an administrative assistant) engaged Rick in activities to help build his self-esteem. In discussing this arrangement, April fully acknowledged her own limitations as well as the limitations stemming from the absence of a "real" father:

> Just this season I've had him help—actually, [the coach] asked to have him be like an assistant manager with the team, because Rick is [*she is at a loss for words*].... He's a very intelligent child, very shy, low self-esteem, and it's hard for a parent that doesn't have a very healthy self-esteem to begin with to try to give it to a child. And there's not that other person there to balance.

When she became a single mother, Sheila Davis made efforts to spend time with members of her extended family because, as she said, "I want my kids to know that they're from something much bigger than the three of us." She had another purpose in mind as well. Because she thought it important for her children "to have that sense of a life outside of themselves," Sheila appreciated the times when her children had contact with their aunt, whose lifestyle was very different from the one she herself had chosen. Valerie Ramsey believed that friends could substitute for extended family to provide security and variety for her adopted daughter, Halley: "I've designed it so that it's a group.... I don't have family living around here...so I have this group of like four or five friends who have been part of her life from the beginning." Megan Paige (who carefully created a friendship circle of single mothers) remembered the extended family of her childhood, which included people of different ages. She tried to recreate that mixture in her children's lives by incorporating an elderly neighbor into her family configuration: "I did that consciously because we need someone in that generation and she needs us."

In making room for such opportunities, these women add to their responsibilities as mothers the new work of selecting and monitoring appropriate influences and of making occasions for these interactions. Much as the middle-class mothers sociologist Annette Lareau describes in *Unequal Childhoods* build a schedule of opportunities as a key element of "concerted cultivation," single mothers learn how to engender and supervise their children's "extracurricular" attachments.[26]

A number of the women worry about the absence of men in their children's lives. Sarah Stanley was among those concerned:

> [My son] had about two years worth of bonding with his dad and it's hard for me to parent him in some ways because he still misses his dad extremely. He talks about his dad every day and I'm not a man so I can't give him what he needs and I find that difficult to be what I'm not. I'm not his dad.

Because of this concern, Sarah enlisted men, as well as women, to babysit for her children. Another woman had purposely sought out a male child-care provider for her (adopted) daughter; she described him as being an easy and comforting presence: "There's a male. He's like popcorn, and he's done a lot of child care over the last five years. So she's had that male influence." Other women who spoke about actively trying to include men in their *children's* lives also talked about how the men present in *their* lives—their fathers, their brothers, and especially their boyfriends—could serve as male role models.[27]

Although some women did purposely seek this "male influence," other women challenged the prevailing discourse that suggests that fathers—or even men in general—are indispensable for the psychological well-being of children. Julie Marshall had mixed, contradictory feelings. At one point, Julie expressed concern over the absence of a man who could provide balance to her heavily female household: "One thing that I really worry about is him not having a dad. I have all sisters. He's got really, really strong female influence coming from my side of the family. I worry about that sometimes." At another point, however, she determined that gender was trumped by care: "I just really feel strongly that Max has a lot of caring people in his life, and I think that's a really good thing. And even though I'm a single *mom* I think he gets what he needs from everyone around him." Julie's good friend Rose Bishop more easily dismissed altogether worries about male models, at least at this stage in her young child's life: "And I think that Hunter is well-rounded even though I'm a single mother [and] he doesn't have a male role model."

To be sure, one motivation for bringing in outsiders—whether they include men or not—rests in material and practical concerns. As shown in previous chapters, single mothers invariably need to draw on a wide variety of resources to ensure the emotional and economic well-being of themselves and their children. But need alone does not determine the shape or meaning of these occasions of expanded sociability: As the women reach out to others, they add to their role as mothers the responsibility of selecting appropriate influences and filling gaps they perceive in their own capabilities.

Not surprising, there are complex aspects to these arrangements. Mothers cannot necessarily control the outside influences that result from their efforts to create a caring community in which to raise their children. And they cannot ensure that the individuals they encourage to become involved will prove to be respectful of the attachments that result. Betsy Black said she had sought to provide her sons with enduring relationships with men, but that, on the whole, she found men to be less reliable than her women friends:

> I had, as a single mom, made it a point to be around men, you know, men friends that would really be able to provide them with some positive role modes. But that didn't [work out]. I mean, it's just different [with men]. They sort of disappeared. We'll see them every now and then, but it's not like—they won't seek the kids out like my women friends do. *They'll* call up and say, "I feel like spending some time with your kids—can I come over?" Men don't do that.

Even if these others *are* reliable, the single mothers might have their own reasons for wanting to create distance. As I show more fully in the next chapter, the attachments between children and men with whom their mothers are (romantically) involved can be sacrificed to the mother's interest in maintaining control over *her* relationships, thus illustrating that the "family" is not necessarily an undifferentiated unit, but instead consists of individuals with competing needs, interests, and desires. In short, expanding the boundaries of the family in a postmodern scenario carries risks as well as benefits, and opportunities for conflict even between mothers and their children.

CONCLUSION

The vision of practical mothering outlined in the beginning of this chapter represents attentiveness to social norms (in its negotiation with the social ideal of intensive mothering and its awareness of "the record") as single mothers raise their children in the context of limited resources and limited time and energy. Although they sometimes are ambivalent about the accommodations they make, single mothers teach their children to be aware of these acute limitations and they use that awareness to develop a model of teamwork.

Many scholars have expressed concern that the growing demands placed on all working mothers will result in a practice of family life where care itself is subsumed by responsibility and where children are treated as miniature adults. In *The Second Shift*, Arlie Russell Hochschild locates her concern within the context of the gendered division of labor in a "traditional" nuclear family. She worries that women will "shut down" when they are asked to carry too great a burden:

> If, in the earlier part of the [twentieth] century, middle-class children suffered from over-attentive mothers ... today's children may suffer from an underestimation of their needs. Our idea of what a *child* needs in each case reflects what *parents* need. The child's needs are thus a cultural football in an economic and marital game.[28]

Another sociologist, Stacey Oliker, locates her concern in a context more explicitly relevant to the lives of single mothers. She notes that the shift from Aid to Families with Dependent Children (AFDC) (which allowed subsidies for the work of mothering itself) to the more stringent requirements of Temporary Assistance to Needy Families (TANF) (which requires employment), could be followed by a shift in what she calls the "moral economy" of mothering itself. She argues that those single mothers who had previously been able to place caregiving ahead of financial goals, might now find that they are able to give less of the former, even as their economic situation improves in conjunction with employment outside the home:

[AFDC] allowed the very poor to adopt an ethos of attentive care-giving that more affluent women pioneered a century before.... [With TANF] work must come first. If work takes inevitable priority, women must surrender caregiving practices that are deeply invested with meaning, that are normative, constitutive of identity in a community, understood to be beneficial, and un-likely to be replaced. Renouncing the priority of care may require psychological denial in order to cope with the pain of loss and failure. Whatever the psychological motives, it seems plausible that the imposition of regular decisions to subordinate caregiving to earning may encourage those who believed in doing otherwise to minimize the damages this causes.[29]

The single mothers interviewed in this study do often hold down full-time jobs and out of necessity leave their children in the care of others for long hours. Their employment rarely produces economic well-being, much less a cushion of luxury. And all single mothers—employed or not—find themselves run ragged at the end of the day. Under these conditions of limited resources and ongoing weariness, it is possible that practical mothering could, indeed, slide into ever-increasing compromises. If her life grew even more challenging than it already is, Grace Jordan, for example, might not only abandon "fuzzy rituals" but all forms of intensive emotional engagement with her daughter. In short, the emphasis on the "practical" leaves room for concern about the norms and practices of mothering itself.

But, though there is room for concern, the adopted stance of the family as a team holds out a promise of optimism on a different front. In an intriguing response to Jerry Jacobs and Kathleen Gerson's, *The Time Divide: Work, Family, and Gender Inequality*, the sociologist Frances Goldscheider commented that "precious but useless children" might well become more engaged in household responsibility to alleviate the time constraints of their parents.[30] Writing in *Unequal Childhoods* about the pattern in working-class and poor families she called "the accomplishment of natural growth," Annette Lareau also identified as valuable the opportunities those children had to take more responsibility for themselves and their siblings. Both Goldscheider and Lareau thus challenge prevailing middle-class norms. The women in this study do the same. They explicitly identify the responsibility that emerges from a "teamwork" model as a moral virtue and even as a social good. They believe that sons and daughters who are taught to understand what it means to respect a mother who needs space in which to repair herself before assuming the "second shift," and children who are taught to understand the burdens of trying to manage on limited incomes, become not only easier to "parent," but also have better characters and a greater social consciousness.[31]

Single mothering shifts in relation to the influence of children's fathers. The women experience little control over these shifts, even as they accumulate new burdens. Vis-à-vis the newly created single-mother family, the role of protector is the most solitary of the identified stances: Single mothers who perceive the father as a threat to their children seek to maintain distance from that influence. Ironically, this stance can also end up as the most "public" when the state intervenes to ensure a continued relationship between a father and his children. Single mothers who perceive fathers as "simply inadequate" shape their mothering to ensure compensatory practices. The "private" mother adjusts her role in response to, and with an eye toward compensating for, the actions of the nonresidential father. She might also take on the additional responsibility of guiding that father into becoming a better parent. Those women who see their children's fathers as adequate and active parents emphasize their complementary skills (and the provision of balance between two households) even as they negotiate through anger and loss and make visible the work that goes into creating parental teamwork. In all of these stances the women mediate among their children's needs, a father's claims, and their own needs and claims. Because these needs and claims do not mesh neatly, single mothers invariably make difficult choices. It is evidence of the truly *moral* nature of their social economies that among these is the frequent choice to forgo financial (and practical) support in order to keep their children safe or, in a different set of circumstances, ensure their children's continued affiliation with their fathers.

When women bring a broader social community into their daily lives, they relieve themselves of the burden of being the only caregiver; they also ensure that their children have opportunities they alone cannot provide. At the same time, this aspect of the social economy—like the component involving the nonresidential father—can create its own contradictory problems. Women may unwittingly cede more control than they wish, and they may subject themselves to negative social appraisal in exchange for material support. And as both Amy and Patsy show, ultimately many single women indicate that they would prefer a more traditional and private family structure, even though achieving that (new) model involves its own efforts of ongoing "emotion work" and of wresting control from others who are involved in their children's care. The next chapter examines how single mothers use a notion of romantic love to achieve this goal.

5

FALLING IN LOVE (AGAIN)[1]

For all the existing scholarship about single mothers, the relations between these women and the men in their lives (as potential or new partners) is a relatively unexplored field. There is much written about how and why women become single mothers, and some scholarship about the relationships between single mothers and the fathers of their children. Little has been written, however, about how single mothers interact with and make sense of their relationships with current boyfriends (especially when those men are *not* the fathers of their children).[2] This is a significant oversight, particularly in the early twenty-first century when the "traditional" family represents an iconic goal in our contemporary welfare system and when the current administration reiterates regularly its view that marriage can solve the problems faced by single mothers.[3]

Those who oppose marriage-promotion policies base their arguments on a wide host of reasons, ranging from concerns about domestic violence to concerns about state interference in private matters. Moreover, they express considerable doubt about whether marriage-promotion initiatives will have their intended effect of reducing women's poverty.[4] At the same time, opponents exercise caution, and perhaps even prudery, in stepping around the fact that single mothers most likely do have men in their lives and in their beds. Indeed, it would be surprising if the women did not, especially because recent research suggests that "a majority of unmarried women, including disadvantaged single and cohabiting mothers, value marriage as a personal goal."[5]

Most scholars who discuss relationships between single mothers and their boyfriends view them through the lens of straightforward social exchange. This is especially true of those who examine single mothers

155

who are very poor. For example, in their study of low-wage and welfare-reliant women, Kathryn Edin and Laura Lein indicate that boyfriends contribute to the survival strategies of both groups of mothers, although, in each case, the cash amount received constitutes but a small portion of overall budgets.[6] The authors state that the single mothers create "obligation by including boyfriends in family life" and that they are critical of those men who do not contribute to the maintenance of the household. Edin and Lein also suggest that women and men equally accept the terms of this exchange: "A mother seldom allowed her boyfriend to stay with her unless he contributed both cash and in-kind goods to the household. Boyfriends, in turn, typically expected to be able to 'stay,' at least occasionally, in return for their cash contributions."[7]

Edin and Lein stress as well the negative dimensions and possible dangers of these "no pay, no stay" relationships. They note that boyfriends "demanded time and energy from women who were short of both," and that "sometimes boyfriends became violent, brought drugs, alcohol, or undesirable companions into the household, or used the household as the headquarters for their illegal activity."[8] And they write about how "the mercenary nature of these relationships occasionally made it difficult for mothers to distinguish between serial boyfriends and outright prostitution."[9] In *"So You Think I Drive a Cadillac?": Welfare Recipients' Perspectives on the System and Its Reform*, Karen Seccombe offers an almost identical analysis, modified by her observation that the mothers did distinguish between "serial boyfriends" and "outright prostitution" on the basis of whether or not they were involved in more than one-night stands.[10] Seccombe thus suggests that ethical concerns can play a role when sex is involved, and that single mothers do not want to confuse a straightforward exchange of sexual services for other goods and services with the moral requirements of relationships with men designated as boyfriends.

Taken as a whole, both sets of authors imply that women are positioned on the cusp of exploitation in their relationships with men. Moreover, they imply that what the women give (which includes the nonmaterial gifts of sex, opportunities for participation in family life, and emotional engagement, in addition to the material benefits of a place to stay, eat, and sleep) is balanced—or, perhaps, more accurately, *returned*—predominantly by the men's exclusively *material* contributions. In fact, there is a deeply gendered (and perhaps even sexist) assumption here: The authors describe the women as providing all the sociable benefits of a relationship without necessarily getting their own delight out of those same elements (including the sex), even as the distinction between "serial boyfriends" and "prostitution" implicitly concedes that the women might derive some pleasure from the relationship itself. Conversely, the men are perceived as being inadequate providers of the nonmaterial relationship benefits, even though they appear to have the capacity to enjoy the sex, companionship, and family life that women supply.

As I will show, the single mothers I interviewed also described relationships within their social economies in which they engaged in calculated trades of sex and companionship for significant contributions to their households, including car repair and financial assistance. The women also indicated that they knew this type of relationship carried dangers of exploitation and abuse by men.[11] At the same time, the women often spoke clearly about the balanced reciprocity involved in these relationships; they were also clear that they subjected these arrangements to the moral judgment of "fair exchange" alone. For some of these women, an exchange involving sex appeared to be relatively easy and straightforward, requiring little more examination or consideration than the exchange of other goods or services.

However, as I explain, the women rely on this language of outright exchange predominantly when accounting for relationships with men in whom they deny having a significant romantic interest. When the women talk about men with whom they are "in love," in contrast, they resist the notion that their relationships are only about economic or material exchange and sex assumes a very different role. In relationships of romantic love the women accept the responsibility of reciprocity with respect to nonmaterial gifts, but they adamantly deny the relevance of that norm in return for material help. Also, in relationships of romantic love, sex becomes a source of pleasure intrinsic to the relationship rather than an item to be exchanged.

In these ongoing relationships, before they have settled into an established practice of cohabitation, the women in this study rely on a vision of romantic love that draws on a dominant cultural paradigm. This paradigm specifies in great detail "with whom one is to fall in love (e.g., opposite-sex age mate), why (e.g., for love, passion), [and] how the relationship is to proceed (e.g., dating, engagement, monogamous lifelong marriage)."[12] The prevailing script gives great power to love itself. Love drives partner selection, offers a reason for continuing the relationship, and legitimizes sexual activity. This vision of love is also highly gendered. It both asks different things of men and women (e.g., more relationship maintenance on the part of women) and, as the sociologist Francesca Cancian suggests, it is measured by the presence of "feminine" qualities such as nurturance, sensitivity, and the expression of feelings.[13] As we will see, these cultural prescriptions are tempered as they are enacted in the deeply encumbered lives of single mothers, even as they provide the groundwork for a woman to make choices and assess potential partners.

Before turning to the two very different kinds of relationships single mothers develop with men, those of exchange and those of love, I want to make a point much like one I made in the previous chapter. There I acknowledged that the women's assessments of their children's fathers might not have been shared by the fathers themselves. Similarly, in what follows, I focus exclusively on the *women's* ideas concerning the content, value, and significance of their relationships with men. Needless to say, the men they describe might have very different notions about the meaning of these relationships. Indeed, it would be surprising if they did not; it would be equally surprising if trouble within these relationships did not turn precisely on those differences.

SINGLE MOTHERS IN RELATIONSHIPS OF OPEN EXCHANGE WITH MEN

As noted, some of the women who were interviewed implied, or even openly acknowledged, that, as Edin and Lein and Seccombe would predict, they currently or previously had established relationships with men primarily for the practical benefits that ensued. Emma Mercier, a never-married mother of two sons, talked about going out and having, "you know, a couple of beers" with a male friend after he fixed her car and only charged a nominal monetary fee; Melissa Henry, the divorced mother of four sons, said that when her boyfriend fixed her car, she only had to pay for "parts." Each of these women made clear that the identified relationship did not have substantial intrinsic value. Emma maintained that her mechanic was "just a friend" and Melissa insisted that the relationship with her boyfriend was insufficiently romantic for the long haul. When asked about the future of this relationship, Melissa said that she did not want to get married for "practical" reasons; she added that she had done so the first time and would not repeat the mistake.

The fact that this kind of exchange relationship did not meet the women's requirements of romance *for its own sake* was made especially apparent in discussions with two women, each of whom was involved with two men at the same time. Joan Meyer, a thirty-three-year-old divorced mother of three children, drew a contrast between two sets of arrangements with men she was "dating." She evaluated the older relationship in strictly "mercenary" terms and she made it clear that she was continuing to see this man solely in return for his financial contributions to her household, even though doing so was costly on other grounds: "I have been staying in a relationship that is not good for myself, not good for my kids, because of financial needs, because I cannot swing it on my own." In her desire to satisfy her children's desires for new bikes, Joan sacrificed their emotional welfare: "Well, I'm trying to get out of the relationship, but I'm staying in the relationship until the end of next week so I can have help finishing paying off my kids' bikes." She also forfeited her own pleasure to meet the sexual demands her boyfriend placed on her as repayment for his help around the house: "Every time he does something around here I feel that I owe him at least in sexual [ways]. That is what I perceive."

When she turned to a description of her newer relationship, Joan implied that it was at this point meeting her expectations for romance and that it did not compel her to fulfill undesirable "obligations." She also depicted the new man as having the characteristics she was "looking for" in a partner and as fulfilling her romantic ideal:

> [The first man] lives at home with his parents, he's thirty years old, he had three DWIs, he can't get himself together. He works full-time but that's about it.... [The other man] has two jobs, is a contractor and a firefighter, owns his own house, is a year older than I am, has never been married, and is just very, very self-dependent, which is something that I was looking for—which is someone who can take care of themselves, because I've got three people to take care of. I can't take care of [another person].

Interestingly, Joan focused on the fact that the first man, in spite of his economic contributions, was "dependent" on her, while the new one was more "independent." Joan clearly had at stake not wanting romance to seduce her into assuming new responsibilities in addition to the costly accommodations she already must make. Creating a social economy can give rise to these complicated circumstances and it can require making painful choices.

Twenty-four-year-old Amanda Swanson also spoke about ending a relationship with one man and starting a new one with another. In retrospect, she judged the older relationship for its practical elements and found it (and the boyfriend) wanting: He didn't ever vacuum or cook when he came to stay with her, even though, she acknowledged, he provided wonderful emotional support to her as she dealt with her son. Amanda consistently referred to the newer man as "Romeo" and explained that she used this term because, "he's not only a good friend [but] he's also more romantic than [the other man] ever thought about being."

SINGLE MOTHERS IN LOVE

In her insightful work on the networks that families establish to ensure the care of school-age children, Karen V. Hansen writes that some of the people she interviewed became irritated by her repeated questions as she probed for clarity about what was given and received in their relationships.[14] I was relieved to read this acknowledgment because I, too, found that many of my respondents became annoyed when urged to explain what they gave and received as they negotiated support. And in contrast to the examples above (where women, like Joan and Amanda, spoke openly about exchange), the annoyance of the single mothers I interviewed often reached its highest pitch precisely when I asked questions about the exchanges in romantic relationships with their "Romeos."

Karen Kelly, who had protested the use of the word *rely* throughout the interview, was particularly bothered when she was asked to explain why the man she called her "beau" helped her out on occasion. Her answer, "That's what people who cherish each other do," left the sarcasm of the trailing, "isn't it?" implicit, but very real. In what follows, I suggest that in this case, what I was getting was not just annoyance, but also a concrete denial that this relationship (or at least the material assistance within this relationship) should be examined predominantly through the lens of calculated exchange. That is, the reluctance to answer was the answer to the question. I'll return to Karen Kelly, but first I will examine how some other single mothers talk about their ongoing relationships with men.

Describing Love

Valerie Ramsey is the thirty-seven-year-old mother of a daughter she adopted as a single woman, following her divorce five years before we spoke. For the previous eight months she had been in a relationship with Jonathan, whom she saw once or twice a week. When asked whether Jonathan helped out in her daily life, Valerie responded affirmatively: "When he's here, he will do the dishes. He helps me clean up, and he mows the lawn. He just started that. And I mean, we're just dating! And he will clean up after I cook. Up at his place, he cooks. He does everything." When asked what she would miss if they stopped seeing each other, however, Valerie focused on the "romance" involved. And she stated explicitly that although she accepted and appreciated Jonathan's daily help, in contrast with the "no pay, no stay" rule, and in contrast with Joan Meyer's outright exchange of sex for practical assistance, she believed that the contributions Jonathan made to her household were neither a necessary component of their relationship, nor were they sufficient reason to stay together:

I think if we broke up, what would be missing would be more the emotional closeness, romantic pleasure, companionship. I mean, you know, it's nice. I would love to have somebody cook me my meal, mow my lawn, but it's not enough. I can do that with friends, my brother does it too. So in terms of those things, it's not enough. But the rest I would [miss] for sure.

As we can see, Valerie placed Jonathan's gifts of assistance outside, or to the side, of what she appreciated most. Although she deemed the actions of practical support as welcome and surprising gifts—"we're just dating"—she also deemed them "not enough" reason to sustain the relationship. Her brother did those things, as did her friends. This was a different relationship within her social economy, pursued and valued more for its (romantic) sociability than for its practical support.

Later in the interview, in the midst of a discussion of how she drew on others for assistance, Valerie made clear her heightened material needs as a single mother. She also made clear her notion of reciprocity and her desire to avoid "overbenefiting" in her exchange relationships:[15] "I usually try to have a trade-off but I hate having an owing." When asked what she did when she perceived herself as "owing," she implied that she would take actions to reestablish equity, even if she was unable to satisfy reciprocity's demands at a moment's notice. She then immediately, and I would say tellingly, turned to the issue of whether or not she *asked* Jonathan to do the tasks he did for her: "Asking [Jonathan] to mow the lawn—that's a big deal to me, to ask him to mow. And so I don't. I guess I could be asking him to do more, but it's like I want it to be like a regular romance—not sort of, you need me to do this and that."

Like Valerie, Megan Paige, the forty-one-year-old mother of three, acknowledged that her boyfriend made substantial efforts to assist her in her daily life. Megan said that she and her boyfriend had originally committed to an equal exchange of visits, thus fairly dividing the practical effort of sustaining their relationship. She also acknowledged that her boyfriend traveled the distance between them more frequently: "It actually turns out through his efforts …. he comes here more often." Recall that Megan had previously been adamant about her commitment to reciprocity and had given a quite economic analysis of its role in her life: "The support thing is like the checking account—first you put the money in and then you make the withdrawal and there's no problem. It's when you do it the other way around [that] there's red ink." Having outlined her philosophy, Megan turned to a discussion of her social network and of the drawing we had asked her to do of it. When she did, she located her boyfriend in a separate sector away from the relationships in which she received financial and even emotional support.

Simultaneously, albeit implicitly, she placed this relationship outside the sphere of reciprocity. This was a place where she did not have to (or even allow herself to) make judgments of balance: "So over here [in the drawing] we have emotional support and that's going two ways [with my friends].... Boyfriend—certain kind of emotional support—*it's a heart, not really support*." (Emphasis added.) When Megan was asked what she would lose if she and her boyfriend broke up, she immediately responded, with a laugh, "the sex." She then added that she would miss enormously the "emotional closeness" of a relationship with another adult. And she, like Valerie, defined romance as being outside of the realm of everyday life, in part because she had fallen in love with a man who lived some distance away: "All my instincts told me not to get involved and not to do this, but as it turns out, just like life isn't about money, relationships are not about real estate; they're not about practicality; they're not about location."

Hannah Warner, a thirty-five-year-old mother of a fifteen-year-old son, similarly explained that in her relationships with friends, she hesitated before making requests: "I think before I ask." She added that she was conscious of the demands of reciprocity in friendship, even as she denied that she precisely monitored give-and-take: "I'm not keeping score, exactly, but I'm there for [my friends] too." She also denied that she depended on her current boyfriend for assistance in the practical demands of daily life, although she indicated that he was helpful in many ways. When she purchased some new crates for her records, she said that she and David had "put together all these cubes from Penney's" and he subsequently "took them all to his house, in his garage, and primed them and painted them." Hannah praised David as well for having done the bulk of the cooking when she hosted a friend's wedding, and she noted that he had recently committed to making the salads for an annual celebration at her workplace. And finally, as Valerie did about Jonathan, Hannah mentioned that David cooked for her when she visited him, and he helped out, sometimes taking over entirely, when he visited her: "When I go to his house, he cooks, and when he comes here, I cook. But sometimes, he cooks." As she discussed her relationship with David, Hannah insisted that she located its greatest value in the fact that he made her feel cherished and loved: She said that she was "blessed" to have him in her life at this time.

In each of these brief accounts a single mother provides evidence that she does indeed derive practical benefits from her relationship with a romantic partner. Each woman thus acknowledges that her relationship has an economic role in her life: Valerie's boyfriend does the mowing; Megan's boyfriend makes the greater effort of traveling the distance between them, and, when he comes, helps out with transportation for her three children, dinner preparation, and other household chores; and Hannah's boyfriend puts together crates and meals.

However the women's responses to these efforts are complex. Karen Kelly's reluctance to even discuss these efforts suggests that a different morality is at work in romantic relationships and that assessment is thus problematic. It is significant that the women insist that these material benefits do not constitute the relationship's central value: Valerie points out that she can find other people to do her mowing within the web of relationships that constitute her social economy. And it is perhaps because she *does* have other resources that she can insist that the contributions Jonathan makes to her material well-being are "not enough" reason to remain involved with him. Even more significant, it turns out that while Valerie demands of herself that she make an equal exchange with Jonathan for those aspects of her relationship that do constitute "enough" reason to maintain it, she does not require the same stance of herself with respect to his mowing. And what is true of Valerie is true as well of the other women who talk of love.

The Exchange of Love

Balance in the Sentiments of Love

In their somewhat fuller accountings, these single mothers do make vivid and articulate assessments of balance in the *nonmaterial* components of their relationships with men.[16] Valerie is ready to judge her boyfriend's gift of emotional closeness as a reason to remain in the relationship and, although she was not pushed to discuss this issue in the interview, it is fair to assume that she believes she returns *that* gift in equal measure, especially since she speaks of mutual "companionship." Megan suggested that she and her boyfriend shared their concerns about their own children and supported each other in that way: "[We provide each other with] someone to talk to about that stuff." Other women as well spoke in the vocabulary of an "exchange." When Hannah Warner described her emotional relationship with David and the way he supported her, she explicitly pointed to the fact that she had drawn "two equally thick arrows" —one from him to her and one from her to him—and she added, "It's the first time in my life I've ever had a relationship with a man where I could have put that down on a chart.... It's the most reciprocal relationship I ever had with a man." (She then noted, with a bit of humor, "You know, men are not that reciprocal.")

Karen Kelly—the woman who was so sarcastic about "what people who cherish each other do"—described in detail the equity in the give and take of the nonmaterial components of her relationship with her "beau":

> I asked my higher powers for a relationship with somebody who had the music inside of them, who walked a spiritual plank, and who honored women as intelligent human beings, someone who knew how to neck, and liked it. And I've received all of those things. It was a good package deal. In return, I think that he feels heard, I think I give him kind of a balancing factor. We're both activists, and his tone is much more angry than mine, and so I sort of add the gentleness. [I also] hold him accountable, as he does me.

In short, the women engage in assessments of balanced reciprocity in the actions and sentiments of romance.

An Imbalance in Practical Affairs

The picture changes utterly when practical affairs are at stake. There is clear evidence that in this realm the women do *not* require reciprocity of themselves. Hannah Warner allows David to cook both at her house and at his; and although Hannah notes that David has become an active participant in her life and that of her son, she mentioned nothing about her responsibilities to his life even though he is the divorced father of several children. Janet Linden, who adopted a daughter on her own, said that she was committed to reciprocity in her exchanges with a female friend ("I want it to be a two-way street"). She also acknowledged that her boyfriend made substantial contributions to her daily life: He mowed the lawn and he entertained her daughter, leaving her free to prepare the evening meal and get done "whatever else needs to be done." But, when asked whether this relationship was balanced, she easily admitted that it was not:

> It really is pretty much a one-way street at this point. I mean, about the only time that I really can say that I'm "helping" him is that I cook some meals. Big deal. And if he needs to get his car into the shop or something like that I will pick him up and take him. It's not a fifty-fifty relationship. Clearly it's not.

Karen Kelly includes in her assessment of accountability promises her beau makes to her children and she holds him to those promises, even when doing so is inconvenient:

The baseball game with the kids—I read the schedule wrong. They were supposed to go last week, according to the schedule that I read. He had made a commitment to take them. His week is overwhelming this week, but he's still honoring his commitment to take them to the baseball game.

But Karen does not suggest that she is similarly beholden to *his* children.

Interpreting Love

In chapter 4 I suggested that the teamwork model emerges when single mothers make the burdens of their daily lives visible to their children. This model has patently practical roots: Single mothers need to have their children become cooperative partners. But the single mothers also elevate the significance of teamwork beyond its merely practical effects and claim that teamwork has a moral component. In an analogous fashion, when single mothers make sense of the gifts that come in relationships with men, they may have utilitarian goals at hand: The help they receive from men relieves them of some daily burdens; if they describe this help as a gift of love, they can ignore making equivalent gifts in exchange. But utility is not the only thing at stake here: Romance also has its own allure, and believing themselves to be worthy recipients of love helps them learn to value themselves.

A Utilitarian Account

Recall that although Valerie indicated that Jonathan helped out in many ways, she was insistent about her reluctance to *ask* for that help: "That's a big deal to me, to ask him to mow." In describing herself in this way, Valerie might well have been implying that asking for the "favor" of participating in her daily routines represented a move toward intimacy, and one that she is hesitant to make with a man she is "just dating." (As Sarah Stanley said of her quite recent relationship with her new boyfriend, "It's the very early stages, so I haven't asked him to help me out with my life.") In reality, however, Valerie has accepted a shift toward greater intimacy and even dependence in her relationship with Jonathan: After all, he does mow her lawn. Thus the fact that the emphasis in her statement is on the issue of "asking" deserves to be taken seriously.

Of course, even within intact marriages, women find it threatening to *have to ask* for the help they need, as the "honeydew" phrasing suggests: "Honey, do you mind taking out the trash?"; "Honey, do you want to put the kids to bed?" But Valerie has more at stake here than an inclination to "honeydew." She might well anticipate that once she has *asked* for help with mowing, rather than simply accepted it as a "gift," she has no choice but to reciprocate. If Valerie requests that Jonathan do something for her, she has to be ready to acknowledge that "giving" and to accept that he may make a similar request in return.

However, as I have demonstrated in previous chapters, Valerie has very good reasons to avoid taking on another set of responsibilities. She already has to manage the ongoing complexities of her daily life, which include a full-time job outside the home, caring for her young daughter, and housework. As I will discuss more fully, at least for the time being, it appears to serve her better to see her boyfriend's cleaning, dish washing, and mowing, as gestures of love rather than as actions emerging out of, or creating, obligation. She does not want to hear herself saying, "I need you to do these things," simply because she fears asking. More important, she does not want to involve Jonathan in the same tangles of obligation that characterize her relationships with friends and family. Quite simply, she does not want to be in the position of "owing."

The Allure of Romance

Valerie might have yet another motivation for not *requesting* help. Recall that Seccombe stated that as an observer she found it "difficult to distinguish between …. serial boyfriends and prostitution" among poor single mothers, even though she believed the women could (and did) make this distinction for themselves.[17] The women in my study appear to want to introduce an additional distinction, namely that between "serial boyfriends" (or men with whom they are up front about requiring an exchange) and true love. In so doing, the women mark off a set of relationships from the "slippery slope of prostitution" and protect an arena of daily life from the nastiness of assessing costs and benefits altogether.[18] Whether they are surviving below "living wage" estimates of self-sufficiency, or in even harsher poverty, daily life for single mothers requires constant attention to the complex strands of relationships within a social economy, as well as to issues that emerge from the complex interconnections among these strands: Can I afford to satisfy my daughter's yearning for Gap jeans? If I get a raise at work, will my new income disqualify me for Medicaid? What will my neighbor want in return if I ask her to watch my children for the afternoon? Should I risk my tenuous peace with my ex-husband, and call him about the late child support payment?

Small wonder that Valerie doesn't want to "ask" for help or even to assess what will be owed in return for Jonathan's mowing. When she says she wants her relationship with Jonathan to be a "regular romance" she suggests, not in spite of, but rather *because* of, the word *regular,* that she wants her relationship to exist outside of, and removed from, the demands and petty calculations of daily life. Romance, not everyday reality, is what she wants now.

Over time, Valerie might learn to read the mowing not only as a concrete manifestation of Jonathan's love but also as being a sufficient demonstration of it. The sociologist Francesca Cancian, for one, would argue that doing so would constitute a healthy move in their relationship.[19] However, Valerie and Jonathan are not quite there yet. For the time being, Valerie wants something else: a regular romance with the trappings of flowers and chocolate as well as companionship and sex. The same is true for Megan, who, when describing her relationship with her boyfriend, said, "It's a heart, not really support." And although Megan said that "relationships are.... not about practicality" in reference to the issue of distance, I think the comment has a broader connotation. She too wants to be involved in a "regular" romance.

First Comes Love

I suggest, then, that these women use a narrative of romance to create a sphere that is both outside of everyday drudgery and free from calculation. They also use this narrative as a way to explain why reciprocity for material assistance is *not* always required, even though when speaking of relations with friends they viewed the give and take of balanced reciprocity both as emerging from, and as creating, friendship.[20] Megan Paige explicitly stated that when she first got divorced she pursued specific friendships in order to fulfill her new needs: "I realized that I particularly needed to be friends with other single parents because they were going to be the people that would be most receptive to having a network of helping each other out." Anne Davenport also reversed causality when she suggested that the bonds of fictive kin followed from obligations rather than created them: "It's always been clear to me that my friends [who are single mothers] are my family here, because I can count on them more than I can count on my own family, often."

In short, in these other relationships the women do not deny either the presence or the significance of utilitarian benefits. They eagerly accept the obligations of reciprocity, even as they stress the intrinsic value of friendship. But, when speaking about relationships with romantic partners, the women reverse causality once again. Now love comes first. The prevailing narrative of "true love" demands that it sustain "an ostentatious manifestation of disinterestedness and appear to short-circuit the economic rationality of profit and loss."[21] If love has priority, both disinterest and the dismissal of economic rationality can be assumed.

Hannah Warner explicitly stated that David's help emerged from his love for her, rather than the other way around:

> I wrote him a card that said, "You know, David, many men—well, not many, but other men—have told me the words, 'I love you.' But you are the only man who has ever also then said to me, 'One, how can I help,' or 'two, what can I do to make you feel better?'" And then when I say what he can do to make me feel better, he does it!

As a specific example of how assistance flowed from love, Hannah described how he made dinner when she was "depressed":

> I have a reaction to sugar. I made the mistake of eating candy from Halloween, and then following it by a day of sugar. And then he came over the next day, and I just cried for two hours for no reason. And he made dinner.

Recall that Megan Paige said that she and her boyfriend had committed to an equal exchange of visits, thus fairly dividing the practical effort of sustaining their relationship. But Megan, who otherwise requires balance, could easily accept the fact that "he comes here more often" because he is motivated by love. As balance goes out the window, Megan says she doesn't have to count who comes more often—even if she does count.

While material assistance that comes from love does not require reciprocity, when love falters, women cannot accept its offerings. Indeed, the women in this study indicate that they believe themselves to have an ethical responsibility to refuse gifts that come with the strings of love attached if they cannot return the love. Sarah Stanley said she could enjoy her relationship with her friend Jack as long as she could believe that she was reciprocating in some equal measure by exchanging friendship for friendship. When Jack fell in love with her, Sarah believed she had to turn down his offerings even though she enjoyed his company and even though her children had become attached to him: "And then he made me pancakes. I think he did that when he was in love with me. I've told him to not come over here as much because I don't want to egg him on.

I don't want him to suffer feelings of pain because he can't have me and my family as his."

Giddy with Love

Two very different scholars provide quite similar frameworks for discussing love. In *The Transformation of Intimacy* Anthony Giddens describes the "pure relationship" as one that is "entered into for its own sake, for what can be derived by each person from a sustained association with another; and which is continued only insofar as it is thought by both parties to deliver enough satisfactions for each individual to stay within it."[22] Although Giddens describes the "active" and "contingent" nature of the "confluent love" that provides the undergirding for the pure relationship as "jarring" with "the for-ever, one-and-only qualities of the romantic love complex," it is quite possible that the two notions merely represent different stages of (or even different moments in) a relationship, rather than directly contradicting each other.[23] This is precisely what Ann Swidler suggests in *Talk of Love: How Culture Matters,* when she argues that, in spite of their contradictions, "two cultures of love" can coexist because they are employed in "two very different contexts":

> When thinking about the choice of whether to marry or stay married, people see love in mythic terms. Love is the choice of one right person whom one will or could marry. Therefore love is all-or-nothing, certain, exclusive, heroic, and enduring. When thinking about maintaining ongoing relationships, however, people mobilize the prosaic-realistic culture of love to understand the varied ways one can manage love relationships. Prosaic love is ambiguous, open-ended, uncertain, and fragile.[24]

But neither of these authors offers insight into how or when single mothers will use each of these two different conceptions of love. Giddens associates a move toward the "pure relationship" as being dependent "on the autonomy of the person" and as being associated with modernism in general, but he does not identify particular moments in particular lives when that move will occur.[25] And although Swidler suggests that during the "unsettled" period of divorce, a woman might "use culture to organize new strategies of action and to model new ways of thinking," and although she identifies love "in its mythic terms" with the process of assessing new marital partners, she does not pursue the issue of just what kinds of shifts divorce will bring about.

The relationships I have described so far certainly have elements of what Giddens might call "confluent love" or what Swidler would identify as "prosaic-realistic" love. For example, as noted, Karen Kelly spoke of "accountability" as a dimension of her relationship with her "beau" and claimed autonomy for each of them; Karen also talked, as Giddens would have predicted, about the intrinsic satisfactions that are sufficient for her to engage in this sustained association. But the evidence from these women suggests that when these relationships are more than "casual," but less than cohabitation, they are better characterized by what Giddens would call "romantic love" or what Swidler would call love in its "mythic" terms.

When asked whether she was currently "seeing" a man, Megan Paige spoke like the giddy teenager her oldest daughter is: "I'm in a relationship—a very romantic relationship. If we'd done this interview the first time you called me the answer would have been no. What a difference six months can make. I am [in a relationship]. Yes!" Hannah Warner was equally giddy when she described how she had fallen in love with David, that most reciprocal of men:

> I fell in love with him when he brought me a picnic. It was really romantic. It was on the green in [the village] and it was in the spring; it was April 30th—no, it was in May and it was a horrible, cold evening....We sat in the middle of the gazebo, and I sat on the bench, and he sat on the floor, and he starts unpacking all these wonderful little containers of all this food that he just made for me. And then he just reached over and he pecked me on the calf. And that was it!

Karen Kelly was irritated when asked about the reciprocity in her relationship, but she spoke of her love as a gift from her "higher powers," because she had met someone with music, someone who knew how to walk along a "spiritual plank." In short, these women do not appear to deny themselves this possibility of falling in love, even if prior relationships have failed them and they are still recovering from the hurt associated with separation or divorce. Indeed, in clinging to love, the women are counting themselves among those with social worth.

Although it seems that both kinds, or both stages, of love could leave lovers with sufficient room to deny that reciprocity around practical matters has any relevance at all to their relationships, these concerns seem especially antagonistic to "romantic" love. If the prosaic-realistic culture of love views inequity as one of the "uncertainties" or "ambiguities" that might be worked out in a relationship, "mythic" love cannot be bothered by concerns about who packed the picnic. As Megan said, "it's a heart," and "relationships are not about real estate, they're not about practicality, they're not about location."

THE CONSEQUENCES OF EXCLUDING ROMANCE
Loving Encumbered Women

What are the consequences of excluding romantic involvements from a required reciprocity around practical matters? These are as varied as the women who use (and perhaps abuse) love in this way. As noted earlier in the chapter, Edin and Lein, along with Seccombe, argue that there *are* great possibilities for exploitation in relationships between single mothers and men, and that these possibilities almost invariably work to the advantage of the men. That is, they imply that unless women establish firm boundaries with respect to what they will give and receive, they may find themselves in highly unequal relationships. In a separate article, Kathryn Edin argues that single women carefully assess what men have to offer before they consider joining them in marriage.[26] And in these assessments single mothers take seriously the possibility of domestic violence as well as other potential costs. Those scholars and politicians who oppose marriage-promotion policies echo the women's own concerns when they raise the fear that pushing poor women into affiliations with men will have negative consequences.

Moreover, the massive literature on the unequal gender division of labor and unequal benefits of marriage would suggest that there *are* significant risks for single mothers in affiliating with men. Giddens too would agree as he describes the very real possibility that subordination emerges from romantic love:

> Romantic love has long had an egalitarian strain, intrinsic to the idea that a relationship can derive from the emotional involvement of two people, rather than from external social criteria. *De facto*, however, romantic love is thoroughly skewed in terms of power. For women dreams of romantic love have all too often led to grim domestic subjection.[27]

But many single mothers have already experienced "grim domestic subjection." And because they now live encumbered lives, all kinds of love—both the "all-or-nothing, certain, exclusive, heroic, and enduring" love and eventually the "prosaic-realistic" relationships—must be accommodated to the demands of those current encumbrances. Single mothers may enter a relationship for their own sakes and to fill their own needs, not only for practical assistance, but also for sex, companionship, and the feeling of being cherished by another adult. Ultimately, however, they will have to assess how well their boyfriends fit into the complex social economies they have created, and they will eventually have to require that these men make significant accommodations and adjustments.

To be sure, becoming involved with a single mother may not entail taking on onerous burdens. Men may well profit from the affiliation with a woman and her children; they may appreciate having a ready-made family handed to them on a silver platter.[28] Many of the women speak in terms that accord significant value to family life, and they openly acknowledge that they are offering men the opportunity to grow as human beings and to expand their range of competence: "He's never had children of his own and never really been around other children, so it's a whole new world for him." Even so, the reality is that a man who becomes involved with a single mother does have to share that woman with her children. Megan Paige explained that a previous romance failed because the man could not make the accommodations necessary to fit into her life as the mother of three children, even as she reiterated her conviction that a heterosexual romantic relationship had its own distinctive place in her cosmology:

> The person that I was in a relationship [with] before this one didn't have kids.... That lasted about two years and the death blow to the whole thing was the fact that he didn't "get" the fact that I had kids. He couldn't get it. He couldn't get that he was always going to be in fourth place. Fourth place is pretty far back. I sympathized, but I couldn't change that. And now I'm with a person who does have kids, [and] he understands that it's not really being in fourth place but [that] they're different kinds of places, a different constellation.

Single mothers who maintain contact with the father of their children have yet another man in their lives; a new romance must accommodate to this reality as well. Jessica Walsh takes delight in her boyfriend's ready participation in her daily life, especially because her ex-husband had never accepted similar responsibilities: "I'm not used to someone helping me. I'm very independent. And it's like when Arnie does even the dishes, it's like 'wow.' I've never had someone do my dishes. It's nice, even though I can do it on my own if he wasn't here." She also calls on Arnie for help with her car, a service that, because he is a mechanic, he is easily able to supply. Even so, Jessica has not fully expunged her ex-husband from her life. She still accepts *his* services as a mechanic

("Kevin still wants to help me like fix my car and stuff like that"), and thus Arnie has to compete even in his own sphere of expertise. Jessica also remains involved in Kevin's life: "[I help him] by letting him see [the baby] whenever, and I still do *little* things [for him], like just reminding when certain bills need to be paid." As a consequence, she has less time and energy than she might have otherwise to do "little things" for her boyfriend. And Kevin still comes to "hang out," sometimes unexpectedly: "He's missing me and [the baby] too. . . . He takes [the baby] every weekend and during the week if he calls. Sometimes he'll even stay here and visit." If Jessica's boyfriend wants to take her bowling, he has to work around the visitation schedule set with Kevin and even around Kevin's unannounced visits. In short, men courting previously attached women cannot easily find opportunities to be alone with those women. Furthermore, if they try to woo women through their relationships with children, they may have to acknowledge that there is a "real" father who is present in those children's lives and therefore, quite possibly, in the lives of the mothers as well.

Given these realities, I want to reemphasize what my evidence so far has shown. At some points in some romantic relationships women are getting the greater (practical) benefit and they can ignore or minimize that reality by emphasizing only the bonds of love and attachment. Therefore, I suggest that many of the women in such romantic relationships deny the need to assess balance in the material realm. This has the consequence of allowing them to accept substantial gifts and services they might never have allowed themselves to accept from others. In addition, it also allows them to require accommodations they might never have asked of others—and do both of these without enmeshing themselves in reciprocal obligation.

Toward the Future

Research on remarriage indicates that there is more equity in these relationships around issues of housework than is found in first marriages. In an analysis of this finding, the sociologist Oriel Sullivan argues that the explanation must be found in "issues of interaction involved in the negotiation of housework responsibilities within new partnerships."[29] The data in this study suggest that preparation for greater equity may well emerge during the period of courtship. A woman's acceptance of a man's washing the dishes and playing with children as gifts of love may make these activities invisible. In the process, women prepare the groundwork for accepting these same activities when in a long-term relationship. (This is similar to the way in which men have traditionally made invisible women's contributions to family survival and explained women's greater participation in housework and child care as an act of love.[30]) Indeed, if these relationships are to survive over the long haul, the men will have to take these tasks on as their own.

In many cases the men with whom single mothers become involved already have their own encumbrances as former husbands and current fathers. In drawing these men into their lives, single mothers may not *encourage* negligence toward prior obligations, but they still might very well create a situation in which those prior obligations *can* be ignored. Ironically, these very women often complain precisely about how an ex-husband's current partner has distracted him away from his obligations to his children. As one woman said, when talking about the father of her son:

> He's henpecked, let's leave it at that. We have seen him, but not a lot. In fact he tried to, he wanted to be part of his [son's] life. He said he was going to be and he really wanted to be. But then he met this other woman and she just couldn't deal with [our son].

The irony deepens when the women boast about a boyfriend's earlier commitment to his wife and children as evidence of reliability, and simultaneously overlook the continued demands of those commitments as they draw that boyfriend further into their own demanding family life. Stephanie Miller described herself as being swept off her feet when she first met Carl. She also decided that he was appropriate marriage material because of his deep involvement with his own child: "He has a thirteen-year-old daughter and he didn't want to leave because he's been a very involved dad with her." Now that he has moved in with Stephanie, Carl is an active participant in her children's lives and makes both practical and financial contributions to the household. But in her cheerful report of these facts, Stephanie never mentions that either of them has ongoing responsibilities to the woman and child he left behind.

Exclusivity

The narrative of romantic love enables women simultaneously to accept gifts and, on occasion, to prepare themselves to make claims that draw attention away from former wives and even former children. But, because that narrative is also exclusive rather than social, it may "wean" women away from those networks that have ensured their survival as single mothers. This is not to say that cohabiting or married women do not sustain social economies.[31] At the same time, when individuals become coupled, the kinds of needs that prompt network formation are likely to change, as are the component members of those networks.

Initially the networks of single mothers are a source of guidance about how to proceed in their new relationships. Megan Paige added to her list of reasons for becoming friends with single mothers the fact that "you need to talk to other single women about the whole dating thing." These networks also clearly *privilege* romance.[32] As one woman said, "I have two other single-mom friends and we have sort of an agreement. You can ask me anytime if you have a date, for example, or if you need help or if you want to go away for the weekend." As they elevate romance to the status of a significant need, these networks prepare the way for, and ironically even hasten, their own demise. To be sure, network members might belatedly express concerns about these consequences. Hannah Warner said as much about her friends: "And my friends were a little worried when I met David, and I fell in love with David. They were a little worried about how it was going to affect them." Although Hannah insisted that her friends had no real cause for concern, and promised to remain loyal to friendship, evidence suggests that her relationship with David did alter the friendship dynamics.

The single mothers in this study reported having, on average, almost four (3.8) different friends from whom they drew support. However, the average conceals patterned variability. The women who were living with men (as members of cohabiting, engaged, or married couples) reported considerably fewer friends (an average of 2.0) than did those who were living alone or with another (nonpartner) adult (an average of 4.5). For some women the rapid reaffiliation with a man following separation or divorce left insufficient time to develop alternative relationships. Stephanie, who so happily met Carl on her fortieth birthday (the same month her divorce became final), illustrates this dynamic. When asked to draw her support network, Stephanie wrote down the names of specific family members (her parents, her siblings) and Carl. She then called another group of people "friends" (without specific names), and she located this group at some distance from the other members of her support network. When asked about her relationships with her "friends," Stephanie explained that they had helped her out during the period when she was mediating her divorce ("I've had friends who've done a lot of free child care for me while I was going to Burlington to meet with the mediator last July"). But Stephanie explained that she had never developed these friendships into reciprocal structures of support (recall that she said she owed a considerable number of hours to her babysitting pool). Instead, she said that her friendships remained casual and that she was not proactive in pursuing them: "There's some friends I see on a regular basis [but] it kind of comes and goes."

For other women, the friendships established while single gave way as they became more absorbed in a "traditional" family structure. Leah Goodman, for example, had been deeply involved in networks of exchange during the years she lived as a single mother. Having recently started living with a man, she found fewer opportunities to maintain these reciprocal friendships. Increasingly she and her partner relied on each other and they got together with other couples for sociability, rather than as individuals involved in the give-and-take of exchange.

There is also evidence that cohabitation can cause a shift in the structure of a support network and in the content of its component relationships. Those who were cohabiting with a romantic partner at the time of the interview included more family members as members of their support networks than did those living just with their children (an average of slightly more than three vs. slightly more than two). The former group of women had more family members from which to draw because they could reach out to those attached to a new partner.[33]

These shifts in support networks are not without their own complications. Patsy Downey's story, discussed in chapter 4, indicates the new tensions that can emerge as women decrease their dependence on previously valued relationships. Following the birth of her children, Patsy relied extensively on her mother to care for her children and to provide her with emotional support. Now that Patsy is living as part of a couple, it is not surprising that she is turning inward to that new relationship for support. Indeed, Patsy now relies heavily on her fiancé for help as she struggles to separate from her mother and to wrest control over her children: "He was really supportive about me really standing up to my mom." Patsy has also made clear that she is willing to cede authority *to him* and that she wants his full engagement in decisions about the children's behavior: "And now he has like an equal input into that, as far as the rules that they follow and the way that we are choosing to teach them."

In the previous chapter I questioned the "legitimacy" of the grounds Patsy gave for her disputes with her mother. Indeed, Patsy's fuller discussion of these disputes suggests that the struggles over the children are only part of a larger issue. In addition to wanting to create a new team for making child-rearing decisions, Patsy wants her mother to accord her new relationship the respect and privacy a marriage "deserves" in our society. Patsy's mother might have good grounds for wanting to remain involved: Patsy chose a violent and abusive man the first time, and although Patsy paid an enormous price for that choice, her mother paid an enormous price as well. She gave up her job as a secretary to become a family day-care provider, she shared her own meager resources with Patsy's family, and she offered the emotional support Patsy needed to recover from her wounds. But now Patsy wants her mother to "back off":

> She must have known that someday I would want to be with somebody else [other than the children's father].... Common sense would tell me that when that time came she would have to step back if she wanted me to be happy. It was that choice—you could keep your nose in there and it's never going to work for me or you can step back and try to give me a chance to let it work.

Patsy has not yet burned her bridges with her mother. If she were to do so, she might be left with no one to turn to because, like other single women who are cohabiting with a man, she has few friends who provide ongoing support. Thus, although Patsy is certainly considerably better off now than she was when she first became a single parent (she has a two-year degree from a local community college and she holds a full-time job), the relationships that enabled at least some of these achievements are now in jeopardy.

CONCLUSION

In this chapter I have argued that single mothers can and do describe relationships with men that include straightforward exchanges and require balanced reciprocity. They trade companionship and sex for car repair and financial assistance; they also fault men for refusing to uphold their ends of these exchanges. But I argued as well that in these cases of open exchange, the single mothers also deliberately denied that the men fulfilled their expectations of love and romance. They do not want to marry for practical reasons alone—nor do they want to believe they would.

When single mothers talk about relationships with the "Romeo" in their lives they provide evidence that these relationships come with significant practical assistance. The need for these contributions itself is not particularly surprising. Because they live encumbered lives, single mothers cannot simply enjoy a dinner date or a night out on the town, but have to include boyfriends in their ongoing activities. And although the women themselves are sometimes astonished to be the recipients of these gestures, it is not so surprising that a man who is eager to make a positive impression on a single mother might soon learn that picking up some of the responsibility for everyday burdens (and establishing good relations with children) is the quickest way to the woman's heart.

Perhaps we shouldn't be surprised to find that these single mothers' accounts of love focus less intensely on the practical contributions than they do on the *other* contributions romantic partners make to their well-being: the emotional connection, the sex (with a laugh), the satisfaction of being cherished by another adult. Especially for those women who have been hurt in prior relationships with men, the love and adoration of a new man can do much to build self-esteem and a sense of self-worth. And, given prevailing contemporary notions about the nature of love, it is not surprising that they spoke of *equal* offerings of emotional closeness, sex, and appreciation.

There is another element that is more surprising than the slighting of practical contributions. The women did not indicate any special obligations resulting from the additional efforts the men made to become helpful participants in their lives. To be sure, these gestures *are* appreciated. (Jessica Walsh, for one, says "wow" when her new boyfriend does the dishes.) But women who were careful about balance in almost every other realm of their lives—and who came up with creative strategic explanations for what might otherwise have been regarded as imbalance—were astonishingly mute on the issue of what they owed in return for mowing, the efforts of travel, and picnics in a gazebo. It is significant that, in contrast to similar instances of imbalance, occasions of imbalance within a romantic relationship appear to require no "strategic explanation." Or, to put it differently, in those cases where there might well be an existing inequality in practical arrangements, romantic love provides the moral basis for an asymmetrical social economy.

Within the framework of romance, single mothers can both avoid assuming responsibilities for another household (e.g., the men's children) and rewrite the script about what it costs a man to assume responsibility for an encumbered woman. A man is eased into making her home and her children his own. His involvement with her children and his mowing her lawn become not things for which she asks or which she requires, but instead they are defined as free and clear gifts of love. And, in the long run, these gifts might transmute into a distribution of domestic labor that is more equitable than that in first-married couples.

If love paves the way for his engagement in her home, love may also pave the way for exclusivity. As a single mother pursues and enacts a more traditional family structure, the elements of support that enabled her to survive on her own give way. The social economy transmutes into a more traditional family economy, with renewed possibilities for both isolation and inequity.

CONCLUSION

This book has explored how the material constraints that characterize the lives of white single mothers living in a rural Vermont county ordinarily give rise to what I call a "social economy." Single mothers cannot survive on their own: To meet their acute needs, they draw on the resources of a wide range of individuals that includes members of their extended family, a network of friends, community services, the state, future (and past) partners, and their own children.[1] Yet, even as they modify the boundaries of family life, single mothers remain attentive to prevailing social norms, especially to those that denigrate the single-parent family and proclaim the necessity of self-sufficiency for all citizens. Single mothers' requests for assistance, whether from family and friends, the state, their own children, or romantic partners, are not only shaped to meet their ongoing needs, but are also designed to avoid condemnation. Only by understanding the whole context within which single mothers construct their daily lives, including their pressing needs and their commitment to social norms, can we understand the choices they make.

I now return to Sarah Stanley, with whom I began. Understanding the constraints in her life in dynamic interaction lends insight into her behaviors: why she was unwilling to accept her father's offer to pay for health insurance and instead drew on state support; why, when it came to daily help with child care and transportation, she worked so hard to find friends in a similar situation rather than relying on her more readily available sister; how she understands and makes adjustments to her notion of a valid family; and why she has refused further material support from a man who has fallen in love with her.

Sociologists frequently debate the relative determinants of what are loosely called "structure" and "agency." Although analyses of structural forces can clearly include "ideology" as well as "material" factors, most scholars (particularly liberal theorists studying the lives of the poor) assume that the latter constitute the bulk of the structural forces that shape, and even determine, behavior. When individual behaviors appear to violate social norms, liberal scholars show how those behaviors emerge from constraints. In this framework, values are either negligible as an independent determinant of action or they are relatively malleable: Presumably they too would change as the structural situation changed.[2] The notion that structure determines behavior is thus quite neatly aligned with a perspective that argues that material forces are more significant than cultural or ideological ones. It is not surprising, then, as will be discussed more fully, liberals propose economic or material solutions for solving the problems that confront single mothers. The implicit assumption is that any lingering value problem manifest in their lives will take care of itself.

When conservative theorists propose policy they often start from a quite different set of assumptions. The welfare restructuring that began in the early to mid-1990s, and remains the policy in the early twenty-first century, assumed that a set of "bad" values underwrote the rise in single parenting and its resulting poverty. As a result, conservatives designed policies to encourage a shift in values, namely programs that include education "on the value of marriage" or counseling on "responsible fatherhood."[3] To be sure, most conservatives are not confident that education or counseling alone can transform "deviant" values; therefore, along with the "carrot," they propose the "stick" of altering incentives and denying access to services when individual behavior violates what they view as acceptable norms. In the harshest state policies, for example, children born while a woman is reliant on welfare are excluded from receiving state benefits. The tacit assumption here is that values do not change easily or through gentle means, but that they respond well to incentives built on crude self-interest or fear. If a woman can get support for her children, she will continue to produce them; when the support is taken away, she will cease.

My argument throughout this book is that even in the midst of the harsh and compelling material conditions of poverty, unpredictability, and remorseless demands, single parents can and do make choices. But, the more closely I looked at the choices single mothers made in every realm of their lives (and perhaps especially in their negotiations for material and emotional support), the more it seemed that those choices were shaped by ideological constraints that single women neither invented nor chose. The fact that they typically enacted behaviors that made adaptations to, and were congenial with, the prevailing social discourse, suggests that the social economy of single mothers is constructed to comply with a public morality, as much as individual circumstances allow. To be sure, as most people can recognize of themselves, single mothers both stretch values (with questionable interpretations of honesty) and apply them selectively (by accepting exchange for some rather than other parts of intimate relations). But public morality matters to single mothers, and it especially matters because of the sharp awareness that their family form is subject to denigration. The lives of the single mothers I studied thus provide evidence of both the effects of structure on decision making and of opportunities to exercise agency. The lives of these women further provide evidence of the impact of both material and ideological worlds. Because these two worlds do not neatly align, however, the social economy of single mothers is composed of the conflicts, complexities, tensions, and contradictions engendered by their collision.

REVIEWING THE SOCIAL ECONOMY
Complex Strands

These conflicts, complexities, tensions, and contradictions emerge even within a single strand of her social economy as a single mother balances competing priorities. It is not surprising that it is respect to the particular issue of care for children that single mothers experience the greatest emotional pinch between what they want and what they have, and between their social ideals and the behavior allowed within a set of very real material constraints. But if this pinch is present in the lives of most parents, who find themselves mediating between responsiveness to their children and the requirements of everyday life, I argue that the poverty of single mothers, especially when combined with the fact that they are frequently the only adult in the household, intensifies the squeeze and the pain. The resulting stance, which I called "practical motherhood," nods to the social norm prescribing "intensive mothering" as "good" mothering, and it acknowledges both woeful inadequacy and great pride in making it through another day. Practical motherhood also paves the way for involving children more fully in the activities of maintaining family life and thus helps relieve at least some of the daily burdens of trying to manage on one's own. As single mothers establish family teamwork as a practical strategy, they (re)gain a sense of their own self-worth as moral actors raising moral children.

In relationships outside the immediate family, single mothers also seek to negotiate among competing priorities, even as these priorities shift and change. Tensions emerge in the set of relationships they value for manifestations of balanced reciprocity amid the exchange of practical services, material goods, and emotional support. Others in the same boat may not understand the tacit rules for membership in a network and thus may ask for more than a friend can easily provide. Single mothers have to weigh the cost of any given exchange against the benefits of the relationship as a whole. If sometimes they find themselves giving more than they want, at other times they withdraw from individuals whose demands (whether emotional or material) they do not have the time or energy to meet. If they free themselves from a specific set of demands, however, they may lose a valuable resource on which their social economy has rested.

Whatever their choice in any given situation, the social economy of single motherhood cannot rely solely on this set of close peer relationships. Other single mothers, who are in the same boat, by definition, cannot satisfy the full range of needs experienced by a single mother, even if they can well understand them. When single mothers draw on family members and friends who are not in similar situations of need, a different set of moral strains emerges even as the available material resources expand. Here women may experience contempt for their poverty, disdain for their family structure, and condemnation for making the decisions that resulted in both poverty and single parenthood. As a result, some avenues of support are quite simply closed, or forgone, as single mothers eschew those needed resources that come with too high a price to their pride.

Even if they can pay that price and slough off the embarrassment and hurtful comments, however, single mothers still have to contend with the morality that requires that, as adult members of their communities, they make at least some return for help received. Single mothers employ a logic of reciprocity that involves "strategic explanations": They draw attention to the nonmaterial gifts they offer in exchange for material resources; they assert that their survival and that of their children should be counted as ample repayment; and they suggest that gift giving is its own reward. But these are not necessarily acceptable strategies to those who offer help; nor can they be achieved without their own costs. Those who are more fortunate, and who have greater resources to share, might not be satisfied with the returns single mothers make and they might demand more (by way of appropriate behavior or deference) than single mothers are comfortable offering in return.[4]

These problems are compounded when single mothers draw outsiders into the intimate dynamics of family life. These involvements originate from necessity (e.g., to meet material needs and by virtue of coresidence) and choice (e.g., to provide children with more bases for emotional support and to broaden a child's sense of the world). No matter what the motivation is, single mothers confront challenges to the assumption that they will have priority in a child's love, receive contradictory (and often unwanted) advice about issues of discipline and character formation, and may even have to rely on people who are not worthy of their trust. Jealousy, disputes about child-rearing styles, and concerns about reliability are thus all byproducts of the close relationships women foster between their children and other individuals.

Women who have experienced welfare reliance (especially after the welfare restructuring of the 1990s) contend with some contradictions similar to those experienced in dependence on informal means of support. As in their relationships with some family members and friends, they must be willing to exhibit deference and endure surveillance, even as they seek autonomy and independence. At a practical or material level, these contradictions ultimately give way to the failed self-sufficiency that leaves former welfare recipients struggling to make do when state support recedes, and dependent on family and friends to help them fill the gap between real needs and real resources.(Thus they circle back to the dilemmas previously discussed.) At a personal level, the women experience a sense of betrayal when state help ends. The new administration of welfare, at least as it is enacted in Vermont, involves intense interaction with an individual caseworker. These bureaucratic representatives are often very clear about their expectations, whereas friends and family members often leave their expectations tacit. As clients seek to meet those state-defined expectations they may have to give up their own dreams and aspirations. And bureaucratic representatives are not there for the long haul, but rather impose discrete time limits on the relationship. Despite the potential negative consequences of working with the state, including having to abandon one's individual ambitions, the loss of a relationship with a caseworker is often depicted as being as devastating as the loss of practical resources; former recipients come to realize that the notion that they were engaged in a "shared" project of progress toward self-sufficiency was a sham.

If welfare is not a way out of daily challenges, conservatives hope that marriage will be. Many of the women in this study shared this hope and actively sought to involve new men in their daily lives. Viewing these relationships through the lens of romantic love helps solve some significant problems: It frees women from requiring reciprocity of themselves when they allow men to make contributions to their households; it makes them feel like real women involved in regular relationships; and it provides an explanation for why men are willing to accept them with all their encumbrances. The outcome is often a newly privatized vision of family life, one underwritten by the exclusivity associated with the traditional script of romance. This exclusivity can be demonstrated by the form of the social economy cohabiting women subsequently establish: In contrast with their peers who live without a romantic partner, those who do live with one report having fewer friends with whom they make daily exchanges. To be sure, cohabiting women do not sever all former ties. But, although cohabiting women still maintain relationships with family members and count them among their significant supporters (and may actually add more family members into their networks as they include a new partner's relatives), they may also alter the nature of these familial relationships as they recreate the nuclear, married-couple family so cherished in the public imagination.[5]

In each set of relationships developed as part of a social economy, be it with children, friends, adult family members, the state, or romantic partners, women are not only trapped between a complex morality and a complex set of material needs, but they are also negatively assessed for the economic rationality that undergirds the choices they make in response to that entrapment. And indeed cold calculation is involved as women weigh the pros and cons of different relationships and different resources. But some of the calculations women make are simply to defend against the condemnation of being calculating, and some of them are required by the situation (or relationship) itself. Sarah Stanley believed that she had to defend against the interviewer's judgment of too much rationality when she described how she decided whom she would call on for support: "But I weigh against, and *this sounds really bad*, but if I need to leave my kids with someone or if I need something from someone, I basically figure out who the last person I asked was and move on to someone else. I try not to overwhelm one particular person with too much." (Emphasis added.) To protect against likely condemnation from her mother, Jackie Ferland picks up the telephone on occasions when she is not in need: "I hate it when I have to call her to ask her to do something and I'll find myself thinking sometimes, even during the day, 'I need to call mom because I don't need anything from her.' I want to call and let her know that I do [call] sometimes not needing something." And the discretion and maternalism embedded in relationships with the state explain why Jackie Porter "begged and pleaded" for additional help from Reach Up when her car broke down. Indeed, it may well be because each relationship takes so much energy from women who have little to spare (including the energy both of making calculated assessments of who is available for what and of protecting against the charge of doing this calculating), that single mothers often idealize a community that responds to need without their having to ask, without requiring anything in return, and without negative judgments about their circumstances.

The Warp and the Woof

The single strands of the social economy do not stand alone, but instead are woven into an entire fabric. An additional set of complexities emerges from the inevitable intersections of these strands. Consider the example of Patsy Downey, whose social economy was discussed in chapter 4 and again in chapter 5. After years of struggle Patsy has completed an associate's degree and has prepared herself for full-time employment. In theory, Patsy suggested, the wages and benefits she receives from her current job should be sufficient to meet her needs. In reality, she insisted, they are not: "I make $10.35 an hour right now and it sounds like a decent minimum wage—I get really good benefits—but if you split $10.35 up three ways, to support three people, there's not enough." Moreover, Patsy is now caught in the all-too-familiar trap between rising wages and de-clining public support. While she does still qualify for Doctor Dynasaur to pay for her children's health insurance, she purchases her own health insurance at a substantial cost through her employment. She receives a modest (one dollar per hour) subsidy for child care for her younger child, but the more she earns the less she receives, and her resentment swells over the "two hours it takes to fill out their paperwork." She has already "outgrown" her Women, Infants and Children (WIC) eligibility, which may explain why she feels especially free to express her frustration with the expense of that practice: "I could have earned four times as much and bought four gallons of milk in the amount of time I spent for me to mess around with them."

This is not the only occasion on which Patsy weighed time against money. For example, she rejected possible self-provisioning activities after assessing their net costs: "I don't make clothes at all because I can make more money if I go to work and work those hours." But Patsy's assessments do not only involve time and money. Instead they include the full range of concerns and issues that emerge by virtue of the fact that her social economy consists of multiple and complex strands and by virtue of the fact that these strands alone and together require practical and moral considerations.

Patsy's mother is a central actor in her web of relationships. While she was getting more support from the state, Patsy would trade some of that support (especially WIC commodities and the monetary subsidy she received for child care) for her mother's regular and sporadic help. Now that she doesn't have that "extra," Patsy finds herself in a more difficult position. She worries about the new trade-offs she has to make between having a sufficient income, getting to work to earn that income, and her mother's tendency to make her "pay" for the support she provides: "If I don't [borrow money] to have the car fixed, then obviously—hello—I need to get to work. But if I borrow money from her to have it fixed, then she's like right there and has that control—a hold over my head." Patsy worries about a different set of trade-offs, which involve her children's emotional and physical needs and her own autonomy, when she uses her mother's washing machine: "[If I go to the Laundromat] it's just like an all-day mess. What do I do with the children? There's nothing for them to do; they don't want to sit there for five years. But [if I use my mother's machines] it's one more hold she has on me."

Important as she is, Patsy's mother is not the only significant actor in Patsy's social economy. Patsy also lives near many members of her extended family. She has asked her cousin to drive her daughter to pre-school along with one of her own. Patsy repays that favor with gestures expected of her as a member of the community: "All of my family, we kind of like help each other. When my cousins moved, we all helped. It's not about like money or anything, it's just about that's what you do. We just offer." Now, however, there is a rumor that the violent man who fathered Patsy's children is back in town, and the cousin is scared to have anything to do with Patsy's family: "My cousin's husband won't allow her to drive [my daughter] back and forth." Patsy believes that her child should have the opportunity to develop her social skills: "My daughter is in preschool, which is really good for her socially to be with the other little kids." Even though Patsy is deeply committed to her daughter's development, she cannot drive her to school herself because doing so would jeopardize her employment: "I can't get her back and forth now, and I can't leave work because I can't afford to take the time off work to bring her to preschool." In this one instance, Patsy navigates among interlocking needs, desires, costs, and resources—her aspirations for her daughter, her obligations to her cousin, the requirements and benefits of her employment, and an old mistake coming back to haunt her—and comes up empty.

Patsy might not recognize herself in the claims of those who argue that marriage-promotion efforts will drive women into hasty relationships with unreliable, and maybe even dangerous, men. She fervently believes that love guided her selection of her current boyfriend as well as her re-cent decision to let him move in with her. Even so, Patsy has embarked on a risky venture. As we saw in previous chapters, she now plays her boyfriend off against her mother, and she could be very vulnerable if the relationship with her boyfriend were to fall on hard times. Patsy openly acknowledges her financial gamble and admits to being demoralized by not being able to live according to the idealized self-sufficiency she had hoped to achieve: "It's like what if something did happen? We seem fine, we're going to try to buy a house, I don't see that we're not going to be together, but realistically, it feels bad to me knowing that I can't do it myself." Patsy does not, however, explicitly acknowledge that she is also in the process of burning bridges that she had previously worked hard to build and that she might need again in the future.

Differences Among Women

Patsy's life history is very different from Sarah Stanley's. Patsy's children were born when she was a teenager and in a relationship with a violent and abusive man. Sarah's children were born when she was in her late twenties and enjoying a relationship she hoped would last a lifetime. Even though the women are similar in that neither can now count on the father of her children, their differing histories present them with differing problems. Patsy has endured the "disgrace" of being a teenage mother and she now worries that the father of her children will reappear and hurt them. Sarah endures the lesser stigma of divorce (albeit with her father's open contempt), and although she worries that the father of her children might never be sufficiently healthy to have an ongoing relationship with them, she does not believe he poses a threat to their well-being.

Patsy and Sarah differ in other ways as well. For much of the time Patsy was a single parent she took for granted her reliance on her mother; after all, Patsy was only a teenager when her children were born. A decade older than Patsy, and having previously achieved independence, Sarah finds her renewed reliance on and closeness to her parents more difficult to endure. Patsy has begun to transition into a new relationship with all its complications and disruptions within her ongoing social economy. Sarah continues to search for a new man and to make the efforts necessary to build and maintain her support network.

Although Sarah and Patsy now experience approximately the same resources (a factor to which I return below), their everyday activities differ greatly. Patsy negotiates employment, complex child-care arrangements, and transportation for her children and herself. Sarah can attend more fully to her children during the day and she can also devote more time and energy to her friendships. These differences (in marital status, age, number of years as a single mother, and labor force involvement), when combined with the other differences among the women in this book (use of means-tested services, education, and living arrangements), determine the shape and contour of the specific social economy each woman develops to meet the challenges of daily life.

Common Themes

Despite the vast differences between Patsy and Sarah's lives, the two women share commonalities with each other and with the other respondents discussed in this book. They are both women and that fact is relevant to the social economy each develops. While gender is an obvious characteristic of single mothers, it is necessary to remember always that gender has a profound effect on daily life experiences. As just one example of this effect, when it comes to involving children in a teamwork approach to housework, men who are single parents appear to have an easier time than do women.[6]This may be because men are less likely to view that work as their responsibility; it may also be because men are less likely to view that work as central to the formation of gender identity. Although both Patsy and Sarah have children too young to be full participants in teamwork, they both acknowledge with some dismay, as do many of their peers, their failings as "housewives." And, as another example of the significance of gender, both women also ask others for help in a manner that reflects the traditional division of household labor between men and women. In so doing, they are absorbed into (and create) a gendered social economy (e.g., they rely on men to repair their cars whereas they rely on women to watch their children). If single mothers can often repay the debts to women by offering "like for like" (e.g., by watching their children), they have to be more inventive in their repayments to men. Neither Sarah nor Patsy acknowledges that her inventiveness entailed exchanging sex for male help, although some of their peers did.

Patsy and Sarah live in the same community in Vermont. The distinctive contours of this community have little impact on some aspects of their daily lives; single mothers everywhere experience very similar conflicts and tensions as they negotiate among competing claims on their time and energies. But the particularities of a rural locale matter in other ways and differentiate the women in this study from those who reside in urban areas. Transportation arrangements stand at the heart of each of their social economies and each of their periodic dilemmas. Both women also experience the downside to rural sociability and visibility. Sarah's mother waves from the kitchen window; Patsy describes her family as "the most nit-picking, into-everybody-else's-business people that I've ever met in my entire life."

Finally, different as they are in so many ways, Sarah's current assets (of approximately $25,000), which are likely to be spent within a single year, are almost equal to Patsy's annual earnings ($21,528), and both women are very close to the state median income for single mothers ($21,125).

Sarah is both learning how to live within straitened circumstances and worried about how long she can make her money last; she also is willing, for now, to forgo employment (and thus potentially having a higher income) in order to stay home with her children. But she is acutely aware of the other deprivations that attend this choice: "The biggest part of my budget goes on food.... There are other families who do more than I do." Patsy, in contrast, finds life easier than when she was living on welfare. During those years she absorbed some bitter costs of poverty while trying to protect her children from material hardship: "Food was a struggle and it was just really hard....I mean, I've gone hungry but my kids never have. They've always had food in their stomachs." Yet, even with her considerably improved situation, she continues to have difficulty making ends meet:

> It got pretty tight a couple of months ago, all the bills came in at the same time, usually they're about two weeks staggered...every bill that I could imagine, my rent was due and electric, the water, the sewer, the heat. I needed gas for my car, cable, everything you could possibly imagine....My god, their sneakers are like $40. Their feet grow really, really fast. I bought my son four new sweat suits, and those are all too short, so he needs four new pairs of jeans.

To be sure, the financial strains that Patsy and Sarah experience are not unique; nor do they compare with the strains that other single mothers face. The two women have higher incomes than half of the single mothers in Vermont, and far more than many of these mothers, and this "more" matters. And some women, like Megan Paige, who bought a pony for her daughter, have still more than either Patsy or Sarah. But, the incomes of single mothers, even those well above the median, rarely stretch so far that they allow for the purchase of significant relief from the relentless demands of trying to get by.

SOCIAL POLICY

Almost every scholarly work on single mothers offers suggestions for social policies that could ease the lives of this group of women. Politicians, regardless of their ideological leanings, do the same. These suggestions fall into two major categories: The first represents the more liberal perspective (insofar as its focus is on material well-being); the second represents the more conservative point of view (insofar as its emphasis is on values). I briefly review and evaluate each of these with respect to its resonance in the voices of single mothers themselves.

A Liberal Perspective: Material Support for Single Mothers

Most of the more liberal policy proposals start by acknowledging that something must be done to address the poverty of single mothers. They identify this poverty as emerging from the fact that the women who earn wages do so within an unequal labor market (and therefore have less than would be available either to a single father or to a couple relying only on a man's earnings) and have but a single source of income (and therefore have less than a married-couple family with two earners). Alternatively, scholars note, among those who rely on welfare, poverty is a consequence of policies enacted to ensure that this practice does not secure a feasible alternative to employment. Proposals intended to ameliorate the conditions facing single mothers revolve around two different goals, each of which is directed to an identified cause of poverty: making employment a possible route to self-sufficiency and making caregiving a viable alternative.

Policies Supporting Employment

Proposals directed at enabling single mothers to support themselves and their families through waged work address both the requirement of access to basic services (such as health insurance, child care, and housing), and the need for cash assistance (either by directly increasing, or by supplementing, women's earnings).[7] The women we interviewed would strongly endorse both sets of proposals.

In fact, given the discussions in previous chapters of this book, it should come as no surprise to find that the respondents in this study expressed considerable concern about their access to basic services. Among these, health insurance often came first. Even though Vermont is more generous than other states in its health care policies, it has its weaknesses. Many women spoke about the hassles of keeping track of benefit cliffs. Some women, like Liz Miles, were bitter when they found that increasing self-reliance was accompanied by major losses in social programs; they resented trading individual autonomy for social support. Others were bitter about what they perceived (whether accurately or not) as the all-or-nothing approach of state programs, whereby they were denied assistance as they watched those with lower or no earnings enjoy full access to these programs. Emily Quesnel, for example, complained,

"If you totally don't work... they'll give you everything. But I don't want everything! I just want, like, maybe a little Medicaid, you know?"

A few women pointed out that their employers' health insurance policies were not only costly (and in some cases beyond their reach), but that they were also founded on a very traditional family structure; as a result, single mothers are poorly served by them. Janet Linden, who had adopted a daughter from China, noted that her employer supported "biological family building" by providing health insurance that covered the expenses associated with pregnancy and childbirth. She proposed an alternative "adoption grant" for those who built a family in a different way. Tiffany Morrow criticized her employer's "family plan" because it did not take into account the special configuration of her family:

> The way my office health care plan is, it's almost like I'm penalized for having one adult and two children. I pay the same premium for my health insurance as I would for two adults and two children. Do you see what I mean? So I'm paying for that perfect family. And I have a great family, but we're not the two-children, two-adults family. So I honestly think there should be exceptions for situations like mine.

If health insurance is a significant concern of these mothers, issues of child care follow closely. Accessible, affordable, and high quality child care underwrites women's employment. The women we interviewed expressed concern about all aspects of the child-care dilemma. They noted, furthermore, that when they failed to solve that dilemma they compromised either their ability to be good mothers to their children or their ability to maintain employment, and sometimes both. Recall, for example, Kitty Thompson, who did not work when her daughter was a baby because frequent asthma attacks disrupted Kitty's employment efforts; recall as well how Melissa Henry worried each morning when she left her four children alone in the house. Another woman, Joan Meyer, suggested that "an after-school program in each town for all ages... subsidized through the state" might allow her to find employment and rest easy about the care her children were receiving when she could not be present.[8]

Several women also mentioned the need for help with the cost of housing. Indeed, Julie Marshall expressly tied her interest in this kind of support to the state's mission of making her self-sufficient. She was mildly sarcastic as she turned the state's emphasis on personal responsibility back on itself:

> I guess [I would like to see the state] making [subsidized hous-
> ing] more available, because everyplace that I've called to ask for
> applications there's like huge, long waiting lists and stuff. And I
> just feel like if you're trying to make somebody get off welfare,
> why don't you put them in a place where they can feel like they're
> being self-sufficient? Because I sure don't feel I'm being self-suf-
> ficient living here in my house with my mother.

The economist Barbara Bergmann would support the respondents'
claims for health insurance, child care, and adequate housing, but she
wants to see the government's reach stretch even further than they
do. For the government to make employment a truly feasible strategy
of self-sufficiency, Bergmann notes, it would have to step in with cash
assistance programs that extend beyond meeting these primary needs.
This assistance, she suggests, "could take the form of children's allowances, tax breaks, wage supplements, government-engineered rises in
the wage rates employers paid, basic income grants, and lump-sum
capital transfers."[9]

Although the single mothers we interviewed are familiar with existing
services, from which they may or may not be able to benefit, they are less
familiar with notions such as Bergmann's, which are largely absent from
the current discourse. Even so, several women did hint at similar ideas
regarding financial support, even as they implied that they believed them
to be in the realm of utopian thinking. For example, Tiffany Morrow
made a very concrete suggestion about health insurance, but she mused
with less certainty about other benefits the state might provide:

> Well, maybe in my fantasy world [you would] get some kind of
> a tax credit, or some kind of a reimbursement thing for the days
> that you've worked, or some kind of an incentive program. Like
> if you have to travel "x" amount of miles to work, give you credit
> for those miles, using the mileage, and using the car manual, and
> that kind of stuff. I mean, I'm talking kind of wild here, and not
> really going anywhere, but it would be nice to just be rewarded
> for the hard work that you do.

In all probability, women like Tiffany understand not only that these
policies would be costly, but that they may very well not be politically
feasible in the United States, even though some are routine components
of the benefits other countries provide.[10]

Supporting Full-Time Mothering

Some social policy analysts hope to create for single mothers the option of full-time caregiving, an option now available to some (albeit only a small proportion of) married women. For example, Kate Green, the former Director of One Parent Families (a UK charity working to tackle problems faced by single-parent families), writing as a citizen of a country that provides greater benefits to all its citizens than the United States does at either the federal or state level, reminds us that we must ask the following question: "Is paid work *desirable* (*or even possible*) for lone parents?" (Emphasis in original.)[11] She argues that the answer is best left to individual single mothers to decide for themselves. In addition, Green argues that supporting single mothers as mothers will recognize the value of parenting. These ideas are echoed by the economist Randy Albelda and the Women's Committee of One Hundred, "a group of U.S. feminist academics, professionals, and activists concerned with the relationship between women, economic survival, and the work of caregiving," who call for a social policy that would "recognize and reward the work of caring for dependents" and replace Temporary Assistance to Needy Families (TANF) "with a guaranteed income for caregivers of minor children and other dependent family members requiring sustained care."[12] Though these scholars also advocate policies that would enable a combination of both employment and caregiving, they want to ensure that caregiving itself can remain a priority and that it can be offered in a way that is humane to both those providing care and those receiving it.

It is interesting to note that, with the exception of the older group of former welfare recipients, who received aid under a policy that allowed mothers to stay home to care for their children (and imposed neither time limits nor work requirements), the majority of the women we interviewed did not mention this potential alternative solution. This is not to say that they do not value caregiving, but rather to suggest that the policy context within which they live does not easily allow them even to contemplate this option. Women who had relied on state support after welfare restructuring did, however, suggest modifying existing welfare policies: They wanted to see Vermont's welfare policies become more flexible, more personalized, and even more extensive; they wanted a reduction in the required paperwork; they wanted changes in procedures to reduce the public stigma associated with being on welfare (e.g., by replacing paper food stamps with swipe cards); and they wanted to see more respectful attitudes on the part of welfare officials. In addition, those women who had recently transitioned off welfare believed that its benefits should be more generous and should extend for a longer period of time. Indeed, some noted that if our social welfare policies were not so stingy (and short-lived), many hardships would be alleviated and women could more easily transition from "dependence" to self-sufficiency.

A Conservative Perspective: Marriage Promotion and Responsible Fatherhood

Neither support for employment nor support for caregiving resonates successfully within the political climate of the early twenty-first century. Since 1993, when president Bill Clinton first announced that he was going to "end welfare as we know it," government policy has only minimally aimed at filling the gaps created by low wages (e.g., through the Earned Income Tax Credit) and has offered fewer allowances for the caregiving needs of single mothers. Instead, it has required them to devote more hours to employment and it has largely ignored the resulting conflicts of care. Moreover, policies today, designed to reduce the number of unwed births (especially by encouraging marriage), are aimed less at alleviating any of the burdens single mothers face than at preventing single parenthood altogether.

Although the original Personal Responsibility and Work Opportunity Responsibility Act (PRWORA) stated that TANF funds could be used to support marriage promotion policies, no separate dedicated funding stream was included in that legislation. The TANF reauthorization proposals debated at the time of writing in 2005 change all that. The Senate bill would provide $500 million "over five years for a competitive matching grant program for 'healthy marriage' promotion." It would provide an additional $500 million over five years to Health and Human Services (HHS) for research demonstrations and technical assistance, 80 percent of which must be spent on marriage promotion activities. The House bill differs slightly; if passed, it would increase the former funding stream to $600 million and loosen the constraints in the HHS component to suggest that the funds must be spent "primarily" on marriage promotion activities.

In contrast with the more liberal policies mentioned in the previous section, this pair of Congressional proposals, which emerge from a more conservative ideology, had almost no resonance in the voices of the single mothers we interviewed. The women did not indicate that they wanted the state to become more involved in their personal lives: They neither wanted advice on how to sustain a flawed marriage nor advice on how to initiate a new relationship. To be sure, many of the women valued the opportunity to receive psychological counseling, and, whether they had or had not been able to do so, many women believed that more public funds should be made available for this service. But, for the most part, the women viewed counseling as a resource to help them make adjustments to being single: They did not want to be counseled to marry the father of a child simply because he was the father, and they did not want to be encouraged to remain in a relationship that they believed had reached its inevitable conclusion.

If the women wanted the government to stay out of their most private affairs, however, they had much to say about how the government could influence the fathers of their children. Most significant, they wanted the state to be of greater assistance in collecting monies owed to them. At the same time, some women were deeply ambivalent about how involved the state should be in the whole matter of child support. A few women complained when the state ate up their current payments because money (from the fathers) was still owed to the Department of Social Welfare; others protested the requirement of revealing paternity; and some believed that when the state interfered men became more resistant to paying. Although almost none of the women directly addressed the issue of "responsible fatherhood," it goes almost without saying that if men truly recognized their responsibilities for the care and nurturance of the children they fathered, the lives of single mothers would be considerably easier.[13] Hence the women might be interested in some of the projects mentioned in TANF reauthorization, which include those involving the promotion of responsible parenting through counseling and those providing men with more education and job training, in turn preparing them to better support their families. At the same time, some of the women might wonder why so much money was being channeled to men, when the mothers were the ones responsible for the daily care of their children.

EVALUATING SOCIAL POLICY FROM THE GROUND UP

Whether taken separately or as a whole, these policy proposals—the material approaches of making employment a more economically viable option for single mothers and of supporting single mothers in their caregiving activities, and the ideological approaches of encouraging marriage and of making fathers more responsible – leave untouched two sets of specific concerns single mothers raise in the discussions of their daily lives.[14]

First, time and energy remain very real issues, especially as they feed into a woman's capacity to provide the care she wants for her children. Indeed, the British sociologist Susan Himmelweit effectively draws our attention to the time constraints within which "lone" mothers live, and she wisely reminds us always to be attentive to the relevant comparison:[15]

> Lone parents who have no outside help must use their time for two competing purposes: to earn an income sufficient to support their families and to care for their children and themselves.... *The gap between the amount of time a lone parent has for these purposes and that available to a couple remains unchanged.* Lone parents face an inevitable dilemma in allocating their time. (Emphasis added.)

This gap cannot be closed simply by increasing a single mother's income either through employment benefits or generous caregiving allowances. Although a woman like Grace Jordan would find in the first of these strategies relief from economic pressures, at the end of the day she might still find herself too tired, and without enough time, to create "fuzzy rituals" for her daughter. And although the opportunity to remain home and provide full-time care for one's child might eliminate significant work/family conflicts for single mothers, as Sarah Stanley reminds us, single mothers will still face stressful, and occasionally heartbreaking, hassles.

A second set of concerns ignored in recent policy proposals has to do with the implicit, and sometimes explicit, condemnation of single-parent families. To be sure, some people (and some communities) do support those mothers who parent alone. And the caregiving allowances proposed by the Women's Committee of One Hundred, for example, would elevate the value of care itself within the contemporary discourse. But even this move would not necessarily relieve Sarah Stanley's anxiety about whether the family she has is a valid one: "I had a hard time in the beginning because family to me signifies a mother and a father with children and a dog and, you know, big household, balanced, happy, fun." Nor would it relieve the shame Amy Phelps felt when her marriage disintegrated before her very eyes: "If things aren't okay in your family, you feel like you've failed and that's exactly what I felt like.... I definitely went through a period when I just felt like I didn't want to be around anybody, I was so embarrassed." Indeed, the marriage promotion policies conservatives propose might actually add to these concerns: Rather than insisting that the single-parent family represents a legitimate alternative, it reiterates the centrality of marriage as the foundation of our society.

As the respondents themselves note, the broad social changes that underlie at least some of the liberal policy suggestions outlined earlier are improbable in today's political climate.[16] But single mothers do not need help in some utopian future: They need it now. The social changes being instituted today do not offer that help. It almost goes without saying that marriage promotion policies do not even consider the substantial stresses that wreak havoc on the lives of single mothers. And even if marriage promotion policies were successful in preventing some out-of-wedlock births, and therefore in reducing the total number of women who experience these stresses, they would do nothing for women who become single parents in other ways. Tiffany Morrow was married and planned to remain married; when her husband died, she was cast into a role she had never anticipated. Telling her she should now remarry is all fine and good, but Tiffany said it was difficult to find a man willing to encumber himself with a special-needs child as well as a rebellious teenager. Furthermore, she added, caring for her children left little time and energy to look for a new partner. The marriage promotion policies also fail to take into account the circumstances of women whose former partners were violent or irresponsible. Of course, a responsible father can provide a woman with vital resources and with a welcome break from the daily care of her children. But single mothers who have already been attached to "irresponsible" men, and women who have already been attached to men whose behavior threatens their safety and that of their children, are better off choosing to remain on their own, even if they are condemned for that choice.

In contrast to those promoting marriage, the women we interviewed make proposals that fill these gaps in policy and help alleviate their two major concerns. They speak about how they could be better supported through gestures that would relieve the burden of being the only adult to care for their children; they also address, albeit somewhat indirectly, how these alternative proposals would change the value structure of the society. While single mothers may want to continue to approach life through the construction of a social economy, they want to build that social economy within a very different material and ideological context.

What a Real Community Could Do

Recall that single mothers repeatedly made reference to an idealized community that would respond with generosity to the needs of its members. The respondents fleshed out their conception of this hopeful vision when they explained how a "real" community could help them resolve the most pressing issues of limited time, energy, and human resources.

Grace Jordan was explicit about the idea that as a matter of course, every community organization should offer child care, thereby enabling her both to meet her social needs and to fulfill her public obligations without having to worry about her child:

> I would want—I'm wishing now—I would want organiza-
> tions . . . to provide day care, babysitting facilities. If you have to go
> to school, for a meeting, it would just be automatic that they make
> that provision that your youngster can be watched and engaged
> while you do it. There are so many times, where there are meet-
> ings to be involved with the community, and I say, "What about?
> May I bring? I'm going to have to bring my child." I have neither
> the interest nor the need to spend money to get a babysitter so I
> can go be civic. I find that frustrating.

If readily available child care would allow Grace to "go be civic," it
would allow other women a break of the sort that is routine for married
women with actively involved partners. Diana Spender would relish
having "some day care that could come to your house, or that could
come [and take] the place of what the other parent would do." Among
the responsibilities of the "other parent" she mentioned, Diana highlighted that of simply playing with her daughter while she attended to
her housework.

Another woman talked about needing extended child-care services
within the community. She believed that the tensions that arose in
relationships with young children could culminate in dangerous
interactions, and she did not want to violate her own norms of good
parenting:

> [There needs to be] somebody in the neighborhood that could be
> like a safe house for your kids, or who could come to your kids
> so that you can take a drive, go down and cool off at the pizza
> parlor or whatever. There is no mechanism for stopping [a] terribly
> destructive dynamic that's happening between you and your kid.
> [There's] absolutely nothing out there.

While the mothers of young children spoke about wanting to see the
community offer opportunities that would allow them to have a break
from their children—be it a dangerous situation or not—the mothers of
older children spoke about wanting the community to develop opportunities that would allow their children to have a break from them. This
was especially true of mothers of teenagers. These parents believed their
children needed access to someone with whom they were not engaged
in struggles of growth and separation. As one woman said, "There has
to be . . . some kind of other support for the kids beside the parents. . . . I
would love for [my daughter] to have someone in the community that
she could really connect with, you know, be there for her." Another

woman echoed this concern: "[I would like to have someone] like my older sisters, just spend some quality time hanging out. Kind of like a big brother, a big sister, a role model."

Kara Lattrell described a place provided by the Visiting Nurses Association (VNA) that she had visited when her child was a baby. She advocated expanding such programs that combine in a single setting relief from the burdens of child care, contact with other mothers in similar situations, and the opportunity to learn more about how to parent:

> [I think we need more] programs that bring parents together, in sort of a learning mode. For instance the VNA had a wonderful place...called the "family room" and parents could just drop in all the time. And when my daughter was really young I dropped in there, and it was really a big help for me because I felt a little cooped up with her sometimes, and it was a way for me to just get out of the room and go to another room while she was still there. I knew she was safe, and I could also sit down, and sit in a rocking chair and have a cup of coffee with somebody else and somebody else will hold my baby. I think programs like that are really valuable for parents being able to value themselves.

As the women express these needs, they invariably make overt both the strain of constant care and the burden of always having to create their own social supports. The community of their imagining responds to these strains and burdens through the provision of day care and respite care, by ensuring that additional role models are available for children, and with the development of opportunities for interaction with other parents. The women do not want or imagine a truly social model of parenting where all the costs and benefits are shared: Rather, they want a form of support for the work they already do, and wish to continue doing, of providing daily care for their own children.

Changing Values

In his first year as president, George W. Bush wrote, "Together, we will address some of society's deepest problems one person at a time, by encouraging and empowering the good hearts and good works of the American people. This is the essence of compassionate conservatism, and it will be a foundation of my administration."[17] At one level, the ideas that the single mothers express might seem to be aligned with this principle: They want help from the community, from the "good hearts and good works of the American people." But there are two differences between what Bush envisioned and what the single mothers propose. First, as has already been shown, these desires for community involvement do not stand alone; single mothers also want the state to help them in material ways. Hence they call for access to organized services, cash assistance, modifications of existing welfare provisions, and help in collecting child support. Second, in calling for this intense community involvement, the single mothers envision not the community President Bush has delineated in his policies—one that disdains single parenthood—but rather a community that accepts this family form as valid, and with that acceptance, makes appropriate and significant adjustments to existing services. That is, they want a change in how the single-parent family is regarded along with the simultaneous enactment of gestures of support that would enable them to be self-sufficient as single parents.

Indeed, the practical solutions these mothers propose clearly rest on a change in values, even if those value changes remain implicit in their recommendations. Evidence of this value change can be found in a fuller consideration of the ideas they offer concerning the actions and attitudes of communities and of the people who reside in them. For example, consider Grace Jordan's suggestion for child care at every community event. The actual provision of such a service would rest entirely on a public awareness that not all households have two adults to share responsibility for civic participation. And as communities make this adjustment in awareness, broader change might ensue. School personnel who came to realize that they had to offer child care at every event might come to realize that they could make life easier for single parents in other ways as well. They might eventually develop additional strategies to enact that realization and encourage others to do the same. Teachers could be taught how to design homework that is responsive to the needs of children in different family structures, for example.[18] A Parent Teacher Association, along with a host of other community institutions, could conduct its fund-raising efforts in ways that actually privileged single parents: Instead of having a bake sale, it could sell the services of teams of "handy-people" at a low hourly rate so that single parents could purchase some needed home repair rather than another plate of brownies; alternatively, single mothers could be invited to contribute their time to such a team and thereby acquire some of the skills they lack rather than being asked to donate scarce financial resources for unnecessary baked goods.

If Samantha Stuart's call for a neighborhood "safe place" were heeded, it would symbolize the community's recognition that it must take the place of the absent father and create a world of real social support to alleviate the strains of single parenthood before crises emerged. The mothers we interviewed are also looking for ways to become better parents, not just safer ones, to their children. This too requires help from the outside. Kara Lattrell noted, for example, that the VNA site she enjoyed visiting "helped parents value themselves."[19] Recall that she had earlier spoken about her anger at a neighbor's disapproval of her yelling at her child. Kara's anger turned both on the fact that her neighbor had never acted to help Kara prevent that behavior and on the fact that her neighbor did not understand that she, too, "has a responsibility to the kids." A number of women would seem to concur with Kara, even if they are not similarly irate. They too proposed that community members could, through formal or informal arrangements, be available not just in crises, but on a routine basis, and not just for young children, but for teenagers as well. And as Kara implies, a community that educated its members to accept responsibility would make them aware of the needs of single parents so that they would cease criticizing a single mother's child-rearing approach and instead step in to provide meaningful help.

Other parents advocated for policies that would make a genuine allowance for variations in family forms. Remember Tiffany Morrow, who spoke of her employer-sponsored health care plan and commented that she did not believe that she should have to pay the same premium as she would for "for two adults and two children." If her employer made adjustments for her "great," albeit not "perfect," family form, it would openly acknowledge that one size does not fit all. And much as the provision of benefits for domestic partners is now widely perceived as undercutting heterosexual privilege, Janet Linden's suggestion—that employers make equal payments for adoption as they do (through health insurance) for biological parenting—would undercut the privilege accorded to the genetic tie.

In short, although the women speak from their own experiences and represent these issues as personal problems that require personal solutions, they also require that we recognize that these are public issues that demand a public response.[20]

No amount of economic support could possibly relieve the full range of material burdens that confront the full range of single mothers. Some women will continue to be poor, and they will find that they cannot meet all of their children's needs and especially not all of their children's yearnings. Like other women (and men) today, some will find that the effort of holding down a full-time job while raising children creates a daily time bind. But some of these burdens and distresses can be alleviated through greater financial support. That is, as a society we could alter what is conceived of as necessary state support by addressing policies to all people through such means as tax credits, living wages, and caregiving allowances. Indeed, the problems that are most apparent among the vulnerable signal difficulties in the overall society: Single mothers are not the only ones who need assistance and protection.[21]

We could also lift the unrealistic burden of self-sufficiency from the shoulders of single mothers as well as from the shoulders of other vulnerable citizens. If we were to shift the terrain encompassed by the ideology of self-sufficiency so as to acknowledge that (out of necessity and choice) most people depend on help from both organizations and individuals, the actions of seeking that help would have to be neither disguised nor concealed.[22] A second ideological shift is imperative. Single mothers both want and need to see their families valued so that they don't have to battle relentlessly against stigma and disdain. However, they do not just want lip service or the gloss of political correctness. They want tangible evidence of that value shift manifest, formally in the way community services are organized, and in less formal gestures that demonstrate both recognition for what they are already doing at great cost and a concrete willingness to support them in those efforts.

Even if both the material and ideological contexts were altered, single mothers would still find themselves having to create a social economy to meet the needs of daily survival. And why would we imagine that they would do otherwise? No amount of support or intervention would change either an individual's need for help from other people or an individual's desire to be sociable, to have friends as a mainstay, to laugh, and to love. Under those conditions, however, single mothers would not be compelled to make their choices simultaneously on the basis of need and on the desire to avoid contempt, and the work of creating a true social economy would no longer fall on their shoulders alone.

NOTES

Notes to Introduction

1. Throughout this book all respondents' names are pseudonyms; place names have also been disguised.
2. Vermont Department of Prevention, Assistance, Transition, and Health Access, "Dr. Dynasaur: Health Care Insurance for Children, Teens Under 18, and Pregnant Women," http://www.dsw.state.vt.us/programs_pages/healthcare/drdynasaur.htm.
3. Not all the single mothers included in this study have sole custody of their children. However, all of them have children living with them at least part of the time.
4. I do not mean to imply here that the two-parent family is *not* social. As Joan Smith and I showed in *Working Hard and Making Do: Surviving in Small Town America*, married-couple families living in the same area of Vermont as this study were deeply involved in networks that served both "social" and "economic" ends: see Margaret K. Nelson and Joan Smith, *Working Hard and Making Do: Surviving in Small Town America* (Berkeley: Univ. of California Press, 1999). For an excellent discussion of this issue, see Karen V. Hansen, *Not-So-Nuclear Families: Class, Gender, and Networks of Care* (New Brunswick, NJ: Rutgers Univ. Press, 2005).
5. There has been a great deal of attention paid to the support networks of single mothers, an issue discussed further in chapter 2. Despite this fact, however, books about single mothers often have titles that convey that single mothers are very much on their own: see, for example, Melissa Ludtke, *On Our Own: Unmarried Motherhood in America* (Berkeley: Univ. of California Press, 1999).
6. On this issue, see Martha Albertson Fineman, *The Neutered Mother, the Sexual Family and Other Twentieth Century Tragedies* (New York: Routledge, 1995).
7. For discussions of this issue see, for example, Deborah Roempke Graefe and Daniel T. Lichter, "Life Course Transitions of American Children: Parental Cohabitation, Marriage, and Single Motherhood," *Demography* 36, no. 2 (May 1999): 205–17; Larry Bumpass and Hsien-Hen Lu, "Trends in Cohabitation and Implications for Children's Family Contexts in the United States," *Population Studies* 54, no. 1 (2000): 29–41; Daniel T. Lichter, Christie D. Batson, and J. Brian Brown, "Welfare Reform and Marriage Promotion: The Marital Expectations and Desires of Single and Cohabiting Mothers," *Social Service Review* March 2004: 2–25. In the late 1990s, when 27 percent of all United

States families were headed by a single mother, half of those single mothers lived on their own, 11 percent lived with parents, 20 percent cohabited with a partner, 8 percent lived with other adults, and 4 percent lived in complex/multigenerational settings; see Gregory Acs and Sandi Nelson, "*Honey, I'm Home*": *Changes in Living Arrangements in the Late 1990's*, The Urban Institute (Washington, DC, June 2001). New Federalism: National Survey of America's Families Series B, no. B-38.

8. Jason Fields, *Children's Living Arrangements and Characteristics: March 2002*, U.S. Census Bureau no. P20-537 (Washington, DC: U.S. Department of Commerce, Economics and Statistics Administration, 2003).

9. In chapter 4 I do look at how living with another adult impacts on relationships between a single mother and her children and between a single mother and the other adult.

10. June Lapidus, "All the Lesbian Mothers Are Coupled, All the Single Mothers Are Straight, and All of Us Are Tired: Reflections on Being a Single Lesbian Mom," *Feminist Economics*, July 2004, 2.

11. The study does *not* include self-defined, lesbian single mothers. I assumed that lesbian mothers confronted a different set of issues than did "straight" mothers and that they might well have different friendship communities. This is not to say that I am certain of, or even interested in, the sexual orientations of the women interviewed for this project. The women might well have had partnerships with other women in the past (and in one case, I know this was so) and they might well have such partnerships again in the future. Rather, I am interested in a particular set of issues that confront single women who have formed sexual partnerships with men and who, for the most part, remain interested in doing so again. For studies of lesbian mothers, see Kath Weston, *Families We Choose: Lesbians, Gays, Kinship* (New York: Columbia Univ. Press, 1991); Ellen Lewin, *Lesbian Mothers: Accounts of Gender in American Culture* (Ithaca, NY: Cornell Univ. Press, 1993); Catherine Donovan, "Who Needs a Father?: Negotiating Biological Fatherhood in British Lesbian Families Using Self-Insemination," *Sexualities* 3, no. 2 (May 2000): 149–64; Jacqui Gabb, "Desirous Subjects and Parental Identities: Constructing a Radical Discourse on (Lesbian) Family Sexuality," *Sexualities* 4, no. 3 (2001): 333–52.

12. The term *social economy* has wide parlance in social scientific literatures (and even a journal devoted entirely to that topic—*The Review of Social Economy*). In common terminology, the concept "encompasses the third sector, the voluntary sector, the cooperative sector, the not-for-profit sector, and the independent sector": see John Burgess, "Tackling Social Exclusion in Europe: The Contribution of the Social Economy (Book Review)," *Labour & Industry* 14, no. 3 (April 2004): 164. Others use the term somewhat differently to describe activities that occur outside of both the public and private sectors, involving the "resources of people and neighborhoods." Colin C. Williams and Richard White, "Evaluating the Role of the Social Economy in Tackling Rural Transport Problems: Some Case Study Evidence from Rural England," *Planning Practice & Research* 16, no. 3/4 (2001): 337. My use of the term differs from both of these insofar as I describe "economic" actions rooted in reliance on others, but conducted by individuals for their own well-being.

In a wonderful article, Stacey J. Oliker has introduced the term *moral economy* to describe how "mothers organize opportunities, obligations, constraints, and commitments in forming work strategies": "The Proximate Contexts of Workfare and Work: A Framework for Studying Poor Women's Economic Choices," *The Sociological Quarterly* 36, no. 2 (Spring 1995): 251–72. She selects that term (first used by E. P. Thompson, "The Moral Economy of the English Crowd in the Eighteenth Century," *Past and Present* 50 [1971]: 76–136) as a way to consider "how investing in full-time domesticity, periodic or interrupted work, or part-time work is purposively rooted in family commitments and communally oriented strategies of contending with market forces" (263). Oliker's term focuses on choices about employment, and she is especially attentive to the "interests of children and the needs of close kin" (266); because I look at not only these interests but also commitments to broad "social" values, I have chosen a different term. Even so, this work conveys an analogous notion: that single mothers, even when they face compelling economic needs, are not simply "rational" actors whose choices always represent a straightforward, or even obvious, cost/benefit analysis.

13. Carmen DeNavas-Walt and Robert Cleveland, *Money Income in the United States: 2001*, U.S. Census Bureau (Washington, DC: U.S. Government Printing Office, 2002). Current Population Reports P60-218.

14. A broad range of studies would fall within this general framework. See, for example, Valerie Polakow, *Lives on the Edge: Single Mothers and Their Children in the Other America* (Chicago: Univ. of Chicago Press, 1992); Virginia E. Schein, *Working from the Margins: Voices of Mothers in Poverty* (Ithaca, NY: ILR Press, 1995); Nancy E. Dowd, *In Defense of Single-Parent Families* (New York: NYU Press, 1997); Kathryn Edin and Laura Lein, *Making Ends Meet: How Single Mothers Survive Welfare and Low-Wage Work* (New York: Russell Sage Foundation, 1997); Karen Seccombe, *"So You Think I Drive a Cadillac?": Welfare Recipients' Perspectives on the System and Its Reform* (Needham Heights, MA: Allyn & Bacon, 1999).

15. For estimates of the financial requirements of households of different sizes and compositions in Vermont, see Ellen Kahler, *The Vermont Job Gap Study, Phase I: Basic Needs and a Livable Wage* (Burlington, VT: Peace & Justice Center, 1997); Vermont State Legislature. Livable Income Study Committee. *Act 21 Research and Analysis in Support of the Livable Income Study Committee* (1999). For a more complete discussion of these issues, see chapter 1.

16. Jason Fields and Lynne M. Casper, *America's Families and Living Arrangements* (Washington, DC: Department of Commerce, U.S. Census Bureau, 2001).

17. Sharon Hays, *Flat Broke with Children: Women in the Age of Welfare Reform* (Oxford: Oxford University Press, 2003), 181–82. As Hays notes, William Julius Wilson argues "that it is precisely this tendency to ignore 'social pathologies' among the poor, and to 'avoid describing any behavior that might be construed as unflattering or stigmatizing to ghetto residents,' that has made the liberal perspective less convincing, and allowed the conservative view of poverty to gain ascendancy." Wilson, *The Truly Disadvantaged: The Inner City, the Underclass, and Public Policy* (Chicago: Univ. of Chicago Press, 1987), 6, quoted in Hays, 256 n. 6.

18. Hays, *Flat Broke with Children*, 12.

19. Edin and Lein, *Making Ends Meet*.

20. Ibid., 193–94. On the issue of overstating choice, see Nicholas Townsend, *The Package Deal: Marriage, Work, and Fatherhood in Men's Lives* (Philadelphia: Temple Univ. Press, 2002).

21. For a discussion of how the members of dual-earner couples envision their own "self-sufficiency" and include within that notion justifications for relying on the services of working-class (and often minority) women, see Rosanna Hertz, "Dual-Career Couples and the American Dream: Self-Sufficiency and Achievement," *Journal of Comparative Family Studies* 22, no. 2 (Summer 1991): 247–63.

22. Shailesh Bhandari and Elizabeth Gilford, *Children with Health Insurance* (Washington, DC: U.S. Census Bureau, U.S. Department of Commerce no. P60-224, August 2003), Current Population Reports. This issue is discussed further below in this introduction and in chapter 1.

23. For historical versions of the "culture of poverty" thesis, see, for example, Daniel Patrick Moynihan, *The Negro Family: The Case for National Action* (Washington, DC: U.S. Government Printing Office, 1965); Ken Auletta, *The Underclass* (New York: Random House, 1982). For more contemporary versions, see Charles Murray, *Losing Ground: American Social Policy 1950–1980* (New York: Basic Books, 1984); Lawrence M. Mead,

New Politics of Poverty: The Nonworking Poor in America (New York: Basic Books, 1992). Insightful reviews of the history of this thought can be found in Joel F. Handler, *The Poverty of Welfare Reform* (New Haven, CT: Yale University Press, 1995); Michael B. Katz, *In the Shadow of the Poorhouse: A Social History of Welfare in America* (New York: Basic Books, 1986 (1996)). For a historical analysis of the specific attitudes toward single mothers in the United States, see Lisa D. Brush, "Worthy Widows, Welfare Cheats: Proper Womanhood in Expert Needs Talk About Single Mothers in the United States, 1900 to 1998," *Gender & Society* 11, no. 6 (December 1997): 720–46.

24. See, for example, Auletta, *The Underclass*; Mead, *New Politics of Poverty*. For evidence that these attitudes are shared widely by the public, see Robert J. Blendon et al., "The Public and the Welfare Reform Debate," *Archives of Pediatric and Adolescent Medicine* 149, no. 10 (1995): 1065–69.

25. See, for example, David Popenoe, "Can the Nuclear Family Be Revived?" *Society* 36, no. 5 (July/August 1999): 28–30. For a discussion about how poor women are perceived as becoming pregnant only to qualify for welfare, see Susan L. Thomas, "Race, Gender, and Welfare Reform: The Antinatalist Response," *Journal of Black Studies* 28, no. 4 (March 1998): 419–47.

26. For a good review of these arguments, see Demie Kurz, *For Richer, for Poorer: Mothers Confront Divorce* (New York and London: Routledge, 1995).

27. Sharon Hays also argues that liberal scholars cannot ignore "values" when she says,

> In this book, I join the conservative critics of welfare in focusing squarely on the question of values. In this case, however, I intend to not only scrutinize the allegedly "bad" values of the poor, but also to critically examine the allegedly "mainstream" values embedded in the newly reorganized welfare system (*Flat Broke with Children*, 12).

My interest here is somewhat different insofar as I am focusing less on the values embedded in welfare per se than on how those values are enacted in the lives of single mothers—whether welfare reliant or not.

28. All interviews followed essentially the same format with an interview guide. The women were asked a series of questions about their background (education, marital history, age at which they had their first child), their current living situation (who lived in the household, whether they owned or rented), and sources of income (jobs, reliance on means-tested programs, child support).

29. The women were also asked about access to a range of material and emotional support that might be necessary in the course of daily life: transportation, home repairs, financial assistance, child care, and comfort or emotional support. More specifically, the women were asked whether they ever needed any of these kinds of assistance and whether they had in fact asked for assistance when it was needed. If they had requested assistance, they were then encouraged to discuss further the situation in which they had done so and to specify whom they had asked (and why) and whether the requested assistance had been received. Follow-up questions probed their feelings about receiving help and their sense of obligation to make a return gesture to those who gave them assistance.(If they did not receive help when they had asked, they were asked about their feelings about refusal.) They were also asked to discuss their broader expectations about what it was appropriate to ask from, and what it was appropriate to give to, neighborhood and communities.

30. Some respondents chose to draw arrows of different lengths between themselves and others, indicating that they believed more was given in one direction than the other [<...... ············>]); some drew arrows with a single point to show that the giving went in one direction alone [------>]; others drew arrows of varying thickness for each side of a relationship and for different kinds of relationships [➔➔]; and still others chose to give

different numbers of points to the arrows when they perceived that the direction of giving was lopsided [<<------->].

31. Nelson and Smith, *Working Hard and Making Do.*

32. For a good discussion of some of these issues, see the debate surrounding Jaber F. Gubrium and James A. Holstein, *The New Language of Qualitative Method* (New York: Oxford Univ. Press, 1997). These debates include the following: Norman K. Denzin, "The New Language of Qualitative Method (Book Review)," *Journal of Contemporary Ethnography* 27, no. 3 (October 1998): 405–15; Robert Dingwall, "The New Language of Qualitative Method (Book Review)," *Journal of Contemporary Ethnography* 27, no. 3 (October 1998): 399–404; Gubrium and Holstein's response: "Standing Our Middle Ground," *Journal of Contemporary Ethnography* 27, no. 3 (October 1998): 416–21; Ann Oakley, "Gender, Methodology and People's Ways of Knowing: Some Problems with Feminism and the Paradigm Debate in Social Science," *Sociology: The Journal of the British Sociological Association* 32, no. 4 (November 1998): 707–31.

33. Ann Oakley, "Interviewing Women: A Contradiction in Terms," 30-61 in *Doing Feminist Research*, ed. Helen Roberts (London: Routledge & Kegan Paul, 1981).

34. For essays that focus more on the process of data collection see Sarah Oerton and Karen Atkinson, "Voices from the Valleys: Researching Lone Mothers' Talk," *Community, Work, and Family* 2, no. 3 (December 1999): 229–56; L. Mun Wong, "The Ethics of Rapport: Institutional Safeguards, Resistance, and Betrayal," *Qualitative Inquiry* 4, no. 2 (June 1998): 178–99.

35. Most of the interviews were conducted by me and my three research assistants. Some of the interviews were conducted by college students as part of their own research projects and they graciously allowed me to share their findings.

36. For an excellent discussion of these issues, see Ruth Frankenberg, *White Women, Race Matters: The Social Construction of Whiteness* (Minneapolis: Univ. of Minnesota Press, 1993).

37. Oerton and Atkinson, "Voices from the Valleys." Although two of the interviewers were themselves the daughters of single mothers, we were all either married or single without children; when asked outright by one respondent whether she was a single mom, one interviewer could only respond that she was "a single friend of other moms."

38. Townsend, *The Package Deal*, 11.

39. In referring to "work" here, I am following the model established by Arlie Russell Hochschild in her discussion of "emotion work," *The Managed Heart: The Commercialization of Human Feeling* (Berkeley: Univ. of California Press, 1983), 7; and of Karla B. Hackstaff in her discussion of "marital work," *Marriage in a Culture of Divorce* (Philadelphia: Temple Univ. Press, 1999).

40. "U.S. Divorce Statistics," *DivorceMagazine.com*, http://www.divorcemag.com/statistics/statsUS.shtml.

41. Ann Swidler, *Talk of Love: How Culture Matters* (Chicago: Univ. of Chicago Press, 2001), 93.

42. For examples of studies that focus on "typical" single mothers see Bette J. Dickerson, *African American Single Mothers: Understanding Their Lives and Families* (Thousand Oaks, CA: Sage, 1995); Bonnie Thornton Dill and Bruce B. Williams, "Race, Gender and Poverty in the Rural South: African American Single Mothers," in *Rural Poverty in America*, ed. Cynthia M. Duncan (New York: Auburn House, 1992), 97–109; Bonnie Thornton Dill, "A Better Life for Me and My Children: Low-Income Single Mothers' Struggle for Self-Sufficiency in the Rural South," *Journal of Comparative Family Studies* 29, no. 2 (Summer 1998): 419–28; Edin and Lein, *Making Ends Meet*; Seccombe, *"So You Think I Drive a Cadillac?"* For studies that examine a different group of single mothers, see Rosanna Hertz and Faith I. T. Ferguson, "Kinship Strategies and Self-Sufficiency Among Single Mothers by Choice: Post Modern Family Ties," *Qualitative Sociology* 20,

no. 2 (Summer 1997): 187–209; Rosanna Hertz and Faith I. T. Ferguson, "Only One Pair of Hands: Ways That Single Mothers Stretch Work and Family Resources," *Community, Work and Family* 1, no. 1 (April 1998): 13–37; Ludtke, *On Our Own*; Kurz, *For Richer, for Poorer*; Yvonne M. Vissing, *Out of Sight, out of Mind: Homeless Children and Families in Small-Town America* (Lexington: Univ. of Kentucky Press, 1996).

43. Fields and Casper, *America's Families and Living Arrangements*.

44. Nelson and Smith, *Working Hard and Making Do*.

45. Men now comprise one sixth of the nation's 11.9 million single parents (Fields and Casper, *America's Families and Living Arrangements*).

46. On premarital pregnancy and gender see Robert D. Plotnick, "The Effects of Attitudes on Teenage Premarital Pregnancy and Its Resolution," *American Sociological Review* 57, no. 6 (December 1992): 800–10. For a broader discussion of the gendered reasons for divorce see Kurz, *For Richer, for Poorer*, 45.

47. Single fathers are considerably less studied. A special issue of the *Journal of Family Issues* did examine the situation of single fathers: D. Terri Heath, ed. Special issue, *A Special Issue on Single Fathers* (1999). See also Lisa C. Hill and Jeanne M. Hilton, "Changes in Roles Following Divorce: Comparison of Factors Contributing to Depression in Custodial Single Mothers and Custodial Single Fathers," *Journal of Divorce and Remarriage* 31, no. 3-4 (July-August 1999): 91–114; Jeanne M. Hilton, Stephan Desrochers, and Esther Devall, "Comparison of Role Demands, Relationships, and Child Functioning in Single-Mother, Single-Father, and Intact Families," *Journal of Divorce and Remarriage* 35, no. 1-2 (March-April 2001): 29–56; Douglas B. Downey, James W. Ainsworth-Darnell, and Mikaela J. Dufur, "Sex of Parent and Children's Well-Being in Single-Parent Households," *Journal of Marriage and the Family* 60, no. 4 (1998): 878–93; Geoffrey D. Paulin and Yoon G. Lee, "Expenditures of Single Parents: How Does Gender Figure In?" *Monthly Labor Review* 25, no. 7 (July 2002): 16–37.

48. See Barbara Reskin, "Sex Segregation in the Workplace," in *Annual Review of Sociology, Volume 19*, ed. Judith Blake and John Hagen (Palo Alto, CA: Annual Reviews, 1993), 241–69. For a discussion of the structural sources of women's poverty see Jacki A. Fitzpatrick and Todd R. Gomez, "Still Caught in a Trap: The Continued Povertization of Women," *Affilia: Journal of Women and Social Work* 12, no. 3 (Fall 1997): 318–41. For a discussion of married women's earnings dependence, and how it is relevant to their status as single mothers, see Suzanne M. Bianchi, Lynne M. Casper, and Pia K. Peltola, "A Cross-National Look at Married Women's Earnings Dependency," *Gender Issues* 17, no. 3 (Summer 1999): 3–33.

49. On the issue of gender see Ann Orloff, "Gender in the Welfare State," in *Annual Review of Sociology, Volume 22*, ed. John Hagan and Karen S. Cook (Palo Alto, CA: Annual Reviews, 1996), 51–78; Stephanie Moller, "Supporting Poor Single Mothers: Gender and Race in the U.S. Welfare State," *Gender & Society* 16, no. 4 (August 2002): 465–83; Linda Gordon, *Pitied but Not Entitled: Single Mothers and the History of Welfare, 1890–1935* (Cambridge, MA: Harvard Univ. Press, 1994). On the issue of race, see Martin Gilens, *Why Americans Hate Welfare: Race, Media, and the Politics of Antipoverty Policy* (Chicago: Univ. of Chicago Press, 1999); Kenneth J. Neubeck and Noel A. Cazenave, *Welfare Racism: Playing the Race Card Against America's Poor* (New York: Routledge, 2001); Jill Quadagno, *The Color of Welfare: How Racism Undermined the War on Poverty* (New York: Oxford Univ. Press, 1996).

50. Jennifer Hamer and Kathleen Marchioro, "Becoming Custodial Dads: Exploring Parenting Among Low-Income and Working-Class African American Fathers," *Journal of Marriage and the Family* 64, no. 1 (February 2002): 116–29.

51. A number of excellent studies remind us that being "white" is also being "raced." As one example, see Frankenberg, *White Women, Race Matters*.

52. Gilens, *Why Americans Hate Welfare*; Neubeck and Cazenave, *Welfare Racism*; Quadagno, *The Color of Welfare*; Alejandra Marchevsky and Jeanne Theoharis, "Welfare

Reform, Globalization, and the Racialization of Entitlement," *American Studies* 41, no. 2-3 (Summer-Fall 2000): 235–54.

53. Karen Brodkin, *How Jews Became White Folks & What That Says About Race in America* (New Brunswick, NJ: Rutgers Univ. Press, 1998, 71.

54. Valerie Polakow, Therese Halskov, and Per Schultz Jorgensen, *Diminished Rights: Danish Lone Mother Families in International Context* (Bristol, UK: The Policy Press, 2001).

55. White single mothers differ substantially from other groups of single mothers in their marital status, poverty status, and location. For statistics see Fields and Casper, *America's Families and Living Arrangements*, 8, table 4.

56. See Matthew D. Bramlett and William D. Mosher, "First Marriage Dissolution, Divorce, and Remarriage: United States," *Advance Data* 323 (May 31, 2001): 1–20.

57. Gordon, *Pitied but Not Entitled*, 19. To be sure, single motherhood is still more commonly found among some groups of women than others: Single parenthood is far more common among African-American families than it is among those who are white; it is also more common among metropolitan populations than among nonmetropolitan ones; and among those who are poor (especially those who are welfare reliant) than among those who are relatively well-off (though with respect to these latter categories, cause and effect are confounded); David T. Ellwood and Christopher Jencks, "The Spread of Single-Parent Families in the United States Since 1960" (working paper no. RWP04-008, Kennedy School of Government, Harvard University, October 2002).

58. Fields and Casper, *America's Families and Living Arrangements*.

59. Stehanie J. Ventura and Christine A. Bachrach, *Nonmarital Childbearing in the United States, 1940–1999* (Centers for Disease Control and Prevention, October 18, 2000), National Vital Statistics Reports.

60. Fields and Casper, *America's Families and Living Arrangements*.

61. For a good overview see Ellwood and Jencks, *The Spread of Single-Parent Families in the United States Since 1960*.

62. Lawrence Mishel, Jared Bernstein, and Heather Boushey, *The State of Working America 2002/2003* (Ithaca, NY: Cornell Univ. Press, 2003).

63. For discussions of this phenomenon in urban areas see Wilson, *The Truly Disadvantaged*; for a study of the same phenomenon in rural areas see Daniel T. Lichter, "Marriage as Public Policy," (policy report, Progressive Policy Institute, (September 10, 2001), http://www.ppionline.org.

64. "Marital Status of Women in the Civilian Labor Force," 2004, http://www.census.gov/statab/hist/HS-30.pdf.

65. For a discussion of historical trends in premarital childbearing, see Amara Bachu, *Trends in Premarital Childbearing: 1930–1994* (Washington, DC: U.S. Census Bureau no. P23-197, October 1999), Current Population Reports.

66. For historical analyses of shifting attitudes toward unwed mothers see Rickie Solinger, *Wake Up Little Susie: Single Pregnancy and Race Before Roe v. Wade* (New York: Routledge, 1992).

67. Sara Eckel, "Single Mothers," *American Demographics* 21, no. 5 (May 1999): 62–66; T. J. Matthews and Brady E. Hamilton, *Mean Age of Mother, 1970–2000*, Centers for Disease Control and Prevention (Atlanta, GA, December 11, 2002). National Vital Statistics Reports 51, Number 1; Jay D. Teachman, Lucky M. Tedrow, and Kyle D. Crowder, "The Changing Demography of America's Families," *Journal of Marriage and the Family* 62, no. 4 (November 2000): 1234–46.

68. Personal Responsibility and Work Opportunity Reconciliation Act of 1996, Public Law 104-193d Cong., H.R. 3734 sess. (1966).

69. For a study that focuses on never-married women alone, see, for example, Elaine Bell Kaplan, *Not Our Kind of Girl: Unraveling the Myths of Black Teenage Motherhood* (Berkeley: Univ. of California Press, 1997). For a study that examines only women who have become single mothers through divorce, see, for example Kurz, *For Richer, for Poorer*.

Chapter 1

1. Portions of chapter 1 were previously published as "How Men Matter: Housework and Self-Provisioning Among Rural-Single-Mother and Married-Couple Families in Vermont, US," *Feminist Economics,* Volume 10, Number 2, July 2004, 9–36. Permission granted by Routledge; reprinted with permission from *Feminist Economics*/International Association for Feminist Economics.

2. The tourism industry says that today there are "almost as many cows as people." "Vermont Tourism Network," 2002, http://www.govtn.com.

3. For an interesting discussion of the myths concerning rural areas and how these myths shape expectations of family life, see Cynthia B. Struthers and Janet L. Bokemeier, "Myths and Realities of Raising Children and Creating Family Life in a Rural County," *Journal of Family Issues* 21, no. 1 (January 2000): 17–46.

4. There is a voluminous literature on economic restructuring in rural areas. Much of it is reviewed in Anthony Winson and Belinda Leach, *Contingent Work, Disrupted Lives: Labour and Community in the New Rural Economy* (Toronto: Univ. of Toronto Press, 2003).

5. "Quick Tables," 2002, http://www.factfinder.census.gov. Stressing these similarities ignores several major differences that have much to do with Vermont's continued "rural" character and so with the conditions that shape the lives of its inhabitants. These differences include higher rates of self-employment, low wages, and a flat income structure. These differences also include the state's deep reliance on seasonal employment associated with tourism (between 1998 and 2000, approximately 19% of the jobs in Vermont were in some way or another associated with the tourism industry) (Nancy E. Wood and Kathleen Liang, "The Impact of Tourism Sector on the Vermont Economy 1999–2000," September 2001, http://www.snr.uvm.edu/vtdc).

6. "UI Covered Wages—Private Industry: Vermont and United States." Vermont Department of Employment and Training, 2002, http://www.vtlmi.info/wage.htm. By virtue of their location in the labor market, Vermont women are especially likely to be engaged in activities affected by seasonal shifts in tourism and thus subject to both layoffs and variable earnings. On this issue, see David Vail and Wade Kavanaugh, "Livable Tourism Wages in Maine's Tight Labor Market," *Choices: Ideas for Shared Prosperity* 6, no. 5 (2000): 1–4.

7. U.S. Department of Labor, *Highlights of Women's Earnings* (2002)*,* 15.

8. "UI Covered Wages- Private Industry Vermont and United States, 1983–2001," 2002, http://www.vtlmi.info/wage.htm.

9. Office of the Assistant Secretary for Planning and Evaluation, *Trends in the Well-Being of America's Children and Youth*, U.S. Department of Health and Human Services http://aspe.hhs.gov/hsp/03trends/index.htm (Washington, D.C., 2004). See also Vicky Lovell, "40-Hour Work Proposal Significantly Raises Mothers' Employment Standard," Institute for Women's Policy Research: Research-in-Brief (Institute for Women's Policy Research, June, 2003), 1–8.

10. See Glenna Spitze and Karyn Loscocco, "Women's Position in the Household—A Crossnational Study," *The Quarterly Review of Economics and Finance* 39, no. 5 (1999): 647–61; Haya Stier, Noah Lewin-Epstein, and Michael Braun, "Welfare Regimes, Family-Supportive Policies, and Women's Employment Along the Life-Course," *The American Journal of Sociology* 106, no. 6 (May 2001): 1731-1761. In general, rural areas appear to have poorer benefits when compared to metropolitan areas (Mark Harvey et al., "The Short-Term Impacts of Welfare Reform in Persistently Poor Rural Areas," in *Rural Dimensions of Welfare Reform*, ed. L. A. Whitener, B. A. Weber and G. Duncan (Kalamazoo, MI: W. E. Upjohn Institute for Employment Research, 2002), 375–412).

11. Margaret K. Nelson and Joan Smith, *Working Hard and Making Do: Surviving in Small Town America* (Berkeley: Univ. of California Press, 1999).

12. Sunhwa Lee, *Women's Work Supports, Job Retention, and Job Mobility: Child Care and Employer-Provided Health Insurance Help Women Stay on Jobs*, Institute for Women's Policy Research no. B244 (Washington, D.C.: Institute for Women's Policy Research, November 2004). For an article that argues that when children are young, the costs of workforce participation are even greater in nonmetropolitan areas than they are in metropolitan areas, see Bradford F. Mills and Gautam Hazarika, "Do Single Mothers Face Greater Constraints to Workforce Participation in Non-Metropolitan Areas?" *American Journal of Agricultural Economics* 85, no. 1 (February 2003): 143–61.

13. For a discussion of the strain of low-wage jobs and their effects on parenting, see Aurora P. Jackson et al., "Single Mothers in Low-Wage Jobs: Financial Strain, Parenting, and Preschoolers' Outcomes," *Child Development* 71, no. 5 (September 2000): 1409–23.

14. Harriet B. Presser, "Shift Work and Child Care Among Young Dual-Earner American Parents," *Journal of Marriage and the Family* 50 (February 1988): 133–48. For a discussion of approaches to child care among dual earner couples, see Rosanna Hertz, "A Typology of Approaches to Child Care: The Centerpiece of Organizing Family Life for Dual-Earner Couples," *Journal of Family Issues* 18, no. 4 (July 1997): 355–85. For shift work see Francine M. Deutsch and Susan E. Saxon, "Traditional Ideologies, Nontraditional Lives," *Sex Roles* 38, no. 5/6 (1998): 331–62.

15. For a general discussion of how child care issues shape women's abilities, and desires, to work outside the home, see Robin Mason, "Listening to Lone Mothers: Paid Work, Family Life, and Childcare in Canada," *Journal of Children & Poverty* 9, no. 1 (2003): 41–54. For discussions of the specific child care problems faced by rural women see J. Halliday and J. Little, "Amongst Women: Exploring the Reality of Rural Childcare," *Sociologia Ruralis* 41, no. 4 (October 2001): 423–37; Carole Cochran et al., "A Rural Road: Exploring Opportunities, Networks, Services, and Supports That Affect Rural Families," *Child Welfare* 81, no. 5 (September 2002): 837–48.

16. Denise Levy and Sonya Michel, "More Can Be Less: Child Care and Welfare Reform in the United States," in *Child Care Policy at the Crossroads: Gender and Welfare State Restructuring*, ed. Sonya Michel and Rianne Mahon (New York: Routledge, 2002), 239–63.

17. The existing child care system is meeting only 65 percent of the estimated need (Windham Child Care Association and Peace & Justice Center, *The Economic Impact of Vermont's Child Care Industry*, June 2002).

18. Only 17 percent of the state's licensed centers open before 7:00 a.m. and only 3 percent offer services after 6:00 p.m. (Windham Child Care Association and Peace & Justice Center, *The Economic Impact of Vermont's Child Care Industry*, 6). Some argue that employed mothers with lower levels of education in the United States tend to have a nonstandard work schedule primarily because of the lack of other options; see Harriet B. Presser and Amy G. Cox, "The Work Schedules of Low-Educated American Women and Welfare Reform," *Monthly Labor Review* 120, no. 4 (April 1997): 25–35. Among former welfare recipients, more than a third of single mothers worked jobs that required evenings or nights, on split or rotating shifts, or on an irregular schedule; see Susan Scrivener et al., *WRP: Final Report on Vermont's Welfare Restructuring Project*, Manpower Demonstration Research Corporation (New York: Manpower Demonstration Research Corporation, September 2002), Appendix Table D.7.

19. Lynet Uttal, "Using Kin for Child Care: Embedment in the Socioeconomic Networks of Extended Families," *Journal of Marriage and the Family* 61, no. 4 (November 1999): 845–57. The literature is divided about whether child care by relatives is a matter of choice and preference or a matter of financial necessity. On this issue see, Peter D. Brandon, "An Analysis of Kin-Provided Child Care in the Context of Intrafamily Exchanges: Linking the Components of Family Support for Parents Raising Young Children," *American Journal of Economics and Sociology* 59, no. 2 (April 2000): 191–216; Karin L. Brewster

and Irene Padavic, "No More Kin Care? Change in Black Mothers' Reliance on Relatives for Child Care, 1977–94," *Gender & Society* 16, no. 4 (August 2002): 546–62.

20. Ellen Kahler, *The Vermont Job Gap Study, Phase I: Basic Needs and a Livable Wage* (Burlington, VT: Peace & Justice Center, 1997); Vermont State Legislature. Livable Income Study Committee. *Act 21 Research and Analysis in Support of the Livable Income Study Committee* (1999)

21. Erica Williams and Anne W. Mitchell, *The Status of Early Care and Education in The States*, Institute for Women's Policy Research (2004).

22. See Annie E. Casey Foundation, "2000 Kids Count Data Online," 2004, http://www.aecf.org/cgi-bin/kc.cgi?action=profile&area=Vermont. In Vermont, out–of-pocket annual child care costs are $2,842 for a family earning $26,000 a year and as much as $6,895 for a family earning $40,000 (Windham Child Care Association and Peace & Justice Center, "The Economic Impact of Vermont's Child Care Industry." 2002:6).

23. Jessica Wasilewski, "Low-Income Credit Rationing and Social Return on Investment: Welfare-to-Work Car Loans in the State of Vermont," Senior Thesis, Department of Economics, Middlebury College, Middlebury, VT, April 5, 2002. Some authors argue that rural women are even more dependent on the car than are urban women and that they make more trips per day than urban women; see Heather MacDonald and Alan H. Peters, "Distance and Labor Force Participation: Implications for Urban and Rural Women," paper presented at the Second National Conference on Women's Travel Issues (October 1996).

24. Mark Lino, "Income and Spending Patterns of Single-Mother Families," *Monthly Labor Review* 117, no. 5 (May 1994): 29–37.

25. In fact, the average commute to work in Vermont is somewhat shorter (21.6 minutes) than it is in the United States. as a whole (25.5 minutes). If the Vermont commute is shorter, in 2000 considerably fewer Vermonters (.8%) relied on public transportation to commute to work than did U.S. residents as a whole (4.9%) ("Vermont; United States").

26. Diana Pearce, "The Feminization of Poverty: Women, Work and Welfare," *Urban and Social Change Review* 11 (February 1978): 28–36. For a good contemporary review of these issues, see Kathryn H. Porter and Allen Dupree, *Poverty Trends for Families Headed by Working Single Mothers: 1993–1999*, Center on Budget and Policy Priorities (August 2001).

27. For the special challenges facing rural single mothers, see Shirley L. Porterfield, "Economic Vulnerability Among Rural Single-Mother Families," *American Journal of Agricultural Economics* 83, no. 5 (November 15, 2001): 1302.

28. Office of the Assistant Secretary for Planning and Evaluation, *Trends in the Well-Being of America's Children and Youth*.

29. U.S. Department of Health and Human Services, "The 1999 HHS Poverty Guidelines," <http://aspe/hhs.gov/poverty/99poverty.htm>, 1999. For a discussion of the "official" measurement of poverty, see Joseph Dalaker and Bernadette D. Proctor, *Poverty in the United States: 1999*, U.S. Census Bureau no. P60-210 (Washington, D.C.: U.S. Government Printing Office, 2000), Current Population Reports.

30. "Vermont; United States."

31. See the discussions in Barbara R. Bergmann, "Deciding Who's Poor," *Dollars and Sense* March/April 2000: 37; Trudi J. Renwick and Barbara R. Bergmann, "A Budget Based Definition of Poverty, with an Application to Single-Parent Families," *Journal of Human Resources* 28, no. 1 (Winter 1993): 1–24. A version of the basic needs budget is used in two Vermont studies to estimate a "livable wage" for urban and rural families of different sizes and configurations. See Kahler, *The Vermont Job Gap Study, Phase I*; Vermont State Legislature, "Livable Income Study Committee." It might be noted as well that some analysis argues that all such measures fail to examine unpaid work and are not sensitive to gender differences (Celia Briar, "In Search of Gender-Sensitive

Concepts and Measures of Poverty, Inequality, and Well-Being," *Social Policy Journal of New Zealand* 14 [July 2000]: 17–29).

32. See Kahler, *The Vermont Job Gap Study, Phase I*; Vermont State Legislature, "Livable Income Study Committee."

33. Not only do few jobs in Vermont pay a "livable wage," but it has been estimated recently that 16.9 percent of all jobs in Vermont pay less than that required to lift an individual above the poverty level; see Tom Waldron, Brandon Roberts, and Andrew Reamor with assistance from Sarah Rab and Steve Ressler, *Working Hard, Falling Short: America's Working Families and the Pursuit of Economic Security* (Annie E. Casey Foundation, 2004, Working Poor Families Project).

34. Lenore Weitzman, *The Divorce Revolution: The Unexpected Social and Economic Consequences for Women and Children in America* (New York: Free Press, 1985). For a more recent discussion of how the end of marriages affects women's labor market involvement and family income mobility, see Katharine Bradbury and Jane Katz, "Women's Labor Market Involvement and Family Income Mobility When Marriages End," *New England Economic Review* 4th Quarter 2002: 41–75.

35. Kathryn Edin and Laura Lein, *Making Ends Meet: How Single Mothers Survive Welfare and Low Wage Work* (New York: Russell Sage Foundation, 1997).

36. Timothy Grall, *Custodial Mothers and Fathers and Their Child Support: 1999*, Census Bureau no. P60-217 (Washington, D.C.: U.S. Department of Commerce; Economics and Statistics Administration, October 2002, Current Population Reports).

37. For a study that shows that Americans are now interested in working fewer hours even if it means less pay, and for a definition of this as "downshifting or personal downsizing," see Juliet B. Schor, "Economic Trend: More Willing to Give Up Pay for Additional Time Off," *Nieman Reports* 49, no. 3 (Fall 1995): 8–9.

38. See, for example, Mary Jane Taylor and Amanda Smith Barusch, "Personal, Family, and Multiple Barriers of Long-Term Welfare Recipients," *Social Work* 49, no. 2 (April 2004): 175–83.

39. See also Raymond Edward Pahl, *Divisions of Labour* (Oxford: Basil Blackwell, 1984).

40. In *Divisions of Labour*, Pahl and Wallace find a similar difference by family structure with only a tenth of households headed by women (in contrast with more than half of the married-couple households) engaging in self-provisioning at a high rate.

41. Nelson and Smith, *Working Hard and Making Do*.

42. For a discussion about how a limited set of financial resources impedes these kinds of "self-help" activities, and *also* limits participation in unpaid community exchange, see Colin C. Williams and Jan Windebank, "Self-Help and Mutual Aid in Deprived Urban Neighbourhoods: Some Lessons from Southampton," *Urban Studies* 37, no. 1 (January 2000): 127–47.

43. Polly A. Fassinger, "Meanings of Housework for Single Fathers and Mothers: Insights into Gender Inequality," in *Men, Work and Family*, ed. Jane C. Hood (Newbury Park, CA: Sage, 1993), 208.

44. Alison Morehead, "Behind the Paid Working Hours of Single Mothers: Managing Change and Constructing Support," *Family Matters* 61 (Autumn 2002): 56–61. Of course multitasking is part of everyone's demands, but competing demands are especially acute problems for single mothers; see Jerry A. Jacobs and Kathleen Gerson, *The Time Divide: Work, Family, and Gender Inequality* (Cambridge, MA: Harvard Univ. Press, 2004).

45. The literature here is almost endless. In addition to the study cited below, see as just one example of this literature the classic study by Arlie Russell Hochschild, *The Second Shift* (New York: Penguin, 1989, 2003).

46. Suzanne M. Bianchi et al., "Is Anyone Doing the Housework?: Trends in the Gender Division of Household Labor," *Social Forces* 79, no. 1 (September 2000): 191–228.

47. Nelson and Smith, *Working Hard and Making Do*.

48. Bianchi et al., "Is Anyone Doing the Housework?"

49. Nelson and Smith, *Working Hard and Making Do*.

50. For a discussion of how this program was implemented, see Margaret K. Nelson, "Declaring Welfare 'Reform' a Success: The Role of Applied Social Science," *Journal of Poverty* 63, no. 3 (2002): 1–27.

51. Stateline.org, "Maximum Monthly Cash Assistance, Family of 3 (Two Kids) (Dollars)," July 17, 2001, http://www.stateline.org/stateline/?pa=fact&sa=showFact&id=125.

52. Stateline.org, "Maximum Monthly Cash Assistance, Family of 3 (Two Kids) (Dollars)"; Jason Gray Zengerle, "Welfare as Vermont Knows It," *The American Prospect*, January-February 1997, 54-57; Eileen Elliott, Commissioner, *Annual Report to the Governor and the General Assembly on Vermont's Reach Up Program*, Department of Prevention, Assistance, Transition and Health Access (Waterbury, VT, January 31, 2002); Jon Margolis, "Vermont: The Greening of Welfare," *The American Prospect* 2000, 34.

53. Scrivener et al., *WRP: Final Report on Vermont's Welfare Restructuring Project*. (Since then, Vermont has instituted a Post-Secondary Education that is even more flexible.)

54. Scrivener et al., *WRP: Final Report on Vermont's Welfare Restructuring Project*. It should be noted that this "generosity" is in part the result of the efforts of "an ad hoc group of low-income women and supporters called the Women's Union [which] organized a highly visible campaign against" harsher measures (Elaine McCrate and Joan Smith, "When Work Doesn't Work: The Failure of Current Welfare Reform," *Gender and Society* 12, no. 1 (February 1998): 61–80).

55. "Vermont; United States."

56. On the argument that rural families turn first to family and informal charities rather than government programs, see Terry K. Adams and Greg J. Duncan, "Long-Term Poverty in Rural Areas," in *Rural Poverty in America*, ed. Cynthia M. Duncan (New York: Auburn House, 1992), 63–93; R. F. Schoeni, *Another Leak in the Bucket?: Public Transfer for Income and Private Family Support*, Population Studies Center Publication no. 92-249 (Ann Arbor: Univ. of Michigan Press, 1992); Harvey et al., "The Short-Term Impacts of Welfare Reform in Persistently Poor Rural Areas"; Maureen Kilkenny and Sonya Kostova Huffman, "Rural/Urban Welfare Program and Labor Force Participation," *American Journal of Agricultural Economics* 85, no. 4 (November 2003): 914–28.

57. Annie E. Casey Foundation, "2000 Kids Count Census Data Online."

58. Williams and Mitchell, *The Status of Early Care and Education in the States*, 11.

59. For an argument that race matters in variability of welfare provisions from state to state and that states with higher proportions of African-Americans on their rolls will have harsher policies, see Matthew C. Fellowes and Gretchen Rowe, "Politics and the New American Welfare States," *American Journal of Political Science* 48, no. 2 (April 2004): 362–73.

60. Valerie Polakow, Therese Halskov, and Per Schultz Jorgensen, *Diminished Rights: Danish Lone Mother Families in International Context* (Bristol, UK: The Policy Press, 2001). On this point see also Sanford F. Schram, *Words of Welfare: The Poverty of Social Science and the Social Science of Poverty* (Minneapolis: Univ. of Minnesota Press, 1995); Nancy Fraser and Linda Gordon, "A Genealogy of Dependency: Tracing a Keyword of the U.S. Welfare State," *Signs: Journal of Women in Culture and Society* 19, No. 2 (1994): 309-336; Gwendolyn Mink, "Aren't Poor Single Mothers Women?: Feminists, Welfare Reform, and Welfare Justice," in *Whose Welfare*, ed. Gwendolyn Mink (Ithaca, NY: Cornell Univ. Press, 1999), 171–88; Randy Albelda and Ann Withorn, *Lost Ground: Welfare Reform, Poverty, and Beyond* (Cambridge, MA: South End Press, 2002).

61. Sam Hemingway, "Dean: He's Quick with a Quote and Brutally Blunt," *Burlington Free Press*, December 15, 2002, 1B.

62. Vermont's "welfare" before restructuring was called Aid to Needy Families with Children (ANFC) rather than the more common Aid to Families with Dependent Children (AFDC). The quote below is from the description of Vermont's Welfare Restructuring

Plan as posted on the Department of Social Welfare Web site "Vermont's Welfare Restructuring Project," 1994, http://www.dsw.state.vt.us/wrp/wrpsum19.htm. In Vermont, the agency responsible for welfare has changed names frequently. When welfare restructuring was initiated, it was under the aegis of the Department of Social Welfare. That agency (under governor Dean) became the Department of Prevention, Assistance, Transition and Health. The agency is now called the Department for Children and Families (under governor James Douglas).

63. Nelson and Smith, *Working Hard and Making Do.*

64. Fraser and Gordon, "A Genealogy of Dependence", 313. Fraser and Gordon point out that dependency was also racialized as "the black, unmarried, teenaged, welfare-dependent mother."

65. Robert Bellah et al., *Habits of the Heart: Individualism and Commitment in American Life* (Berkeley: Univ. of California Press, 1985).

66. Nelson and Smith, *Working Hard and Making Do,* 163; Nancy A. Naples, "Contradictions in Agrarian Ideology: Restructuring Gender, Race, Ethnicity, and Class," *Rural Sociology* 59, no. 1 (Spring 1994): 110–35; Struthers and Bokemeier, "Myths and Realities of Raising Children and Creating Family Life in a Rural County"; Barbara Wells, "Women's Voices: Explaining Poverty and Plenty in a Rural Community," *Rural Sociology* 67, no. 2 (2002): 234–54.

67. Sharon Hays, *Flat Broke with Children: Women in the Age of Welfare Reform* (New York: Oxford Univ. Press, 2003).

68. For an overview, see Robin Toner and Robert Pear, "Bush Urges Work and Marriage Programs in Welfare Plan," *New York Times,* February 27, 2002, A18.

69. "Research: Family," 2003, http://www.heritage.org/research/family/index.cfm http://marriage.rutgers.edu.

70. Erving Goffman, *Stigma: Notes on the Management of Spoiled Identity* (New York: Simon & Schuster, 1963), 16.

71. Similarly, a colleague with whom I was discussing my research at a professional meeting said that even in the far more progressive Scandinavian country in which she lived, people believed they could ask invasive questions about the details of her personal life as a single mother: Why did you and your husband break up? Does your ex-husband pay child support? How much? What kind of a relationship do you have with him? What are the custody and visitation arrangements? Comments by her colleagues brought her personal life into a professional environment. It is interesting to note that she was *not* in a position to retaliate: Why do you stay with such a drip? How much does your husband earn? How much of it does he give you for housekeeping money? How much do your children like their father?

72. For excellent discussions of these issues, see Dorothy E. Smith, *Writing the Social: Critique, Theory, and Investigations* (Toronto: Univ. of Toronto Press, 1999), 151–71; Kari Moxnes, "What Are Families After Divorce?" *Marriage & Family Review* 28, no. 3/4 (199): 105–20.

73. See, for example, J. Ross Eshleman, *The Family,* 9th ed. (Needham Heights, MA: Allyn & Bacon, 2000). To be sure, some college textbooks offer more balance. The At Issue series, part of the Opposing Viewpoints Series of Greenhaven Press, offers a volume on single-parent families: Karen L. Swisher, ed., *Single-Parent Families* (1997), as well as other topics like smoking, domestic violence, and rape on campus. Chapters are devoted to the harmfulness of single-parent families and divorce, the contribution of single-parent families to crime and the breakdown of society, and, of course, the significance of fathers to families. The more "positive" chapters suggest that the harmful effects are "exaggerated"; that single-parent families are "unfairly" blamed for poverty and "unfairly" stigmatized"; and, in a short piece by Katha Pollitt, that "single motherhood is a legitimate choice." While this book does offer a range of opinions (though there is little *positive* to be said about single parents), until "two-parent families" are also considered "at issue,"

we might view single-parent families as being stigmatized—unfairly or not. For a good review of "paradigm shifts" in family sociology, see Susan A. Mann et al., "Paradigm Shifts in Family Sociology? Evidence from Three Decades of Family Textbooks," *Journal of Family Issues* 18, no. 3 (May 1997): 315–50.

74. The literature here is almost endless, as are the particular "problems" seen to be connected with single parenting. A good, very brief review of these issues can be found in David T. Ellwood and Christopher Jencks, "The Spread of Single-Parent Families in the United States Since 1960," (working paper no. RWP04-008, Kennedy School of Government, Harvard University (October 2002). For an interesting discussion that argues that feminists have not altered the "deficit" model of single parenting, see Joy Puls, "Poor Women and Children," *Australian Feminist Studies* 17, no. 37 (March 2002): 65–80.

75. Emma Ross, "Kids of Single Parents Face Struggles: Mental Problems, Addiction Twice as Common, Study Says," *Burlington Free Press*, January 24, 2003, A1; Associated Press, "Children in Single-Parent Homes Found at Risk of Mental Illness," *New York Times*, January 24, 2003, A21.

76. Smith, *Writing the Social*, 163.

77. Smith, *Writing the Social*, 164.

78. Rita Rhodes and Miriam McNown Johnson, "Students' Perceptions of Single Parents and Social Injustice: A Women's Issue," *Affilia* 15, no. 3 (August 2000): 434.

79. Martha Albertson Fineman, *The Neutered Mother, the Sexual Family and Other Twentieth Century Tragedies* (New York: Routledge, 1995).

80. In a poll conducted for *Time* and CNN almost two thirds of all single women between the ages of eighteen and fifty answered "yes" when asked whether they themselves would consider rearing a child on their own: see Jodie Hannaman, "Flying Solo," *Time* (August 28, 2000): 9.

81. Hannaman, "Flying Solo"; Sara Eckel, "Single Mothers," *American Demographics* 21, no. 5 (May 1999): 62–66. For a discussion of how Hollywood portrays single mothers as being "good" if they obey conservative social norms and find an appropriate man and "bad" if they remain single, see Angharad N. Valdivia, "Clueless in Hollywood: Single Moms in Contemporary Family Movies," *Journal of Communication Inquiry* 22, no. 3 (July 1998): 272–93.

82. "Vermont: The State That Says We Do," 2004, http://www.vermontcivilunion.com.

83. David Brooks, *Bobos in Paradise: The New Upper Class and How They Got There* (New York: Touchstone, 2000), 104.

84. David Moats, *Civil Wars: A Battle for Gay Marriages* (New York: Harcourt, 2004).

85. For a marvelous study that covers some of these issues, see Arlene Stein, *The Stranger Next Door: The Story of a Small Community's Battle over Sex, Faith, and Civil Rights* (Boston: Beacon Press, 2001).

86. The poor are also dispersed more: In Vermont only 5 percent of children live in neighborhoods with a high poverty rate (above 18.6%) in comparison with 23 percent of children nationwide (Annie E. Casey Foundation, "2000 Kids Count Census Data Online").

87. Kahler, *The Vermont Job Gap Study, Phase I*.

88. Theodora Ooms, Stacey Bouchet, and Mary Parke, "Beyond Marriage Licenses: Efforts in States to Strengthen Marriage and Two-Parent Families: A State-by-State Snapshot," Center for Law and Social Policy (April 2004).

Chapter 2

1. Portions of this chapter were previously published as "Single Mothers and Social Support: The Commitment to, and Retreat from, Reciprocity." *Qualitative Sociology*, 23, no. 3 (Fall 2000): 291–317. Permission granted by Kluwer Academic/Plenum Publishers.

2. Alvin W. Gouldner, "The Norm of Reciprocity: A Preliminary Statement," *American Sociological Review* 25, no. 2 (April 1960): 170; Karen V. Hansen, *Not-So-Nuclear*

Families: Class, Gender and Networks of Care (New Brunswick, NJ: Rutgers Univ. Press, 2005).

3. Hansen, *Not-So-Nuclear Families*.

4. Carol Stack, *All Our Kin: Strategies for Survival in a Black Community* (New York: Harper & Row, 1974).

5. Ibid., 14.

6. For studies of rural poverty see Virginia E. Schein, *Working from the Margins: Voices of Mothers in Poverty* (Ithaca, NY: ILR Press, 1995); Marion H. Wijnberg and Kathleen M. Reding, "Reclaiming a Stress Focus: The Hassles of Rural, Poor Single Mothers," *Families in Society* 80, no. 5 (1999): 506–15. On the issue of "romanticizing" rural relations, see Lois Levitan and Shelley Feldman, "For Love or Money: Nonmonetary Economic Arrangements Among Rural Households in Central New York," in Daniel C. Clay and Harry K. Schwarzweller, *Research in Rural Sociology and Development*, vol. 5, *Household Strategies* (Greenwich, CT: JAI Press, 1991), 149–72.

7. Dennis P. Hogan, Lingxin Hao, and William L. Parish, "Race, Kin Support and Mother Headed Families," *Social Forces* 68 (1990): 810.

8. Dennis P. Hogan, David J. Eggebeen, and Clifford C. Clogg, "The Structure of Inter-generational Exchange in American Families," *American Journal of Sociology* 98, no. 6 (May 1993): 1444–45.

9. Anne R. Roschelle, *No More Kin: Exploring Race, Class, and Gender in Family Networks* (Thousand Oaks, CA: Sage, 1997).

10. See, for example, Carol B. Stack and Linda M. Burton, "Kinscripts," *Journal of Comparative Family Studies* 24, no. 2 (Summer 1993): 157–70; Walter R. Allen, "Class Culture and Family Organization: The Effects of Class and Race on Family Structure in Urban America," *Journal of Comparative Family Studies* 10, no. 3 (1979): 301–13; H. P. McAdoo, "Black Mothers and the Extended Family Support Network," in *The Black Woman*, ed. L. Rodgers-Rose (Beverly Hills, CA: Sage, 1980), 67–87. A number of scholars compare single and married mothers with respect to three interrelated issues: the amount of support received, the composition of networks, and the content of the support that emerges from kin and family. For good, relatively recent reviews, see Roschelle, *No More Kin*; Karen Pugliesi and Scott L. Shook, "Gender, Ethnicity and Network Characteristics: Variation in Social Support Resources," *Sex Roles* 38, no. 3-4 (February 1998): 215–38; Catherine M. Lee and Linda Duxbury, "Employed Parents' Support from Partners, Employers, and Friends," *The Journal of Social Psychology* 138, no. 3 (June 1998): 303–22; Anita F. Flowers, H. G. Schneider, and H. A. Lidtke, "Social Support and Adjustment in Mothers with Young Children," *Journal of Divorce and Remarriage* 25, no. 3-4 (1996): 69–83; Candan Duran-Aydintug, "Emotional Support During Separation: Its Sources and Determinants," *Journal of Divorce and Remarriage* 29, no. 3-4 (1998): 121–41; Mary Benin and Verna M. Keith, "The Social Support of Employed African American and Anglo Mothers," *Journal of Family Issues* 16, no. 3 (May 1995): 275–97.

11. Roschelle, *No More Kin*, 193.

12. Hogan, Eggebeen, and Clogg, for example, do examine reciprocity and they report mixed results: "Nearly half of all persons receiving intergenerational support also give support"; the other half do not. Hogan, Eggebeen, and Clogg, "The Structure of Intergenerational Exchange in American Families," 1445.

13. Bronislaw Malinowski, *Crime and Custom in Savage Society* (London: Routledge & Kegan Paul, 1926); Marcel Mauss, *The Gift: The Form and Reason of Exchange in Archaic Societies* (Glencoe, IL: Free Press, 1954); Claude Lévi-Strauss, *The Elementary Structures of Kinship* (London: Eyre & Spottiswoode, 1969); George C. Homans, *Social Behavior: Its Elementary Forms* (New York: Harcourt Brace Jovanovich, 1974); Marshall Sahlins, *Stone Age Economics* (Chicago: Aldine Atherton, 1972); Gouldner, "The Norm of Reciprocity: A Preliminary Statement."

14. Sahlins, *Stone Age Economics*, 195–96.

15. See Stacey Oliker, "The Proximate Contexts of Workfare and Work: A Framework for Studying Poor Women's Economic Choices," *The Sociological Quarterly* 36, no. 2 (Spring 1995): 251–72.

16. Aafke Elisabeth Komter, "Reciprocity as a Principle of Exclusion: Gift Giving in the Netherlands," *Sociology: The Journal of the British Sociological Association* 30, no. 2 (1996): 299–316; Raymond Edward Pahl, *Divisions of Labour* (Oxford: Basil Blackwell, 1984), 25.

17. Janet Finch and Jennifer Mason, *Negotiating Family Responsibilities* (London/New York: Tavistock/Routledge, 1993), 1972.

18. For this concept of "overbenefiting," see Edwina S. Uehara, "Reciprocity Reconsidered: Gouldner's 'Moral Norm of Reciprocity' and Social Support," *Journal of Social and Personal Relationships* 12, no. 4 (1995): 483–502.

19. For Vermont see Margaret K. Nelson and Joan Smith, *Working Hard and Making Do: Surviving in Small Town America* (Berkeley: Univ. of California Press, 1999). For single mothers see Bonnie Thornton Dill, "A Better Life for Me and My Children: Low-Income Single Mothers' Struggle for Self-Sufficiency in the Rural South," *Journal of Comparative Family Studies* 29, no. 2 (Summer 1998): 419–28; Rosanna Hertz, "A Typology of Approaches to Child Care: The Centerpiece of Organizing Family Life for Dual-Earner Couples," *Journal of Family Issues* 18, no. 4 (July 1997): 355–85; Prohanta K. Nandi and Hugh Harris, "The Social World of Female-Headed Black Families: A Study of Quality of Life in a Marginalized Neighborhood," *International Journal of Comparative Sociology* 40, no. 2 (May 1999): 195–214. For the society as a whole, see Robert Bellah et al., *Habits of the Heart: Individualism and Commitment in American Life* (Berkeley: Univ. of California Press, 1985); Hertz, "A Typology of Approaches to Child Care."

20. Hertz and Ferguson have suggested that single mothers can be roughly classified with respect to their access to social and material resources to create four different groupings. And they suggest that the type of tight network of mutual support (described here for the relationships with other single mothers) is found predominantly among those who have high social resources but low material resources. Rosanna Hertz and Faith I.T. Ferguson, "Only One Pair of Hands: Ways That Single Mothers Stretch Work and Family Resources," *Community, Work and Family* 1, no. 1 (April 1998): 13–37. Given these findings, the question arises of whether in describing the different logics of reciprocity I am really describing different people. The data suggest otherwise. Both Anne Davenport and Sheila Davis, to pick the two examples with which the chapter began, are deeply bound in intense relationships with other single mothers, even though Anne Davenport relies on a combination of Aid for Needy Families with Children (ANFC) and self-employment while Sheila Davis holds down a secure, relatively well-paying position. Moreover, both of these women also rely on other people with whom they use quite different logics of reciprocity.

21. Stack, *All Our Kin.*

22. Sahlins, *Stone Age Economics.*

23. As I show below, while women include others within their networks of balanced reciprocity, the members of tight friendship circles are quite homogenous on a number of different levels. On these issues, see Susan McRae, "Lone Mothers and European Welfare Regimes" (Book Review), *The British Journal of Sociology* 49, no. 4 (December 1998): 675; J. Jill Suitor, Karl Pillemer, and Shirley Keeton, "When Experience Counts: The Effects of Experiential and Structural Similarity on Patterns of Support and Interpersonal Stress," *Social Forces* 73, no. 4 (June 1995): 1573–89.

24. For an interesting variation on this, see Karen V. Hansen, "The Asking Rules of Reciprocity: Negotiating Need and Obligation in Networks of Care for Children," *Qualitative Sociology* 27, no. 4 (2004): 421-437.

25. Micaela di Leonardo, "The Female World of Cards and Holidays: Women, Families and the Work of Kinship," *Signs* 12, no. 3 (1987): 440–53.

26. Marjorie DeVault, *Feeding the Family: The Social Organization of Caring as Gendered Work* (Chicago: Univ. of Chicago Press, 1991).

27. Both theory and research suggest that family has a special place in relationships of reciprocity, and that the normative obligations of kinship help sustain generalized reciprocity over long periods of time. The question might well be raised of whether the women in this study distinguish between family and friends in their strategic explanations and believe themselves less obligated to make returns to the former. The answer is complex. On the one hand, assumed family obligation clearly is a factor insofar as respondents appear to find it easier to come up with a strategic explanation for making returns to family members. On the other hand, the respondents did require that explanation of themselves—suggesting that the normative obligation of family is not in and of itself a sufficient basis for receiving unreciprocated assistance—and they could satisfy themselves with the same kind of explanations in their relationships with those bound neither by fictive nor factual kinship.

28. I am indebted to an anonymous reviewer for *Qualitative Sociology* (where the original version of this chapter was first published for this term [see note 1]). After I had used it, I ran across Uehara's phrase *strategic interpretation,* which is used quite similarly (Uehara, "Reciprocity Reconsidered"). See also the notion of "waived" reciprocity in Anne Neufeld and Margaret J. Harrison, "Reciprocity and Social Support in Caregivers' Relationships: Variations and Consequences," *Qualitative Health Research* 5, no. 3 (1995): 348–65.

29. To the degree that this undermining occurs in relationships with "real" family members, it highlights the fact that the inequalities that so commonly exist in marriage can be found, as well, in the cross-generational and sibling relationships of which individuals are a part.

30. This term comes from Arlie Russell Hochschild, *The Second Shift* reissue edition (New York: Penguin, 2003).

31. Arlie Russell Hochschild, *The Managed Heart: The Commercialization of Human Feeling* (Berkeley: Univ. of California Press, 1983).

32. Judith Rollins, *Between Women: Domestics and Their Employers* (Philadelphia: Temple Univ. Press, 1985); Mary Romero, *Maid in the U.S.A.* (New York: Routledge, 1992); Pierrette Hondagneu-Sotelo and Ernestine Avila, "'I'm Here, But I'm There': The Meanings of Latina Transnational Motherhood," *Gender and Society* 11, no. 5 (October 1997): 548–71.

33. Margaret K. Nelson, *Negotiating Care: The Experience of Family Day Care Providers* (Philadelphia: Temple Univ. Press, 1990), 86.

34. Ann Swidler, *Talk of Love: How Culture Matters* (Chicago: Univ. of Chicago Press, 2001).

35. Stack, *All Our Kin.*

36. Kathryn Edin and Laura Lein, *Making Ends Meet: How Single Mothers Survive Welfare and Low-Wage Work* (New York: Russell Sage Foundation, 1997), 209.

Chapter 3

1. Portions of chapter 3 were previously published as "The Challenge of Self-Sufficiency: Women on Welfare Redefining Independence," *Journal of Contemporary Ethnography* 31, no. 5 (October 2002): 582–615. Permission granted by Sage Publications.

2. William M. Epstein, *Welfare in America: How Social Science Fails the Poor* (Madison: Univ. of Wisconsin Press, 1997), 41.

3. Charles Murray, *Losing Ground: American Social Policy 1950–1980* (New York: Basic Books, 1984). As commentators have noticed, liberals did little to undercut the conflation of poverty and dependence on welfare that asserts that dependence itself is the "principal problem of the welfare system": see Ann R. Tickamyer et al., "Voices of Welfare Reform:

Bureaucratic Rationality Versus the Perceptions of Welfare Participants," *Affilia* 15, no. 2 (Summer 2000): 173–92. Many feminists even viewed dependence as a problem for welfare recipients insofar as they became subject to control by the state—the public husband—as a substitution for control by the family—the private husband: see Mimi Abramovitz, *Regulating the Lives of Women: Social Welfare Policy from Colonial Times to the Present* (Boston: South End Press, 1988); Carol Brown, "Mothers, Fathers and Children: From Private to Public Patriarchy," in *Women and Revolution*, ed. Lydia Sargent (Boston: South End Press, 1981), 239–67; Nancy Fraser, "Struggle over Needs: Outline of a Socialist–Feminist Critical Theory of Late-Capitalist Political Culture," in *Women, the State and Welfare*, ed. Linda Gordon (Madison: Univ. of Wisconsin Press, 1990), 199–225. However, as Tickamyer et al. note, there is also a critique in the feminist literature that "has contested the dominant framework that juxtaposes the norm of independence against the deviance of dependence.... This work has proposed a model that starts from an assumption of universal vulnerability, rather than autonomy, which normalizes interdependence" (Tickamyer et al., "Voices of Welfare Reform," 175).

4. For an oft-cited example, see vice president Dan Quayle's casual comment about Murphy Brown and the 1993 *Atlantic Monthly* article that asserted that Dan Quayle was "right": Barbara Defoe Whitehead, "Dan Quayle Was Right," *Atlantic Monthly* 271, no. 4 (April 1993, 47–53). For comments, see Judith Stacey, "The New Family Values Crusaders: Dan Quayle's Revenge," *The Nation* 259, no. 4 (July 25, 1994): 119–22.

5. The striking effectiveness of this political rhetoric rested in part on its capacity to draw on and reinforce racism. The American public largely believes that most welfare recipients are African-Americans and it draws on "the centuries-old stereotype of blacks as lazy": see Martin Gilens, *Why Americans Hate Welfare: Race, Media, and the Politics of Antipoverty Policy* (Chicago: Univ. of Chicago Press, 1999), 3. On this point see also Kenneth J. Neubeck and Noel A. Cazenave, *Welfare Racism: Playing the Race Card Against America's Poor* (New York: Routledge, 2001). Such notions extend to *all* welfare recipients, who are viewed as looking for a free ride, thereby not only violating social mandates to be independent and self-sufficient but relying on resources provided (through taxes) by those who have chosen the route of hard work. Conversely, the benefits that accompany good jobs (e.g., health insurance underwritten by employers) and high incomes (e.g., tax deductions for the interest on mortgages) are cast as personal achievements and as rights rather than forms of dependence. Independence—and dependence—it seems, are in the eye of the beholder. And middle-class beholders often define the latter as reliance on means-tested programs while preserving the accolade of independence for their own private and public practices of claiming necessary assistance. For an excellent discussion of this point, see Stephanie Coontz, *The Way We Never Were: American Families and the Nostalgia Trap* (New York: Basic Books, 1992).

6. Scott Briar, "Welfare from Below: Recipients' View of the Public Welfare System," in "Symposium: Law of the Poor," ed. Jacobus ten Broek, special issue, *California Law Review* 54 (1966): 37–388.

7. Harold R. Kerbo, "The Stigma of Welfare and a Passive Poor," *Sociology and Social Research* 60, no. 2 (1976): 173–87.

8. Nancy Goodban, "The Psychological Impact of Being on Welfare," *Social Service Review* 59, no. 3 (1985): 403–22.

9. Liane V. Davis and Jan L. Hagan, "Stereotypes and Stigma: What's Changed for Welfare Mothers," *Affilia* 11, no. 3 (Fall 1996): 334.

10. Karen Seccombe, Delores James, and Kimberly Battle Walters, "'They Think You Ain't Much of Nothing': The Social Construction of the Welfare Mother," *Journal of Marriage and the Family* 60, no. 4 (November 1998): 849–65.

11. Tickamyer et al., "Voices of Welfare Reform," 4. For a fuller discussion of the manner in which members of other stigmatized groups rely on both distancing and differentiation, see Nelson, "The Challenge of Self-Sufficiency."

12. John Michael Hall, Commissioner, "Annual Report to the Governor and the General Assembly on Vermont's Reach Up Program," Department of Prevention, Assistance, Transition, and Health Access (Waterbury, VT, January 31, 2004), 6. Although the number of families relying on welfare has declined substantially in Vermont (as it has elsewhere) from 10,006 families in 1994 to but 4,987 families in 2003, the vast majority continue to be headed by single mothers; ibid., 13.

13. Annie E. Casey Foundation, "2000 Kids Count Census Data Online," 2004, http://www.aecf.org/cgi-bin/kc.cgi?action=profile&area=Vermont.

14. See the discussion and endnotes 52 and 53 in the Introduction.

15. Prue Rains, Linda Davies, and Margaret McKinnon, "Taking Responsibility: An Insider View of Teen Motherhood," *Families in Society* 79, no. 3 (May-June 1998): 308–19.

16. Margaret K. Nelson and Joan Smith, *Working Hard and Making Do: Surviving in Small Town America* (Berkeley: Univ. of California Press, 1999).

17. We might think of the dramatic vision of self-sufficiency represented in the children's books written by Laura Ingalls Wilder, such as *Little House in the Big Woods* (New York: Harper Trophy, 1953).

18. For historical studies of these issues, see Linda Gordon, *Pitied but Not Entitled: Single Mothers and the History of Welfare, 1890–1935* (Cambridge, MA: Harvard Univ. Press, 1994); Michael B. Katz, *In the Shadow of the Poorhouse: A Social History of Welfare in America* (1986; repr., New York: Basic Books, 1996).

19. Several of these women were active in the Women's Union in Burlington, which was actively opposing the new welfare rules. On this issue, the stance of the women who were politically engaged was no different from that of women who were not involved in political resistance. For a discussion of this activism, see Elaine McCrate and Joan Smith, "When Work Doesn't Work: The Failure of Current Welfare Reform," *Gender & Society* 12, no. 1 (February 1998): 61–80.

20. See note 2 above.

21. Recall that Sarah Stanley *did* make claims to entitlement that rested on the needs of her children (see Introduction). Sarah, however, had not been involved with the administration of welfare in Vermont. Had she been, she too might have learned to align her claims within the confines of the institutionalized discourse.

22. A Manpower Demonstration Research Corporation report makes a similar point about clients in Florida and Connecticut: see Amy Brown, Dan Bloom, and David Butler, *The View from the Field: As Time Limits Approach, Welfare Recipients and Staff Talk About Their Attitudes and Expectations* (New York: Manpower Demonstration Research Corporation, October 1997):

> There is also some evidence that time limits may keep some recipients on welfare longer. In the Florida and Connecticut studies, small numbers of program and control group members were surveyed by telephone about three months after their random assignment date and asked how long they expected to remain on welfare. Many program group members gave an answer that corresponded roughly to the length of their time limit, while control group members were more likely to predict a shorter stay. In other words, it appeared that some clients had adopted the time limit as their personal schedule for leaving welfare, rather than trying to leave earlier. This may be because clients wanted to take advantage of training opportunities or earned income disregards and, as discussed above, did not believe they would need welfare again in the future.

23. For the specific report discussed below, see Dan Bloom et al., *WRP: Implementation and Early Impacts of Vermont's Welfare Restructuring Project* (New York: Manpower Demonstration Research Corporation, October 1998). Vermont's welfare has been studied extensively by MDRC and the reports are available on its Web site (http://www.mdrc.org).

24. Ibid., 56.
25. Ibid., 33, 60. A difference between the "eligibility specialists" and the "Reach Up case managers" is perceived by the respondents who believe the latter are more attentive to, and supportive of, their individual cases. On this issue see also Steven G. Anderson, "Welfare Recipient Views About Caseworker Performance: Lessons for Developing TANF Case Management Practices," *Families in Society: The Journal of Contemporary Human Services* 82, no. 2 (March 2001): 165–74; Yeheskel Hasenfeld, "Social Service and Welfare-to-Work: Prospects for the Social Work Profession," *Administration in Social Work* 23, no. 3–4 (2000): 185–99.
26. http://www.path.state.vt.us/wrp/tanf_stp.htm.
27. This surveillance is associated with increased "work" of maintaining benefits. Although the welfare offices in Vermont are more conveniently located (and more efficiently run) than are those in urban areas, women still have to find time out of their busy lives to make appointments and complete the paperwork required to keep their benefits current: see Lynnell Hancock, *Hands to Work: The Stories of Three Families Racing the Welfare Clock* (New York: William Morrow, 2002); Sharon Hays, *Flat Broke with Children: Women in the Age of Welfare Reform* (New York: Oxford Univ. Press, 2003). Not surprisingly, given these demands, some women cease drawing benefits before their "official" location on a transition calculus requires them to do so. Other means-tested programs entail similar tedious paperwork (although somewhat less surveillance). The cost of *not* making the effort to maintain engagement in these programs, however, can be considerable, though individuals close to a benefit cliff might be willing to risk those costs.
28. Sanford F. Schram, *After Welfare: The Culture of Postindustrial Social Policy* (New York: NYU Press, 2000), 29. See also Sanford F. Schram, *Words of Welfare: The Poverty of Social Science and the Social Science of Poverty* (Minneapolis: Univ. of Minnesota Press, 1995); Fraser, "Struggle over Needs."
29. Hays, *Flat Broke with Children*.
30. Ibid., 48–49.
31. Ibid., 65.
32. Vermont is one of the few states that actually allow college attendance instead of employment while a person is receiving welfare. On the importance of education, see Ellen K. Scott, Andrew S. London, and Kathryn Edin, "Looking to the Future: Welfare-Reliant Women Talk About Their Job Aspirations in the Context of Welfare Reform," *Journal of Social Issues* 56, no. 4 (Winter 2000): 727–46.
33. Hays, *Flat Broke with Children*, 90.
34. Julie says "master's" here although she probably means a bachelor's degree. But the reference to a master's degree is in keeping with the import of what she is saying, which is that she would like to see the state be even more expansive than it currently is.
35. Kathryn Edin and Laura Lein, *Making Ends Meet: How Single Mothers Survive Welfare and Low-Wage Work* (New York: Russell Sage Foundation, 1997).
36. Ibid.
37. Sandra L. Hofferth et al., "Achievement and Behavior Among Children of Welfare Recipients, Welfare Leavers, and Low-Income Single Mothers," *Journal of Social Issues* 56, no. 4 (Winter 2000): 747–74.
38. Murray, *Losing Ground*; Lawrence M. Mead, *New Politics of Poverty: The Nonworking Poor in America* (New York: Basic Books, 1992).
39. Hays, *Flat Broke with Children*, 90–91.
40. Assessing the consequences of welfare "reform" is a major business these days. Up-to-date information can be found on the sites of the following organizations: the Urban Institute (http://www.urban.org), Institute for Women's Policy Research (http://www.IWPR.org); Manpower Demonstration Research Corporation (http://www.MDRC.org); Office of the Assistant Secretary for Planning and Evaluation, Health and Human Services (http://www.aspe.hhs.gov); the Welfare Information Network of the Finance

Project (http://www.financeprojectinfor.org); the Center for Law and Social Policy (http://www.clasp.org); and the Center on Budget and Policy Priorities (http://www.cbpp.org).

41. While the respondents in this study who had recently been on welfare, had higher incomes than those who were currently on welfare, on average their incomes were lower than those who had not been on welfare at all.

Chapter 4

1. For examples among wealthier single mothers of a pattern of hiring caregivers, see Melissa Ludtke, *On Our Own: Unmarried Motherhood in America* (Berkeley: Univ. of California Press, 1999); Karen V. Hansen, *Not-So-Nuclear Families: Class, Gender and Networks of Care* (New Brunswick, NJ: Rutgers Univ. Press, 2005). For a discussion of outsourcing among families of different social classes, see Michael Bittman, "Parenthood Without Penalty: Time Use and Public Policy in Australia and Finland," *Feminist Economics* 5, no. 3 (1999): 27–42.

2. Federerman et al. report that 67.5 percent of single-parent poor families have a washing machine in contrast with 92.7 percent of other poor families and 92.7 percent of non-poor families; for a clothes dryer the figures are 43.9 percent (among poor families), 40.2 percent (among single- parent poor families), and 87.3 percent (among nonpoor); see Maya Federerman et al., "What Does It Mean to Be Poor in America?" *Monthly Labor Review* 119, no. 5 (May 1996): 3–17.

3. For reviews of these shifts, see Sharon Hays, *The Cultural Contradictions of Motherhood* (New Haven, CT: Yale Univ. Press, 1996); Ann Hulbert, *Raising America: Experts, Parents and a Century of Advice About Children* (New York: Alfred Knopf, 2003).

4. Hays, *The Cultural Contradictions of Motherhood*, 86.

5. Ibid., 8; A. Viviana Zelizer, *Pricing the Priceless Child: The Changing Social Value of Children* (New York: Basic Books, 1985). Lareau's groundbreaking ethnographic study *Unequal Childhoods* highlights the fact that "how parents *enacted* their visions of what it meant to be a good parent" differ radically by social class. Even so, Lareau suggests that when she looked at attitudes—as did Hays and as I do here—she "saw fewer differences; for example, all exhibited the desire to be a good mother and to have their children grow and thrive." *Unequal Childhoods: Class, Race, and Family Life* (Berkeley: Univ. of California Press, 2003), 290 n. 5.

6. Hays, *The Cultural Contradictions of Motherhood*.

7. For a similar point see Anita Ilta Garey, *Weaving Work and Motherhood* (Philadelphia: Temple Univ. Press, 1999).

8. Allison Pugh, "Windfall Child Rearing: Low-Income Care and Consumption," Department of Sociology, University of California, Berkeley, January 2004.

9. Lareau, *Unequal Childhoods*; Zelizer, *Pricing the Priceless Child*.

10. Lareau, *Unequal Childhoods*.

11. For information on how this model is adopted by single fathers, see Polly A. Fassinger, "Meanings of Housework for Single Fathers and Mothers: Insights into Gender Inequality," in *Men, Work and Family*, ed. Jane C. Hood (Newbury Park, CA: Sage, 1993), 195–216.

12. On this issue of difference, see Stacey R. Bloomer, Theresa Ann Sipe, and Danielle E. Ruedt, "Child Support Payment and Child Visitation: Perspectives from Nonresident Fathers and Resident Mothers," *Journal of Sociology & Social Welfare* 29, no. 2 (June 2002): 77–91.

13. Sara McLanahan and Gary D. Sandefur, *Growing up with a Single Parent: What Hurts, What Helps* (Cambridge, MA: Harvard Univ. Press, 1994).

14. I include here women who considered the fathers of their children so unreliable that they never lived with those men or refused to name the fathers of their children.

15. Sara Ruddick, "Maternal Thinking," *Rethinking the Family: Some Feminist* Questions, ed. Barrie Thorne, with Marilyn Yalom (New York: Longman, 1982), 76–94.

16. Although the focus here is on comparisons with fathers, it is also the case that some of these women had to argue with their own parents about the reasonableness of going through with a pregnancy. In discussing the issue of abortion, I do not mean to imply anything about attitudes toward abortion among the women in this study. Several women said that they had earlier had abortions. Even so, their focus in the present context is on the pregnancies they have chosen to carry to term and how that demonstrates a willingness to "protect" a child.

17. A widely documented dynamic in violent relationships is the "honeymoon period" that follows a beating: Neil Jacobson and John Gottman, *When Men Batter Women: New Insights into Ending Abusive Relationships* (New York: Simon & Schuster, 1998); Julia T. Wood, "'That Wasn't the Real Him': Women's Dissociation of Violence from the Men Who Enact It," *Communication Quarterly* 47, no. 3 (Summer 1999): S1-S7. For evidence that formerly battered women experience increased closeness with their family of origin and support from friends and relatives, and believe that they have improved in their parental capabilities following their divorce from an abusing partner, see Dorit Eldar-Avidan and Muhammad M. Haj-Yahia, "The Experience of Formerly Battered Women with Divorce: A Qualitative Descriptive Study," *Journal of Divorce and Remarriage* 32, no. 3-4 (2000): 19–40.

18. The term *hard living*, used initially by Joseph Howell, is useful as a description of a predominant reason for divorce and separation among this sample of single mothers: Joseph T Howell, *Hard Living on Clay Street: Portraits of Blue Collar Families* (Garden City, NY: Anchor Press, 1973). For an excellent discussion of the role of "hard living" in divorce, see Demie Kurz, *For Richer, for Poorer: Mothers Confront Divorce* (New York and London: Routledge, 1995).

19. See, for example, E. Mavis Hetherington, "Marriage and Divorce American Style: A Destructive Marriage Is Not a Happy Family," *The American Prospect* 13, no. 7 (April 8, 2002): 62–63.

20. Judith Stacey, *Brave New Families: Stories of Domestic Upheaval in Late-Twentieth-Century America* (New York: Basic Books, 1990).

21. Single mothers negotiate different issues when they share a residence with other single mothers to whom they are not necessarily related by bonds of kinship. A series of articles and Web sites describe coresidential arrangements as only offering benefits. As one example, see Jennifer Wolcott, "Single Moms Find Roommates," *Christian Science Monitor*, March 12, 2003, 11. The single mothers in this study who had opted for this arrangement gave widely varying accounts.

22. Indeed, for one of the major kinds of support, offering a home to an adult child, children's marital status is the strongest predictor of coresidence: William S. Aquilino, "The Likelihood of Parent–Adult Child Coresidence: Effects of Family Structure and Parental Characteristics," *Journal of Marriage and the Family* 52 (1990): 405. See also Lynn White and Debra Peterson, "The Retreat from Marriage: Its Effect on Unmarried Children's Exchange with Parents," *Journal of Marriage and the Family* 57 (May 1995): 428–34. In 1997, 2.5 percent of all children lived in a home with a grandparent and a single mother: see Ken Bryson and Lynne M. Casper, "Coresident Grandparents and Grandchildren," *Current Population Reports: Special Studies* P213-198 (May 1999).

23. June Lapidus, "All the Lesbian Mothers Are Coupled, All the Single Mothers Are Straight, and All of Us Are Tired: Reflections on Being a Single Lesbian Mom," *Feminist Economics* (July 2004): 227–236.

24. On relationships between parents and grandparents, see Jeanne L. Thomas, "The Grandparent Role: A Double Bind," *International Journal of Aging and Human Development* 31, no. 3 (October 1990): 169–77.

25. In *All Our Kin*, Carol Stack describes a pattern of shared child rearing where other adults are given the "right" and privilege to become disciplinarians: see *All Our Kin: Strategies for Survival in a Black Community* (New York: Harper & Row, 1974). This strategy was not found among the single mothers I interviewed. For further discussions of variation in the way mothering has been constructed among different groups see Evelyn Nakano Glenn, "Social Constructions of Mothering: A Thematic Overview," in *Mothering: Ideology, Experience, and Agency*, ed. Evelyn Nakano Glenn, Grace Chang, and Linda Rennie Forcey (New York: Routledge, 1994), 1–32. Research suggests that cohabitation with a new partner has relatively little influence on most aspects of mothering, with the exception that women reduce the time they spend with their own children and become less harsh disciplinarians: see Elizabeth Thomson et al., "Remarriage, Cohabitation, and Changes in Mothering Behavior," NSFH Working Paper No, 80, A National Survey of Families and Households (Center for Demography and Ecology, University of Wisconsin, Madison, May 1998).
26. Lareau, *Unequal Childhoods*.
27. Karen Hansen argues that a concern about providing a male role model was more a working-class concern than it was a middle-class one among those she interviewed: see "Men in Networks of Care for Children" (paper presented at the Carework, Inequality and Advocacy Conference at the University of California, Irvine, August 17, 2001). I did not find a similar difference based in social class among the respondents in this study.
28. Arlie Russell Hochschild, *The Second Shift* (New York: Penguin, 2003), 241.
29. Stacey Oliker, "Challenges for Studying Care After AFDC," *Qualitative Sociology* 23, no. 4 (2000): 293.
30. Jerry A. Jacobs and Kathleen Gerson, *The Time Divide: Work, Family, and Gender Inequality* (Cambridge, MA: Harvard Univ. Press, 2004). Goldscheider's comments were made at the Eastern Sociological Society's annual meetings in New York City, March 2004.
31. Acock and Demo report not only that children under the age of nineteen do considerably more work in families of divorce and in continuously single families than they do in families of a first marriage, but that they continue to do more work in stepfamily situations than they do in first-married situations: see Alan C. Acock and David H Demo, *Family Diversity and Well-Being* (Thousand Oaks, CA: Sage, 1994), 82.

Chapter 5

1. Portions of chapter 5 were previously published as "Reciprocity and Romance," *Qualitative Sociology* 27, no. 4 (Winter 2004). Permission granted by Kluwer Academic/Plenum Publishers.
2. On the issue of how and why some women become single mothers, see Kathryn Edin, "What Do Low-Income Single Mothers Say About Marriage?" *Social Problems* 47, no. 1 (2000): 112–33. On the issue of relationships between single mothers and fathers of children, see Rosanna Hertz, "The Father as an Idea: A Challenge to Kinship Boundaries by Single Mothers," *Symbolic Interaction* 25, no. 1 (2002): 1–31; Elaine Bell Kaplan, *Not Our Kind of Girl: Unraveling the Myths of Black Teenage Motherhood* (Berkeley: Univ. of California Press, 1997); Melissa Ludtke, *On Our Own: Unmarried Motherhood in America* (Berkeley: Univ. of California Press, 1999). Increasingly there is also scholarship about men's attitudes toward the children they have fathered outside of marriage: see, for example, Sara McLanahan et al., *The Fragile Families and Child Wellbeing Study Baseline Report*, Princeton, NJ: Center for Research on Child Wellbeing, Princeton Univ., 2001); Maureen R. Waller, *My Baby's Father: Unmarried Parents and Paternal Responsibility* (Ithaca, NY: Cornell Univ. Press, 2002).
3. Sharon Hays, *Flat Broke with Children: Women in the Age of Welfare Reform* (New York:

Oxford Univ. Press, 2003); Robert Pear and David D. Kirkpatrick, "Bush Plans $1.5 Billion Drive for Promotion of Marriage," *New York Times*, January 14, 2004, A1.

4. For additional reviews of these issues, see the special issue of *The American Prospect* 12, no. 7 (April 2002). See also Scott Coltrane, "Marketing the Marriage 'Solution': Misplaced Simplicity in the Politics of Fatherhood," *Sociological Perspectives* 44, no. 4 (2001): 287–418; Robert Lerman, "Should Government Promote Healthy Marriages?" (working Paper no. 5, Short Takes on Welfare Policy, Urban Institute, Washington, DC, 2002); Hedieh Rahmanou and Amy LeMar, "Marriage and Poverty: An Annotated Bibliography," (IWPR Publication #B239, Assessing the New Federalism, Institute for Women's Policy Research, Washington, DC, April 16, 2002).

5. Daniel T. Lichter, Christie D. Batson, and J. Brian Brown, "Welfare Reform and Marriage Promotion: The Marital Expectations and Desires of Single and Cohabiting Mothers," *Social Service Review* 78, no. 1 (March 2004): 2.

   Many will achieve this goal of marriage: Although women who have given birth outside of marriage are slightly less likely than those who have not to be married by the age of forty, the majority of them ultimately do marry: see Deborah Roempke Graefe and Daniel T. Lichter, "Marriage Among Unwed Mothers: Whites, Blacks and Hispanics Compared," *Perspectives on Sexual and Reproductive Health* 34, no. 6 (November-December 2002): 286–93. Although divorced women are somewhat less likely than divorced men to remarry, the vast majority of them do so: see Elizabeth Thomson et al., "Remarriage, Cohabitation, and Changes in Mothering Behavior" (NSFH Working Paper no. 80, A National Survey of Families and Households, Center for Demography and Ecology, University of Wisconsin, Madison, May 1998).

6. Kathryn Edin and Laura Lein, *Making Ends Meet: How Single Mothers Survive Welfare and Low-Wage Work* (New York: Russell Sage Foundation, 1997).

7. Ibid., 155.

8. Ibid., 158.

9. Ibid., 157.

10. Karen Seccombe, *"So You Think I Drive a Cadillac?": Welfare Recipients' Perspectives on the System and Its Reform* (Needham Heights, MA: Allyn & Bacon, 1999).

11. Some of the women interviewed also implied that when sex was cheap to them, the exploitation could go in the opposite direction, and they could get significant payback at relatively little cost.

12. Suzanna Rose, "Heterosexism and the Study of Women's Romantic and Friend Relationships," *Journal of Social Issues* 56, no. 2 (Summer 2000): 315–28.

13. Francesca Cancian, *Love in America: Gender and Self-Development* (New York: Cambridge Univ. Press, 1987). See also discussions in Michael S. Kimmel, *The Gendered Society* (New York: Oxford Univ. Press, 2000), 216–20; Karla B. Hackstaff, *Marriage in a Culture of Divorce* (Philadelphia: Temple Univ. Press, 1999), 52–53.

14. Karen V. Hansen, "Staging Reciprocity and Mobilizing Networks in Working Families" (working paper, Department of Sociology, Brandeis University, Waltham, MA, 2002), 31.

15. Edwina S. Uehara, "Reciprocity Reconsidered: Gouldner's 'Moral Norm of Reciprocity' and Social Support," *Journal of Social and Personal Relationships* 12, no. 4 (1995): 483–502.

16. In chapter 2 I argued that in relationships with family members, single mothers also established realms in which there was balance as well as realms within which imbalance occurred. I also pointed out that the imbalance was repaid with such actions as those entailed in gratitude and deference. In describing relationships with men, I am making a similar point about the complexity of assessing balance. At the same time, I am also making a *different* point here. In the former set of relationships (with those who were more fortunate than they), single mothers often repaid an imbalance, where the flow of

material goods pointed toward them, with "immaterial" actions. In the set of relationships under consideration here, the immaterial aspects of the relationship are balanced while the material imbalance is explained away.

17. Seccombe, *"So You Think I Drive a Cadillac?"* 138.
18. I am grateful to Naomi Gerstel (personal communication) for this phrase and these insights.
19. Cancian argues that since the nineteenth century, prevailing notions of love have excluded qualities associated with masculinity while focusing on "feminine" qualities. She argues as well that a new standard is needed that measures more fully male contributions to relationships; see Cancian, *Love in America.*, 88-90.
20. I am grateful to Robert Zussman (personal communication) for this interpretation.
21. Eve Illouz, *Consuming the Romantic Utopia: Love and the Cultural Contradictions of Capitalism* (Berkeley: Univ. of California Press, 1997), 141.
22. Anthony Giddens, *The Transformation of Intimacy: Sexuality, Love and Eroticism in Modern Societies* (Stanford, CA: Stanford Univ. Press, 1992), 58.
23. Giddens, *The Transformation of Intimacy,* 61.
24. Ann Swidler, *Talk of Love: How Culture Matters* (Chicago: Univ. of Chicago Press, 2001), 129.
25. Illouz, *Consuming the Romantic Utopia,* 206.
26. Edin, "What Do Low-Income Single Mothers Say About Marriage?"
27. Giddens, *The Transformation of Intimacy,* 62.
28. William Marsiglio, *Stepdads: Stories of Love, Hope, and Repair* (Lanham, MD: Rowman & Littlefield, 2004).
29. Oriel Sullivan, "The Division of Housework Among 'Remarried' Couples," *Journal of Family Issues* 18, no. 2 (1997): 221. For a similar point see also Masako Ishii-Kuntz and Scott Coltrane, "Remarriage, Stepparenting and Household Labor," *Journal of Family Issues* 13, no. 2 (June 1992): 215–33. Studies also suggest that premarital cohabitation gives rise to more equity in household labor. As in the remarriage studies, it is possible that women are assessing men's contributions before making the decision to "tie the knot." See Jeanne A. Batalova and Philip N. Cohen, "Premarital Cohabitation and Housework: Couples in Cross-National Perspective," *Journal of Marriage and Family* 64, no. 3 (August 2002): 743–54.
30. As Rosanna Hertz (private communication) has noted, love has traditionally been the explanation for women's unequal contributions to housework and carework. The early efforts on the part of feminists to view housework as work were often critiqued on the grounds that women were engaging in these activities out of "love" rather than obligation or subordination. In this context it is particularly ironic that the women I interview perceive men's contributions toward their households and men's involvement in their children's lives as being motivated by love and therefore not being something they have to count.
31. For a full discussion of this issue, see Karen V. Hansen, *Not-So-Nuclear Families: Class, Gender and Networks of Care* (New Brunswick, NJ: Rutgers Univ. Press, 2004).
32. Hackstaff, *Marriage in a Culture of Divorce.*
33. Naomi Gerstel, "Divorce and Kin Ties: The Importance of Gender," *Journal of Marriage and the Family* 50, no. 1 (1988): 209–19.

Conclusion

1. Once again, I want to reiterate that I do not believe that it is only single mothers who establish a "social economy." On this point, see Karen V. Hansen, *Not-So-Nuclear Families: Class, Gender and Networks of Care* (New Brunswick, NJ: Rutgers Univ. Press, 2005). However, I do believe that the social economies single mothers establish have

different contours, and arise from different circumstances, than do those established by married-couple families. Not the least of these differences emerges from the fact that single mothers bear the entire responsibility for reciprocity on their own shoulders rather than sharing it with others.

2. Annette Lareau, *Unequal Childhoods: Class, Race, and Family Life* (Berkeley: Univ. of California Press, 2003).

3. See "IWPR's Statement on Marriage Promotion and TANF Reauthorization" (working paper, Institute for Women's Policy Research, Washington, DC, December 2001).

4. Kanchana N. Ruwanpura and Jane Humphries, "Mundane Heroines: Conflict, Ethnicity, Gender, and Female Headship in Eastern Sri Lanka," *Feminist Economics* 10, no. 2 (July 2004): 173–206. Moreover, as Stacey Oliker suggests, over time these networks might well disintegrate when single mothers are unable to make any appropriate reciprocal gesture: see "Family Care After Welfare Ends," *National Forum* 80, no. 3 (Summer 2000): 27–33.

5. Throughout these chapters it has become clear that the privatized system of support on which single mothers depend in the absence of adequate state support involves considerable effort on the part of friends and family members; this is because single mothers must seek to meet both their ongoing needs and exceptional needs that arise unexpectedly (e.g., a flat tire). Although I have not stressed the attitudes and actions of those who help to sustain single parents, it is worth noting that the costs of single parenthood do extend outward from a single-mother family to her extended family, her friends, and even to the community at large. In some cases, these costs are burdensome and have significant repercussions in the lives of those who, for whatever reasons—love, obligation, or some combination of the two—engaged in such activities as housing their grown daughters and grandchildren, providing child care on a regular or irregular basis, digging into savings or retirement funds to support their daughters' families, or simply serving as a source of comfort and emotional support. Indeed, not the least of these costs is the disruption caused by involvement in the daily care of children who are not their own. In measuring the costs of single parenthood and the costs of policies urging marriage, we should not forget these other costs.

6. Polly A. Fassinger, "Meanings of Housework for Single Fathers and Mothers: Insights into Gender Inequality," in *Men, Work and Family*, ed. Jane C. Hood (Newbury Park, CA: Sage, 1993), 195–216.

7. See, for example, Paula England and Nancy Folbre, "Who Pays for Raising the Next Generation of Americans—Women, Men, or State?" *EurAmerica* 32, no. 2 (June 2002): 187–208; Harrell Rodgers, "Welfare Reform: Making Work Really Work," *The Policy Studies Journal* 31, no. 1 (2003): 89–100.

8. Although Joan Meyer's proposal would meet the needs of many working women, other women made suggestions that might work at cross-purposes with broader goals of quality care. For example, Anne Davenport criticized the state's inflexibility in only providing subsidies for child care in licensed facilities and argued that she should be able to use those subsidies to hire teenage babysitters in her home.

9. Barbara R. Bergmann, "What Policies Toward Lone Mothers Should We Aim For?" *Feminist Economics* 10, no. 2 (July 2004): 240–45.

10. D. Stanley Eitzen and Craig S. Leedham, *Solutions to Social Problems: Lessons from Other Societies* (Boston: Allyn & Bacon, 2004).

11. Kate Green, "Is Work Worth It for Lone Parents," *Feminist Economics* 10, no. 2 (July 2004): 251.

12. Randy Albelda and the Women's Committee of One Hundred, "An Immodest Proposal," *Feminist Economics* 10, no. 2 (July 2004): 246–57.

13. For programs addressed to men as fathers, see Laura Curran, "Social Work and Fathers: Child Support and Fathering Programs," *Social Work* 48, no. 2 (April 2003): 219–27.

14. I do not mean to discount either of these as being of ideological value: Clearly, if money were set aside to support single mothers (whether predominantly as caregivers or not), that would represent a significant shift in *public* valuation of that family form. In drawing the distinction I do, however, I am focusing on whether the proposals address the mothers' material needs or their (presumed to be deficient) values.

15. Susan Himmelweit, "Introduction: Lone Mothers—What Is to Be Done?" *Feminist Economics* 10, no. 2 (July 2004): 237–39.

16. On this issue, see Bergmann, "What Policies Toward Lone Mothers Should We Aim For?"

17. "Compassionate Conservatism," 2004, http. www://compassionate.conservative.com.

18. For wonderful discussions of the possibility of schools becoming more attentive to different family forms see Stephanie Coontz, *The Way We Never Were: American Families and the Nostalgia Trap* (New York: Basic Books, 1992); Diane Lewis, "Flat-Out Parents Can Help with Homework—On the Fly," *The Boston Globe*, July 1, 1997, D5. For discussions of how schools now disadvantage children from single-parent homes, see Kay Standing, "Lone Mothers and 'Parental' Involvement: A Contradiction in Policy?" *Journal of Social Policy* 28, no. 3 (July 1999): 479–495; Kay Standing, "Lone Mothers' Involvement in Their Children's Schooling: Towards a New Typology of Maternal Involvement," *Gender and Education* 11, no. 1 (March 1, 1999): 57–73; Katherine D. Newman and Margaret M. Chin, "High Stakes, Hard Choices: When School Reformers Demand That Parents Spend More Time on Homework and Welfare Reformers Demand More Time at Work, What's Supposed to Give?" *The American Prospect* 13, no. 13 (July 15, 2002): A14–18.

19. Support groups for single women would provide occasions in which women were linked with others in similar situations. These linkages, in turn, could easily give rise to the women becoming more active agents in their own lives: Kathleen M. Blee, ed., *No Middle Ground: Women and Radical Protest* (New York: NYU Press, 1998); Nancy Naples, ed., *Community Activism and Feminist Politics: Organizing Across Race, Class, and Gender* (New York: Routledge Kegan Paul, 1998); Helen Icken Safa, "Women's Social Movements in Latin America," in *Women in the Latin American Development Process*, ed. Christine E. Bose and Edna Acosta-Belen (Philadelphia: Temple Univ. Press, 1995), 227–41. Indeed, some of the women who *are* political actors became politicized through just these kinds of opportunities; see Jennifer LaBrecque, "A Process of Becoming: Understanding the Political Activism of Women on Welfare" (Senior Thesis, Department of Sociology/Anthropology, Middlebury College, Middlebury, VT, 2000).

20. I might note here that academic scholars have a role too in providing needed background. At the very least, we need more studies that compare single-parent and married-couple households, not just with respect to income levels or even housework, but with respect to the full range of activities that enable a household to get by.

21. On this point, see Lani Guinier and Gerrald Torres, *The Miner's Canary* (Cambridge, MA: Harvard Univ. Press, 2003).

22. For a proposal that takes into account the constraints of achieving self-sufficiency while taking a moral stance on what people who make up a society owe to one another, and in particular to its most vulnerable citizens, see Amy L. Wax, "Social Welfare, Human Dignity, and the Puzzle of What We Owe Each Other," *Harvard Journal of Law & Public Policy* 27, no. 1 (Fall 2003): 121–37.

BIBLIOGRAPHY

Abramovitz, Mimi. 1988. *Regulating the Lives of Women: Social Welfare Policy from Colonial Times to the Present.* Boston: South End Press.

Acock, Alan C. and David H. Demo. 1994. *Family Diversity and Well-being.* Thousand Oaks, CA: Sage.

Acs, Gregory and Sandi Nelson. 2001. *"Honey, I'm Home": Changes in Living Arrangements in the Late 1990s,* The Urban Institute. New Federalism: National Survey of America's Families Series B, No. B-38. Washington, D.C.

Adams, Terry K. and Greg J. Duncan. 1992. Long-term Poverty in Rural Areas. In *Rural poverty in America,* edited by Cynthia M. Duncan, 63–93. New York: Auburn House.

Albelda, Randy and the Women's Committee of One Hundred. 2004. An Immodest Proposal. *Feminist Economics* 10, no. 2, July: 246–57.

Albelda, Randy and Ann Withorn. 2002. *Lost Ground: Welfare Reform, Poverty, and Beyond.* Cambridge, MA: South End Press.

Allen, Walter R. 1979. Class Culture and Family Organization: The Effects of Class and Race on Family Structure in Urban America. *Journal of Comparative Family Studies* 10, no. 3: 301–13.

Anderson, Steven G. 2001. Welfare Recipient Views About Caseworker Performance: Lessons for Developing TANF Case Management Practices. *Families in Society: The Journal of Contemporary Human Services* 82, no. 2, March: 165–74.

Annie E. Casey Foundation. 2004. 2000 Kids Count Census Data Online, http://www.aecf.org/cgi-bin/kc.cgi?action=profile&area=Vermont.

Aquilino, William S. 1990. The Likelihood of Parent-adult Child Coresidence: Effects of Family Structure and Parental Characteristics. *Journal of Marriage and the Family* 52: 405–19.

Associated Press. 2003. Children in Single-Parent Homes Found at Risk of Mental Illness. *New York Times,* January 24, A21.

Auletta, Ken. 1982. *The Underclass.* New York: Random House.

Bachu, Amara. 1999. *Trends in Premarital Childbearing: 1930–1994,* U.S. Census Bureau no. P23-197. Current Population Reports.

Batalova, Jeanne A. and Philip N. Cohen. 2002. Premarital Cohabitation and Housework: Couples in Cross-national Perspective. *Journal of Marriage and Family* 64, no. 3, August: 743–54.

Bellah, Robert, Richard Madsen, William M. Sullivan, Ann Swidler, and Steven M. Tipton. 1985. *Habits of the Heart: Individualism and Commitment in American Life*. Berkeley: University of California Press.

Benin, Mary and Verna M. Keith. 1995. The Social Support of Employed African American and Anglo Mothers. *Journal of Family Issues* 16, no. 3, May: 275–97.

Bergmann, Barbara R. 2000. Deciding Who's Poor. *Dollars and Sense*, March/April: 36–38.

———. 2004. What Policies Toward Lone Mothers Should We Aim For? *Feminist Economics* 10, no. 2, July: 240–45.

Bhandari, Shailesh and Elizabeth Gilford. 2003. *Children with Health Insurance*, U.S. Census Bureau, U.S. Department of Commerce no. P60–224. Current Population Reports.

Bianchi, Suzanne M., Lynne M. Casper, and Pia K. Peltola. 1999. A Cross-National Look at Married Women's Earnings Dependency. *Gender Issues* 17, no. 3, Summer: 3–33.

Bianchi, Suzanne M., Melissa A. Milkie, Liana C. Sayer, and John P. Robinson. 2000. Is Anyone Doing the Housework?: Trends in the Gender Division of Household Labor. *Social Forces* 79, no. 1, September: 191–228.

Bittman, Michael. 1999. Parenthood Without Penalty: Time Use and Public Policy in Australia and Finland. *Feminist Economics* 5, no. 3: 27–42.

Blee, Kathleen M., ed. 1998. *No Middle Ground: Women and Radical Protest*. New York: NYU Press.

Blendon, Robert J., Drew E. Altman, John Beson, Mollyann Brodie, Matt James, and Gerry Chervinsky. 1995. The Public and the Welfare Reform Debate. *Archives of Pediatric and Adolescent Medicine* 149, no. 10: 1065–69.

Bloom, Dan, Charles Michalopoulos, Johanna Walter, and Patricia Auspos. 1998. *WRP: Implementation and Early Impacts of Vermont's Welfare Restructuring Project*, Manpower Demonstration Research Corporation. New York: Manpower Demonstration Research Corporation.

Bloomer, Stacey R., Theresa Ann Sipe, and Danielle E. Ruedt. 2002. Child Support Payment and Child Visitation: Perspectives from Nonresident Fathers and Resident Mothers. *Journal of Sociology & Social Welfare* 29, no. 2, June: 77–91.

Bradbury, Katharine and Jane Katz. 2002. Women's Labor Market Involvement and Family Income Mobility When Marriages End. *New England Economic Review*, 4th Quarter: 41–75.

Bramlett, Matthew D. and William D. Mosher. 2001. First Marriage Dissolution, Divorce, and Remarriage: United States. *Advance Data*, 323 (31 May): 1–20.

Brandon, Peter D. 2000. An Analysis of Kin-Provided Child Care in the Context of Intrafamily Exchanges: Linking the Components of Family Support for Parents Raising Young Children. *American Journal of Economics and Sociology* 59, no. 2, April: 191–216.

Brewster, Karin L. and Irene Padavic. 2002. No More Kin Care?: Change in Black Mothers' Reliance on Relatives for Child Care, 1977–94. *Gender & Society* 16, no. 4, August: 546–62.

Briar, Celia. 2000. In Search of Gender-Sensitive Concepts and Measures of Poverty, Inequality, and Well-Being. *Social Policy Journal of New Zealand* 14 (July): 17–29.

Briar, Scott. 1966. Welfare from Below: Recipients' View of the Public Welfare System. In *The Law of the Poor*, edited by Jacobus ten Broek. San Francisco: Chandler.

Brodkin, Karen. 1998 . *How Jews Became White Folks & What That Says About Race in America*. New Brunswick, NJ: Rutgers University Press.

Brooks, David. 2000. *Bobos In Paradise: The New Upper Class and How They Got There*. New York: Touchstone.

Brown, Amy, Dan Bloom, and David Butler. 1997. *The View from the Field: As Time Limits Approach, Welfare Recipients and Staff Talk About Their Attitudes and Expectations*, Manpower Demonstration Research Corporation. New York: Manpower Demonstration Research Corporation.

Brown, Carol. 1981. Mothers, Fathers and Children: From Private to Public Patriarchy. In *Women and Revolution*, edited by Lydia Sargent, 239–67. Boston: South End Press.

Brush, Lisa D. 1997. Worthy Widows, Welfare Cheats: Proper Womanhood in Expert Needs Talk About Single Mothers in the United States, 1900 to 1998. *Gender & Society* 11, no. 6, December: 720–46.

Bryson, Ken and Lynne M. Casper. 1999. Coresident Grandparents and Grandchildren. *Current Population Reports: Special Studies* P213–198 (May).

Bumpass, Larry and Hsien-Hen Lu. 2000. Trends in Cohabitation and Implications for Children's Family Contexts in the United States. *Population Studies* 54, no. 1: 29–41.

Burgess, John. 2004. Tackling Social Exclusion in Europe: The Contribution of the Social Economy (Book Review). *Labour & Industry* 14, no. 3, April: 164–66.

Cancian, Francesca. 1987. *Love in America: Gender and Self -Development*. New York: Cambridge University Press.

Cochran, Carole, Gemma D. Skillman, Richard W. Rathge, Kathy Moore, Janet Johnston, and Ann Lochner. 2002. A Rural Road: Exploring Opportunities, Networks, Services, and Supports That Affect Rural Families. *Child Welfare* 81, no. 5, September: 837–48.

Coltrane, Scott. 2001. Marketing the Marriage "Solution": Misplaced Simplicity in the Politics of Fatherhood. *Sociological Perspectives* 44, no. 4: 287–418.

Compassionate Conservatism. 2004. http://www.compassionate.conservatism.com. Accessed July 11, 2004.

Coontz, Stephanie. 1992. *The Way We Never Were: American Families and the Nostalgia Trap*. New York: Basic Books.

Curran, Laura. 2003. Social Work and Fathers: Child Support and Fathering Programs. *Social Work* 48, no. 2, April: 219–27.

Dalaker, Joseph and Bernadette D. Proctor. 2000. *Poverty in the United States: 1999*, U.S. Census Bureau no. P60–210. Washington, DC: U.S. Government Printing Office. Current Population Reports.

Davis, Liane V. and Jan L. Hagan. 1996. Stereotypes and Stigma: What's Changed for Welfare Mothers. *Affilia* 11, no. 3, Fall: 319–37.

DeNavas-Walt, Carmen, and Robert Cleveland. 2002. *Money Income in the United States: 2001*, U.S. Census Bureau. Washington, DC: U.S. Government Printing Office. Current Population Reports P60–218.

Denzin, Norman K. 1998. The New Language of Qualitative Method (book review). *Journal of Contemporary Ethnography* 27, no. 3, October: 405–15.

Deutsch, Francine M., and Susan E. Saxon. 1998. Traditional Ideologies, Nontraditional Lives. *Sex Roles* 38, no. 5/6: 331–62.

DeVault, Marjorie. 1991. *Feeding the Family: The Social Organization of Caring as Gendered Work*. Chicago: University of Chicago Press.

Di Leonardo, Micaela. 1987. The Female World of Cards and Holidays: Women, Families and the Work of Kinship. *Signs* 12, no. 3: 440–53.

Dickerson, Bette J. 1995. *African American Single Mothers: Understanding Their Lives and Families*. Thousand Oaks, CA: Sage.

Dill, Bonnie Thornton. 1998. A Better Life for Me and My Children: Low-Income Single Mothers' Struggle for Self-Sufficiency in the Rural South. *Journal of Comparative Family Studies* 29, no. 2, Summer: 419–28.

Dill, Bonnie Thornton and Bruce B. Williams. 1992. Race, Gender and Poverty in the Rural South: African American Single Mothers. In *Rural Poverty in America*, edited by Cynthia M. Duncan, 97–109. New York: Auburn House.

Dingwall, Robert. 1998. The New Language of Qualitative Method (book review). *Journal of Contemporary Ethnography* 27, no. 3, October: 399–404.

DivorceMagazine.com. 2004. U.S. Divorce Statistics, http://www.divorcemag.com/statistics/statsUS.shtml. Accessed October 19, 2004.

Donovan, Catherine. 2000. Who Needs a Father?: Negotiating Biological Fatherhood in British Lesbian Families Using Self-Insemination. *Sexualities* 3, no. 2, May: 149–64.

Dowd, Nancy E. 1997. *In Defense of Single-Parent Families*. New York: NYU Press.

Downey, Douglas B., James W. Ainsworth-Darnell, and Mikaela J. Dufur. 1998. Sex of Parent and Children's Well-Being in Single-Parent Households. *Journal of Marriage and the Family* 60, no. 4: 878–93.

Dr. Dynasaur: Health Care Insurance for Children, Teens Under 18, and Pregnant Women. 2004. http://www.dsw.state.vt.us/programs_pages/healthcare/drdynasaur.htm. Accessed October 18, 2004.

Duran-Aydintug, Candan. 1998. Emotional Support During Separation: Its Sources and Determinants. *Journal of Divorce and Remarriage* 29, no. 3-4: 121–41.

Eckel, Sara. 1999. Single Mothers. *American Demographics* 21, no. 5, May: 62-66.

Edin, Kathryn. 2000. What Do Low-Income Single Mothers Say About Marriage? *Social Problems* 47, no. 1: 112–33.

Edin, Kathryn and Laura Lein. 1997. *Making Ends Meet: How Single Mothers Survive Welfare and Low-Wage Work*. New York: Russell Sage Foundation.

Eldar-Avidan, Dorit and Muhammad M. Haj-Yahia. 2000. The Experience of Formerly Battered Women with Divorce: A Qualitative Descriptive Study. *Journal of Divorce and Remarriage* 32, no. 3-4: 19–40.

Elliott, Eileen, Commissioner. 2002. *Annual Report to the Governor and the General Assembly on Vermont's Reach Up Program*, Department of Prevention, Assistance, Transition and Health Access. Waterbury, VT.

Ellwood, David T. and Christopher Jencks. 2002. *The Spread of Single-Parent Families in the United States Since 1960*, working paper no. RWP04-008, Kennedy School of Government. Harvard University.

England, Paula and Nancy Folbre. 2002. Who Pays for Raising the Next Generation of Americans—Women, Men, or State? *EurAmerica* 32, no. 2, June: 187–208.

Epstein, William M. 1997. *Welfare in America: How Social Science Fails the Poor*. Madison: University of Wisconsin Press.

Eshleman, J. Ross. 2000. *The Family* (9th ed.). Needham Heights, MA: Allyn & Bacon.

Fassinger, Polly A. 1993. Meanings of Housework for Single Fathers and Mothers: Insights into Gender Inequality. In *Men, Work and Family*, edited by Jane C. Hood, 195–216. Newbury Park, CA: Sage.

Federman, Maya, Thesia I. Garner, Kathleen Short, W. Boman Cutter IV, John Kiely, David Levine, Duane McGough, and Marilyn McMillen. 1996. What Does It Mean to Be Poor in America? *Monthly Labor Review* 119, no. 5, May: 3–17.

Fellowes, Matthew C. and Gretchen Rowe. 2004. Politics and the New American Welfare States. *American Journal of Political Science* 48, no. 2, April: 362–73.

Fields, Jason. 2003. *Children's Living Arrangements and Characteristics: March 2002*, U.S. Census Bureau no. P20-537. Washington DC: U.S. Department of Commerce, Economics and Statistics Administration.

Fields, Jason and Lynne M. Casper. 2001. *America's Families and Living Arrangements* Department of Commerce, U.S. Census Bureau.

Finch, Janet and Jennifer Mason. 1993. *Negotiating Family Responsibilities*. London/New York: Tavistock/Routledge.

Fineman, Martha Albertson. 1995. *The Neutered Mother, the Sexual Family and Other Twentieth Century Tragedies*. New York: Routledge.

Fitzpatrick, Jacki A. and Todd R. Gomez. 1997. Still Caught in a Trap: The Continued Povertization of Women. *Affilia Journal of Women and Social Work* 12, no. 3, Fall: 318–41.

Flowers, Anita F., H. G. Schneider, and H. A. Lidtke. 1996. Social Support and Adjustment in Mothers with Young Children. *Journal of Divorce and Remarriage* 25, no. 3-4: 69–83.

Frankenberg, Ruth. 1993. *White Women, Race Matters: The Social Construction of Whiteness*. Minneapolis: University of Minnesota Press.

Fraser, Nancy. 1990. Struggle over Needs: Outline of a Socialist-feminist Critical Theory of Late-capitalist Political Culture. In *Women, the State and Welfare*, edited by Linda Gordon, 199–225. Madison: University of Wisconsin Press.

Fraser, Nancy and Linda Gordon. 1994. "A Genealogy of Dependency: Tracing a Keyword of the U.S. Welfare State. *Signs: Journal of Women in Culture and Society* 19, no. 2.: 309-36.

Gabb, Jacqui. 2001. Desirous Subjects and Parental Identities: Constructing a Radical Discourse on (Lesbian) Family Sexuality. *Sexualities* 4, no. 3: 333–52.

Garey, Anita Ilta. 1999. *Weaving Work and Motherhood*. Philadelphia: Temple University Press.

Gerstel, Naomi. 1988. Divorce and Kin Ties: The Importance of Gender. *Journal of Marriage and the Family* 50, no. 1: 209–19.

Giddens, Anthony. 1992. *The Transformation of Intimacy: Sexuality, Love and Eroticism in Modern Societies*. Stanford, CA: Stanford University Press.

Gilens, Martin. 1999. *Why Americans Hate Welfare: Race, Media, and the Politics of Antipoverty Policy*. Chicago: University of Chicago Press.

Glenn, Evelyn Nakano. 1994. Social Constructions of Mothering: A Thematic Overview. In *Mothering: Ideology, Experience, and Agency*, edited by Evelyn Nakano Glenn, Grace Chang, and Linda Rennie Forcey, 1–32. New York: Routledge.

Goffman, Erving. 1963. *Stigma: Notes on the Management of Spoiled Identity*. New York: Simon & Schuster.

Goodban, Nancy. 1985. The Psychological Impact of Being on Welfare. *Social Service Review* 59, no. 3: 403–22.

Gordon, Linda. 1994. *Pitied but Not Entitled: Single Mothers and the History of Welfare, 1890-1935*. Cambridge, MA: Harvard University Press.

Gouldner, Alvin W. 1960. The Norm of Reciprocity: A Preliminary Statement. *American Sociological Review* 25, no. 2, April: 161–78.

Graefe, Deborah Roempke and Daniel T. Lichter. 1999. Life Course Transitions of American Children: Parental Cohabitation, Marriage, and Single Motherhood. *Demography* 36, no. 2, May: 205-17.

———. 2002. Marriage Among Unwed Mothers: Whites, Blacks and Hispanics Compared. *Perspectives on Sexual and Reproductive Health* 34, no. 6, November-December: 286–93.

Grall, Timothy. 2002. *Custodial Mothers and Fathers and Their Child Support: 1999*, Census Bureau no. P60–217. Washington, DC: U.S. Department of Commerce; Economics and Statistics Administration. Current Population Reports.

Green, Kate. 2004. Is Work Worth It for Lone Parents. *Feminist Economics* 10, no. 2, July: 246–50.

Gubrium, Jaber F. and James A. Holstein. 1997. *The New Language of Qualitative Method*. New York: Oxford University Press.

———. 1998. Standing Our Middle Ground. *Journal of Contemporary Ethnography* 27, no. 3, October: 416–21.

Guinier, Lani and Gerrald Torres. 2003. *The Miner's Canary*. Cambridge, MA: Harvard University Press.

Hackstaff, Karla B. 1999. *Marriage in a Culture of Divorce*. Women in the Political Economy. Philadelphia: Temple University Press.

Hall, John Michael, Commissioner. 2004. *Annual Report to the Governor and the General Assembly on Vermont's Reach Up Program*, Department of Prevention, Assistance, Transition, and Health Access. Waterbury, VT.

Halliday, J. and J. Little. 2001. Amongst Women: Exploring the Reality of Rural Childcare. *Sociologia Ruralis* 41, no. 4, October: 423–37.

Hamer, Jennifer and Kathleen Marchioro. 2002. Becoming Custodial Dads: Exploring Parenting Among Low-Income and Working-Class African American Fathers. *Journal of Marriage and the Family* 64, no. 1, February: 116–29.

Hancock, Lynnell. 2002. *Hands to Work: The Stories of Three Families Racing the Welfare Clock.* New York: William Morrow.

Handler, Joel F. 1995. *The Poverty of Welfare Reform.* New Haven, CT: Yale University Press.

Hannaman, Jodie. 2000. Flying Solo. *Time,* August 28, 9.

Hansen, Karen V. 2001. Men in Networks of Care for Children. Paper presented at the Carework, Inequality and Advocacy Conference at the University of California, Irvine, August 17.

———. 2002. Staging Reciprocity and Mobilizing Networks in Working Families, Working Paper Series, no. 33, Center for Working Families, University of California, Berkeley, April.

———. 2004. The Asking Rules of Reciprocity: Negotiating Need and Obligation in Networks of Care for Children. *Qualitative Sociology* 27, no. 4, December: 419-37.

———. 2005. *Not-So-Nuclear Families: Class, Gender and Networks of Care.* New Brunswick, NJ: Rutgers University Press.

Harvey, Mark, Gene Summers, Kathleen Pickering, and Patricia Richards. 2002. The Short-term impacts of welfare reform in persistently poor rural areas. In *Rural dimensions of welfare reform,* edited by L. A. Whitener, B. A. Weber and G. Duncan, 375–412. Kalamazoo, MI: W. E. Upjohn Institute for Employment Research.

Hasenfeld, Yeheskel. 2000. Social Service and Welfare-to-Work: Prospects for the Social Work Profession. *Administration in Social Work* 23, no. 3-4: 185–99.

Hays, Sharon. 1996. *The Cultural Contradictions of Motherhood.* New Haven, CT: Yale University Press.

———. 2003. *Flat Broke with Children: Women in the Age of Welfare Reform.* New York: Oxford University Press.

Heath, D. Terri, ed. 1999. *Journal of Family Issues.* Special issue of *A Special Issue on Single Fathers.*

Hemingway, Sam. 2002. Dean: He's Quick with a Quote and Brutally Blunt. *Burlington Free Press,* December 15, 1B.

Hertz, Rosanna. 1991. Dual-career Couples and the American Dream: Self-sufficiency and Achievement. *Journal of Comparative Family Studies* 22, no. 2, Summer: 247–63.

———. 1997. A Typology of Approaches to Child Care: The Centerpiece of Organizing Family Life for Dual-Earner Couples. *Journal of Family Issues* 18, no. 4, July: 355–85.

———. 2002. The Father as an Idea: A Challenge to Kinship Boundaries by Single Mothers. *Symbolic Interaction* 25, no. 1: 1–31.

Hertz, Rosanna and Faith I. T. Ferguson. 1997. Kinship Strategies and Self-Sufficiency Among Single Mothers by Choice: Post Modern Family Ties. *Qualitative Sociology* 20, no. 2, Summer: 187–209.

———. 1998. Only One Pair of Hands: Ways That Single Mothers Stretch Work and Family Resources. *Community, Work and Family* 1, no. 1, April: 13–37.

Hetherington, E. Mavis. 2002. Marriage and Divorce American Style: A Destructive Marriage is Not a Happy Family. *The American Prospect* 13, no. 7, April 8: 62–63.

Hill, Lisa C. and Jeanne M. Hilton. 1999. Changes in Roles Following Divorce: Comparison of Factors Contributing to Depression in Custodial Single Mothers and Custodial Single Fathers. *Journal of Divorce and Remarriage* 31, no. 3-4, July-August: 91–114.

Hilton, Jeanne M., Stephan Desrochers, and Esther Devall, L. 2001. Comparison of Role Demands, Relationships, and Child Functioning in Single-Mother, Single-Father, and Intact Families. *Journal of Divorce and Remarriage* 35, no. 1-2, March-April: 29–56.

Himmelweit, Susan. 2004. Introduction: Lone Mothers—What Is to Be Done? *Feminist Economics* 10, no. 2, July: 237–39.

Hochschild, Arlie Russell. 1983. *The Managed Heart: The Commercialization of Human Feeling.* Berkeley: University of California Press.

———. 1989, 2003. *The Second Shift.* New York: Penguin.

Hofferth, Sandra L., Julia Smith, Bonnie C. McLoyd, and Jonathon Finkelstein. 2000. Achievement and Behavior Among Children of Welfare Recipients, Welfare Leavers, and Low-Income Single Mothers. *Journal of Social Issues* 56, no. 4, Winter: 747–74.

Hogan, Dennis P., David J. Eggebeen, and Clifford C. Clogg. 1993. The Structure of Intergenerational Exchange in American Families. *American Journal of Sociology* 98, no. 6, May: 1428–58.

Hogan, Dennis P., Lingxin Hao, and William L. Parish. 1990. Race, Kin Support and Mother Headed Families. *Social Forces* 68: 797–812.

Homans, George C. 1974. *Social Behavior: Its Elementary Forms.* New York: Harcourt Brace Jovanovich.

Hondagneu-Sotelo, Pierrette and Ernestine Avila. 1997. I'm Here, but I'm There: The Meanings of Latina Transnational Motherhood. *Gender and Society* 11, no. 5, October: 548–71.

Howell, Joseph T. 1973. *Hard Living on Clay Street: Portraits of Blue Collar Families.* Garden City, NY: Anchor Press.

Hulbert, Ann. 2003. *Raising America: Experts, Parents and a Century of Advice About Children.* New York: Alfred Knopf.

Illouz, Eve. 1997. *Consuming the Romantic Utopia: Love and the Cultural Contradictions of Capitalism.* Berkeley, CA: University of California Press.

Institute for Women's Policy Research. 2001. IWPR's Statement on Marriage Promotion and TANF Reauthorization.

Ishii-Kuntz, Masako and Scott Coltrane. 1992. Remarriage, Stepparenting and Household Labor. *Journal of Family Issues* 13, no. 2, June: 215–33.

Jackson, Aurora P., Jeanne Brooks-Gunn, Chien-Chung Huang, and Marc Glassman. 2000. Single Mothers in Low-Wage Jobs: Financial Strain, Parenting, and Preschoolers' Outcomes. *Child Development* 71, no. 5, September: 1409–23.

Jacobs, Jerry A. and Kathleen Gerson. 2004. *The Time Divide: Work, Family, and Gender Inequality.* Cambridge, MA: Harvard University Press.

Jacobson, Neil and John Gottman. 1998. *When Men Batter Women: New Insights to Ending Abusive Relationships.* New York: Simon & Schuster.Kahler, Ellen. 1997. *The Vermont Job Gap study, Phase I: Basic Needs and a Livable Wage.* Burlington, VT: Peace & Justice Center.

Kaplan, Elaine Bell. 1997. *Not Our Kind of Girl: Unraveling the Myths of Black Teenage Motherhood.* Berkeley: University of California Press.

Katz, Michael B. 1986 (1996). *In the Shadow of the Poorhouse: A Social History of Welfare in America.* New York: Basic Books.

Kerbo, Harold R. 1976. The Stigma of Welfare and a Passive Poor. *Sociology and Social Research* 60, no. 2: 173–87.

Kilkenny, Maureen and Sonya Kostova Huffman. 2003. Rural/Urban Welfare Program and Labor Force Participation. *American Journal of Agricultural Economics* 85, no. 4, November: 914–28.

Kimmel, Michael S. 2000. *The Gendered Society.* New York: Oxford University Press.

Komter, Aafke Elisabeth. 1996. Reciprocity as a Principle of Exclusion: Gift Giving in the Netherlands. *Sociology: The Journal of the British Sociological Association* 30, no. 2: 299–316.

Kurz, Demie. 1995. *For Richer, for Poorer: Mothers Confront Divorce.* New York and London: Routledge.

LaBrecque, Jennifer. 2000. A Process of Becoming: Understanding the Political Activism of Women on Welfare. Senior Thesis, Department of Sociology/Anthropology, Middlebury College.

Lapidus, June. 2004. All the Lesbian Mothers Are Coupled, All the Single Mothers Are Straight, and All of Us Are Tired: Reflections on Being a Single Lesbian Mom. *Feminist Economics*, July, 2.

Lareau, Annette. 2003. *Unequal Childhoods: Class, Race, and Family Life*. Berkeley: University of California Press.

Lee, Catherine M. and Linda Duxbury. 1998. Employed Parents' Support from Partners, Employers, and Friends. *The Journal of Social Psychology* 138, no. 3, June: 303–22.

Lee, Sunhwa. 2004. *Women's Work Supports, Job Retention, and Job Mobility: Child Care and Employer-Provided Health Insurance Help Women Stay on Jobs*, Institute for Women's Policy Research no. #B244. Washington, DC: Institute for Women's Policy Research.

Lerman, Robert. 2002. Should Government Promote Healthy Marriages? Short Takes on Welfare Policy no. 5. Washington, DC: Urban Institute.

Levi-Strauss, Claude. 1969. *The Elementary Structures of Kinship*. London: Eyre and Spottiswoode.

Levitan, Lois and Shelley Feldman. 1991. For Love or Money: Nonmonetary Economic Arrangements Among Rural Households in Central New York, in *Research in Rural Sociology and Development*, Vol. 5: *Household Strategies*, edited by Daniel C. Clay, and Harry K. Schwarzweller, 149–72. Greenwich, CT: JAI Press.

Levy, Denise and Sonya Michel. 2002. More Can Be Less: Child Care and Welfare Reform in the United States. In *Child Care Policy at the Crossroads: Gender and Welfare State Restructuring*, edited by Sonya Michel and Rianne Mahon, 239–63. New York: Routledge.

Lewin, Ellen. 1993. *Lesbian Mothers: Accounts of Gender in American Culture*. Ithaca, NY: Cornell University Press.

Lewis, Diane. 1997. Flat-out Parents Can Help with Homework — On the Fly. *The Boston Globe*, July 1, D5.

Lichter, Daniel T. 2001. *Marriage as Public Policy*, Progressive Policy Institute, http://www.ppionline.org/documents/marriage_lichter.pdf.

Lichter, Daniel T., Christie D. Batson, and J. Brian Borwn. 2004. Welfare Reform and Marriage Promotion: The Marital Expectations and Desires of Single and Cohabiting Mothers. *Social Service Review*, March: 2–25.

Lino, Mark. 1994. Income and Spending Patterns of Single-Mother Families. *Monthly Labor Review* 117, no. 5, May: 29–37.

Lovell, Vicky. 2003. 40-hour Work Proposal Significantly Raises Mothers' Employment Standard. Institute for Women's Policy Research: Research-in-Brief, 1–8. Washington, DC: Institute for Women's Policy Research.

Ludtke, Melissa. 1999. *On Our Own: Unmarried Motherhood in America*. Berkeley: University of California Press.

MacDonald, Heather and Alan H. Peters. 1996. Distance and Labor Force Participation: Implications for Urban and Rural Women. Paper presented at the Second National Conference on Women's Travel Issues.

Malinowski, Bronislaw. 1926. *Crime and Custom in Savage Society*. London: Routledge and Kegan Paul.

Mann, Susan A., Michael D. Grimes, Alice Abel Kemp, and Pamela J. Jenkins. 1997. Paradigm Shifts in Family Sociology? Evidence from Three Decades of Family Textbooks. *Journal of Family Issues* 18, no. 3, May: 315–50.

Marchevsky, Alejandra and Jeanne Theoharis. 2000. Welfare Reform, Globalization, and the Racialization of Entitlement. *American Studies* 41, no. 2-3, Summer-Fall: 235–54.

Margolis, Jon. 2000. Vermont: The Greening of Welfare. *The American Prospect*, 34.

Marital Status of Women in the Civilian Labor Force: 1900-2002. 2003. U.S. Census Bureau Census Abstract no. HS-30, http://www.census.gov/statab/hist/HS-30.pdf. Accessed October 20, 2004.

Marsiglio, William. 2004. *Stepdads: Stories of Love, Hope, and Repair*. Lanham, MD: Rowman & Littlefield.

Mason, Robin. 2003. Listening to Lone Mothers: Paid Work, Family Life, and Childcare in Canada. *Journal of Children & Poverty* 9, no. 1: 41–54.

Matthews, T. J. and Brady E. Hamilton. 2002. *Mean Age of Mother, 1970-2000*, Centers for Disease Control and Prevention. National Vital Statistics Reports 51, no. 1. Atlanta: Centers for Disease Control and Prevention.

Mauss, Marcel. 1954. *The Gift: The Form and Reason of Exchange in Archaic Societies*. Glencoe, IL: Free Press.

McAdoo, H. P. 1980. Black Mothers and the Extended Family Support Network. In *The Black Woman*, edited by L. Rodgers-Rose, 67-87. Beverly Hills, CA: SAGE.

McCrate, Elaine and Joan Smith. 1998. When Work Doesn't Work: The Failure of Current Welfare Reform. *Gender and Society* 12, no. 1, February: 61–80.

McLanahan, Sara. and Gary D. Sandefur. 1994. *Growing Up with a Single Parent: What Hurts, What Helps*. Cambridge, MA: Harvard University Press.

McLanahan, Sara, Irwin Garfinkel, Nance E. Reichman, Julien Teitler, Marica Carloson, and Christina Norland Audigier. 2001. *The Fragile Families and Child Wellbeing Study Baseline Report*, Princeton University Center for Research on Child Wellbeing. Princeton, NJ: Princeton University.

McRae, Susan. 1998. Lone Mothers and European Welfare Regimes (book review). *The British Journal of Sociology* 49, no. 4, December: 675.

Mead, Lawrence M. 1992. *New Politics of Poverty: The Nonworking Poor in America*. New York: Basic Books.

Mills, Bradford F., and Gautam Hazarika. 2003. Do Single Mothers Face Greater Constraints to Workforce Participation in Non-metropolitan Areas? *American Journal of Agricultural Economics* 85, no. 1, February: 143–61.

Mink, Gwendolyn. 1999. Aren't Poor Single Mothers Women?: Feminists, Welfare Reform, and Welfare Justice. In *Whose Welfare*, edited by Gwendolyn Mink, 171–88. Ithaca, NY: Cornell University Press.

Mishel, Lawrence, Jared Bernstein, and Heather C. Boushey. 2003. *The State of Working America 2002/2003*. Ithaca, NY: Cornell University Press.

Moats, David. 2004. *Civil Wars: A Battle for Gay Marriages*. New York: Harcourt.

Moller, Stephanie. 2002. Supporting Poor Single Mothers: Gender and Race in the U.S. Welfare State. *Gender & Society* 16, no. 4, August: 465–83.

Morehead, Alison. 2002. Behind the Paid Working Hours of Single Mothers: Managing Change and Constructing Support. *Family Matters* 61 (Autumn): 56–61.

Moxnes, Kari. 199. What are Families After Divorce? *Marriage & Family Review* 28, no. 3/4: 105–20.

Moynihan, Daniel Patrick. 1965. *The Negro Family: The Case for National Action*. Washington, DC: U.S. Government Printing Office.

Murray, Charles. 1984. *Losing Ground: American Social Policy 1950-1980*. New York: Basic Books.

Nandi, Prohanta K. and Hugh Harris. 1999. The Social World of Female-Headed Black Families: A Study of Quality of Life in a Marginalized Neighborhood. *International Journal of Comparative Sociology* 40, no. 2, May: 195–214.

Naples, Nancy, ed. 1998. *Community Activism and Feminist Politics: Organizing Across Race, Class, and Gender*. New York: Routledge Kegan Paul.

Naples, Nancy A. 1994. Contradictions in Agrarian Ideology: Restructuring Gender, Race, Ethnicity, and Class. *Rural Sociology* 59, no. 1, Spring: 110–35.

National Marriage Project. 2003. http://marriage.rutgers.edu/ Rutgers University.

Nelson, Margaret K. 1990. *Negotiating Care: The Experience of Family Day Care Providers*. Philadelphia: Temple University Press.

———. 2000. Single Mothers and Social Support: The Commitment to and Retreat from Reciprocity. *Qualitative Sociology* 23, no. 3, Fall: 291–319.

———. 2002. Declaring Welfare "Reform" A Success: The Role of Applied Social Science. *Journal of Poverty* 63, no. 3: 1–27.

———. 2002. The Challenge of Self-Sufficiency: Women on Welfare Redefining Independence. *Journal of Contemporary Ethnography* 31, no. 5, October: 582–614.

Nelson, Margaret K. and Joan Smith. 1999. *Working Hard and Making Do: Surviving in Small Town America*. Berkeley: University of California Press.

Neubeck, Kenneth J. and Noel A. Cazenave. 2001. *Welfare Racism: Playing the Race Card Against America's Poor*. New York: Routledge.

Neufeld, Anne and Margaret J. Harrison. 1995. Reciprocity and Social Support in Caregivers' Relationships: Variations and Consequences. *Qualitative Health Research* 5, no. 3: 348–65.

Newman, Katherine D. and Margaret M. Chin. 2002. High Stakes, Hard Choices: When School Reformers Demand that Parents Spend More Time on Homework and Welfare Reformers Demand More Time at Work, What's Supposed to Give? *The American Prospect* 13, no. 13, July 15: A14–18.

Oakley, Ann. 1981. Interviewing Women: A Contradiction in Terms. In *Doing Feminist Research*, edited by Helen Roberts. London: Routledge & Kegan Paul.

———. 1998. Gender, Methodology and People's Ways of Knowing: Some Problems with Feminism and the Paradigm Debate in Social Science. *Sociology: The Journal of the British Sociological Association* 32, no. 4, November: 707–31.

Oerton, Sarah and Karen Atkinson. 1999. Voices from the Valleys: Researching Lone Mothers' Talk. *Community, Work, and Family* 2, no. 3, December: 229–56.

Office of the Assistant Secretary for Planning and Evaluation, U.S. Department of Health and Human Services. 2004. Trends in the Well-Being of America's Children and Youth. http://aspe.hhs.gov/hsp/03trends/index.htm.

Oliker, Stacey. 1995. The Proximate Contexts of Workfare and Work: A Framework for Studying Poor Women's Economic Choices. *The Sociological Quarterly* 36, no. 2, Spring: 251–72.

———. 2000. Challenges for Studying Care After AFDC. *Qualitative Sociology* 23, no. 4: 453–66.

———. 2000. Family Care After Welfare Ends. *National Forum* 80, no. 3, Summer: 27–33.

Ooms, Theodora, Stacey Bouchet, and Mary Parke. 2004. Beyond Marriage Licenses: Efforts in State to Strengthen Marriage and Two-Parent Families: A State-by-State Snapshot, Center for Law and Social Policy, http://www.clasp.org/publications/beyond_marr.pdf.

Orloff, Ann. 1996. Gender in the Welfare State. In *Annual Review of Sociology*, Vol. 22, edited by John Hagan and Karen S. Cook, 51–78. Palo Alto, CA: Annual Reviews.

Pahl, Raymond Edward. 1984. *Divisions of Labour*. Oxford: Basil Blackwell.

Paulin, Geoffrey D. and Yoon G. Lee. 2002. Expenditures of Single Parents: How Does Gender Figure In? *Monthly Labor Review* 25, no. 7, July: 16–37.

Pear, Robert and David D. Kirkpatrick. 2004. Bush Plans $1.5 Billion Drive for Promotion of Marriage. *New York Times*, January 14, A1.

Pearce, Diana. 1978. The Feminization of Poverty: Women, Work and Welfare. *Urban and Social Change Review* 11 (February): 28–36.

Personal Responsibility and Work Opportunity Reconciliation Act of 1996, Public Law 104-193d Cong., H.R. 3734 sess. (1966)

Plotnick, Robert D. 1992. The Effects of Attitudes on Teenage Premarital Pregnancy and Its Resolution. *American Sociological Review* 57, no. 6, December: 800–10.

Polakow, Valerie. 1992. *Lives on the Edge: Single Mothers and Their Children in the Other America*. Chicago: University of Chicago Press.

Polakow, Valerie, Therese Halskov, and Per Schultz Jorgensen. 2001. *Diminished Rights: Danish Lone Mother Families in International Context.* Bristol, UK: The Policy Press.

Popenoe, David. 1999. Can the Nuclear Family Be Revived? *Society* 36, no. 5, July/August: 28–30.

Porter, Kathryn H. and Allen Dupree. 2001. *Poverty Trends for Families Headed by Working Single Mothers: 1993–1999.* Washington, DC: Center on Budget and Policy Priorities.

Porterfield, Shirley L. 2001. Economic Vulnerability Among Rural Single-Mother Families. *American Journal of Agricultural Economics* 83, no. 5, November 15: 1302.

Presser, Harriet B. 1988. Shift Work and Child Care Among Young Dual-Earner American Parents. *Journal of Marriage and the Family* 50 (February): 133–48.

Presser, Harriet B. and Amy G. Cox. 1997. The Work Schedules of Low-Educated American Women and Welfare Reform. *Monthly Labor Review* 120, no. 4, April: 25–35.

Pugh, Allison. 2004. Windfall Child Rearing: Low-Income Care and Consumption. *Journal of Consumer Culture* 4, no. 2, July: 229–49.

Pugliesi, Karen and Scott L. Shook. 1998. Gender, Ethnicity and Network Characteristics: Variation in Social Support Resources. *Sex Roles* 38, no. 3-4, February: 215–38.

Puls, Joy. 2002. Poor Women and Children. *Australian Feminist Studies* 17, no. 37, March: 65–80.

Quadagno, Jill. 1996. *The Color of Welfare: How Racism Undermined the War on Poverty.* New York: Oxford University Press.

Rahmanou, Hedieh and Amy LeMar. 2002. *Marriage and Poverty: An Annotated Bibliography*, IWPR Publication #B239. Washington, DC: Institute for Women's Policy Research.

Rains, Prue, Linda Davies, and Margaret McKinnon. 1998. Taking Responsibility: An Insider View of Teen Motherhood. *Families in Society* 79, no. 3, May-June: 308–19.

Renwick, Trudi J. and Barbara R. Bergmann. 1993. A Budget-Based Definition of Poverty, with an Application to Single-Parent Families. *Journal of Human Resources* 28, no. 1, Winter: 1–24.

Research: The Heritage Foundation: Family. Policy Research and Analysis, http://www.heritage.org/research/family/index.cfm. Accessed May 11, 2003.

Reskin, Barbara. 1993. Sex Segregation in the Workplace. In *Annual Review of Sociology, Volume 19*, edited by Judith Blake and John Hagen, 241–69. Palo Alto, CA: Annual Reviews.

Rhodes, Rita and Miriam McNown Johnson. 2000. Students' Perceptions of Single Parents and Social Injustice: A Women's Issue. *Affilia* 15, no. 3, August: 434–46.

Rodgers, Harrell. 2003. Welfare Reform: Making Work Really Work. *The Policy Studies Journal* 31, no. 1: 89–100.

Rollins, Judith. 1985. *Between Women: Domestics and Their Employers.* Philadelphia: Temple University Press.

Romero, Mary. 1992. *Maid in The U.S.A.* New York: Routledge.

Roschelle, Anne R. 1997. *No More Kin: Exploring Race, Class, and Gender in Family Networks.* Thousand Oaks, CA: Sage.

Rose, Suzanna. 2000. Heterosexism and the Study of Women's Romantic and Friend Relationships. *Journal of Social Issues* 56, no. 2, Summer: 315–28.

Ross, Emma. 2003. Kids of Single Parents Face Struggles: Mental Problems, Addiction Twice as Common, Study Says. *Burlington Free Press*, January 24, A1.

Ruddick, Sara. 1982. Maternal Thinking, In *Rethinking the Family: Some Feminist Questions*, edited by Barrie Thorne, with Marilyn Yalom, 76–94. New York: Longman.

Ruwanpura, Kanchana N. and Jane Humphries. 2004. Mundane Heroines: Conflict, Ethnicity, Gender, and Female Headship in Eastern Sri Lanka. *Feminist Economics* 10, no. 2, July: 173–206.

Safa, Helen Icken. 1995. Women's Social Movements in Latin America. In *Women in the Latin*

American Development Process, edited by Christine E. Bose and Edna Acosta-Belen, 227–41. Philadelphia: Temple University Press.

Sahlins, Marshall. 1972. *Stone Age Economics*. Chicago: Aldine Atherton.

Schein, Virginia E. 1995. *Working from the Margins: Voices of Mothers in Poverty*. Ithaca, NY: ILR Press.

Schoeni, R. F. 1992. *Another Leak in the Bucket?: Public Transfer for Income and Private Family Support*, Population Studies Center Publication no. 92-249, Institute for Social Research, University of Michigan, Ann Arbor.

Schor, Juliet B. 1995. Economic Trend: More Willing to Give Up Pay for Additional Time Off. *Nieman Reports* 49, no. 3, Fall: 8–9.

Schram, Sanford F. 1995. *Words of Welfare: The Poverty of Social Science and the Social Science of Poverty*. Minneapolis: University of Minnesota Press.

———. 2000. *After Welfare: The Culture of Postindustrial Social Policy*. New York: NYU Press.

Scott, Ellen K., Andrew S. London, and Kathryn Edin. 2000. Looking to the Future: Welfare-Reliant Women Talk About Their Job Aspirations in the Context of Welfare Reform. *Journal of Social Issues* 56, no. 4, Winter: 727–46.

Scrivener, Susan, Richard Hendra, Cindy Redcross, Dan Bloom, Charles Michalopoulos, and Johanna Walter. 2002. *WRP: Final Report on Vermont's Welfare Restructuring Project*, Manpower Demonstration Research Corporation. New York: Manpower Demonstration Research Corporation.

Seccombe, Karen. 1999. *"So You Think I Drive a Cadillac?": Welfare Recipients' Perspectives on the System and Its Reform*. Needham Heights, MA: Allyn & Bacon.

Seccombe, Karen, Delores James, and Kimberly Battle Walters. 1998. "They Think You Ain't Much of Nothing": The Social Construction of the Welfare Mother. *Journal of Marriage and the Family* 60, no. 4, November: 849–65.

Smith, Dorothy E. 1999. *Writing the Social: Critique, Theory, and Investigations*. Toronto: University of Toronto Press.

Solinger, Rickie. 1992. *Wake Up Little Susie: Single Pregnancy and Race Before Roe v. Wade*. New York: Routledge.

Spitze, Glenna and Karyn Loscocco. 1999. Women's Position in the Household: A Crossnational Study. *The Quarterly Review of Economics and Finance* 39, no. 5: 647–61.

Stacey, Judith. 1990. *Brave New Families: Stories of Domestic Upheaval in Late-Twentieth-Century America*. New York: Basic Books.

———. 1994. The New Family Values Crusaders: Dan Quayle's Revenge. *The Nation* 259, no. 4, July 25: 119–22.

Stack, Carol. 1974. *All Our Kin: Strategies for Survival in a Black Community*. New York: Harper and Row.

Stack, Carol B. and Linda M. Burton. 1993. Kinscripts. *Journal of Comparative Family Studies* 24, no. 2, Summer: 157–70.

Standing, Kay. 1999. Lone Mothers and "Parental" Involvement: A Contradiction in Policy? *Journal of Social Policy* 28, no. 3, July: 479.

———. 1999. Lone Mothers' Involvement in their Children's Schooling: Towards a new Typology of Maternal Involvement. *Gender and Education* 11, no. 1, March 1: 57–73.

Stateline.org. 2001. Maximum Monthly Cash Assistance, Family of 3 (Two Kids) (dollars). http://www.stateline.org/stateline/?pa=fact&sa=showFact&id=125. Accessed July 17 2001.

Stein, Arlene. 2001. *The Stranger Next Door: The Story of a Small Community's Battle over Sex, Faith, and Civil Rights*. Boston: Beacon Press.

Stier, Haya, Noah Lewin-Epstein, and Michael Braun. 2001. Welfare Regimes, Family-Supportive Policies, and Women's Employment Along the Life-Course. *The American Journal of Sociology* 106, no. 6, May: 1731-60.

Struthers, Cynthia B. and Janet L. Bokemeier. 2000. Myths and Realities of Raising Children and Creating Family Life in a Rural County. *Journal of Family Issues* 21, no. 1, January: 17–46.

Suitor, J. Jill, Karl Pillemer, and Shirley Keeton. 1995. When Experience Counts: The Effects of Experiential and Structural Similarity on Patterns of Support and Interpersonal Stress. *Social Forces* 73, no. 4, June: 1573–89.

Sullivan, Oriel. 1997. The Division of Housework Among "Remarried" Couples. *Journal of Family Issues* 18, no. 2: 205–23.

Swidler, Ann. 2001. *Talk of Love: How Culture Matters*. Chicago: University of Chicago Press.

Swisher, Karen L., ed.. 1997. *Single-Parent Families*. San Diego: Greenhaven Press.

Taylor, Mary Jane and Amanda Smith Barusch. 2004. Personal, Family, and Multiple Barriers of Long-Term Welfare Recipients. *Social Work* 49, no. 2, April: 175–83.

Teachman, Jay D., Lucky M. Tedrow, and Kyle D. Crowder. 2000. The Changing Demography of America's Families. *Journal of Marriage and the Family* 62, no. 4, November: 1234–46.

Thomas, Jeanne L. 1990. The Grandparent Role: A Double Bind. *International Journal of Aging and Human Development* 31, no. 3, October: 169–77.

Thomas, Susan L. 1998. Race, Gender, and Welfare Reform: The Antinatalist Response. *Journal of Black Studies* 28, no. 4, March: 419–47.

Thompson, E. P. 1971. The Moral Economy of the English Crowd in the Eighteen Century. *Past and Present* 50: 76–136.

Thomson, Elizabeth, Jane Mosley, Thomas L. Hanson, and Sara S. McLanahan. 1998. *Remarriage, Cohabitation, and Changes in Mothering Behavior*, Center for Demography and Ecology, NSFH Working Paper no. 80. A National Survey of Families and Households, University of Wisconsin, Madison.

Tickamyer, Ann R., Debra A. Henderson, Julie Anne White, and Barry L. Tadlock. 2000. Voices of Welfare Reform: Bureaucratic Rationality Versus the Perceptions of Welfare Participants. *Affilia* 15, no. 2, Summer: 173–92.

Toner, Robin and Robert Pear. 2002. Bush Urges Work and Marriage Programs in Welfare Plan. *New York Times*, February 27, A18.

Townsend, Nicholas. 2002. *The Package Deal: Marriage, Work, and Fatherhood in Men's Lives*. Philadelphia: Temple University Press.

U.S. Census Bureau, Quick Tables (profile of selected economic characteristics in Vermont, 2000). http://factfinder.census.gov/bf/_lang=en_vt_name=DEC_2000_SF3_U_DP3_geo_id=04000US50.html. Accessed December 15, 2002.

U.S. Department of Health and Human Services. 1999. The 1999 HHS Poverty Guidelines, http://aspe/hhs.gov/poverty/99poverty.htm. Accessed October 22, 2004.

U.S. Department of Labor. 2002. Highlights of Women's Earnings.

Uehara, Edwina S. 1995. Reciprocity Reconsidered: Gouldner's 'Moral Norm of Reciprocity' and Social Support. *Journal of Social and Personal Relationships* 12, no. 4: 483–502.

Uttal, Lynet. 1999. Using Kin for Child Care: Embedment in the Socioeconomic Networks of Extended Families. *Journal of Marriage and the Family* 61, no. 4, November: 845–57.

Vail, David and Wade Kavanaugh. 2000. Livable Tourism Wages in Maine's Tight Labor Market. *Choices: Ideas for shared prosperity* 6, no. 5, (July 31 2000) 1-4..

Valdivia, Angharad N. 1998. Clueless in Hollywood: Single moms in contemporary family movies. *Journal of Communication Inquiry* 22, no. 3, July: 272–93.

Ventura, Stephanie J. and Christine A. Bachrach. 2000. *Nonmarital Childbearing in the United States, 1940–1999*. Centers for Disease Control and Prevention. National Vital Statistics Reports.

Vermont Office of Employment & Training. 2002. UI Covered Wages- Private Industry Vermont and United States, 1983–2001. http://www.vtlmi.info/wage.htm. Accessed

December 14, 2002. Vermont Office of Employment & Training. 2004. UI Covered Wages- Private Industry Vermont and United States, 1983–2003. http://www.vtlmi.info/wage.htm. Accessed October 22, 2004.

Vermont State Legislature, Livable Income Study Committee. 1999. *Act 21 Research and Analysis in Support of the Livable Income Study Committee*. Vermont Tourism Network. 2002. http://www.govtn.com. Accessed June 25, 2002.

Vermont's Welfare Restructuring Project. 1994. http://www.dsw.state.vt.us/wrp/wrpsum19.htm. Accessed January 18, 2000.

Vermont: The State That Says We Do (civil union resource guide). 2004. http://www.vermontcivilunion.com/. Accessed November 10, 2004.

Vissing, Yvonne M. 1996. *Out of Sight, Out of Mind: Homeless Children and Families in Small-Town America*. Lexington: University of Kentucky Press.

Waldron, Tom, Brandon Roberts, and Andrew Reamer (with assistance from Sarah Rab and Steve Ressler). 2004. Working Hard, Falling Short: America's Working Families and the Pursuit of Economic Security. Working Poor Families Project, Annie E. Casey Foundation.

Waller, Maureen R. 2002. *My Baby's Father: Unmarried Parents and Paternal Responsibility*. Ithaca, NY: Cornell University Press.

Wasilewski, Jessica. 2002. Low-Income Credit Rationing and Social Return on Investment: Welfare-to-Work Car Loans in the State of Vermont. Senior Thesis, Department of Economics, Middlebury College, Middlebury, VT, April 5.

Wax, Amy L. 2003. Social Welfare, Human Dignity, and the Puzzle of What We Owe Each Other. *Harvard Journal of Law & Public Policy* 27, no. 1, Fall: 121–37.

Weitzman, Lenore. 1985. *The Divorce Revolution: The Unexpected Social and Economic Consequences for Women and Children in America*. New York: Free Press.

Wells, Barbara. 2002. Women's Voices: Explaining Poverty and Plenty in a Rural Community. *Rural Sociology* 67, no. 2: 234-54.

Weston, Kath. 1991. *Families We Choose: Lesbians, Gays, Kinship*. (Between Men—Between Women.) New York: Columbia University Press.

White, Lynn and Debra Peterson. 1995. The Retreat from Marriage: Its Effect on Unmarried Children's Exchange with Parents. *Journal of Marriage and the Family* 57, May: 428-34.

Whitehead, Barbara Defoe. 1993. Dan Quayle was Right. *Atlantic Monthly* 271, no. 4, April: 47–53.

Wijnberg, Marion H., and Kathleen M. Reding. 1999. Reclaiming a Stress Focus: The Hassles of Rural, Poor Single Mothers. *Families in Society* 80, no. 5: 506–15.

Wilder, Laura Ingalls. 1953. *Little House in the Big Woods*. New York: Harper Trophy.

Williams, Colin C., and Richard White. 2001. Evaluating the Role of the Social Economy in Tackling Rural Transport Problems: Some Case Study Evidence from Rural England. *Planning Practice & Research* 16, no. 3/4: 337–48.

Williams, Colin C. and Jan Windebank. 2000. Self-Help and Mutual Aid in Deprived Urban Neighbourhoods: Some Lessons from Southampton. *Urban Studies* 37, no. 1, January: 127-47.

Williams, Erica and Anne W. Mitchell. 2004. *The Status of Early Care and Education in the States*, Institute for Women's Policy research.

Wilson, William Julius. 1987. *The Truly Disadvantaged: The Inner City, the Underclass, and Public Policy*. Chicago: University of Chicago Press.

Windham Child Care Association, and Peace & Justice Center. 2002. *The Economic Impact of Vermont's Child Care Industry*.

Winson, Anthony and Belinda Leach. 2003. *Contingent Work, Disrupted Lives: Labour and Community in the New Rural Economy*. Toronto: University of Toronto Press.

Wolcott, Jennifer. 2003. Single Moms Find Roommates. *Christian Science Monitor*, March 12, 11.

Wong, L. Mun. 1998. The Ethics of Rapport: Institutional Safeguards, Resistance, and Betrayal. *Qualitative Inquiry* 4, no. 2, June: 178-99.

Wood, Julia T. 1999. "That Wasn't the Real Him": Women's Dissociation of Violence from the Men Who Enact it. *Communication Quarterly* 47, no. 3, Summer: S1.

Wood, Nancy E. and Kathleen King, eds. 2001. The Impact of the Tourism Sector on the Vermont Economy 1999–2000. Vermont Tourism Data Center, University of Vermont, http://www.uvm.edu/~snrvtdc/publications/2000_Economic_Impact_Report.pdf.

Zelizer, Viviana, A. 1985. *Pricing the Priceless Child: The Changing Social Value of Children.* New York: Basic Books.

Zengerle, Jason Gray. 1997. Welfare as Vermont Knows It. *The American Prospect*, January-February, 54(2).

INDEX